THE OLD
TESTAMENT
and ETHICS

THE OLD TESTAMENT
and ETHICS

A BOOK-BY-BOOK SURVEY

EDITED BY
JOEL B. GREEN
AND JACQUELINE E. LAPSLEY

Baker Academic
a division of Baker Publishing Group
Grand Rapids, Michigan

Published by Baker Academic
a division of Baker Publishing Group
P.O. Box 6287, Grand Rapids, MI 49516-6287
www.bakeracademic.com

Printed in the United States of America

The Old Testament and Ethics first published in 2013. Chapters for this volume previously appeared in Joel B. Green, ed., *Dictionary of Scripture and Ethics* (Baker Academic, 2011).

Library of Congress Cataloging-in-Publication Data
    The Old Testament and ethics : a book-by-book survey / Joel B. Green and Jacqueline E. Lapsley, editors.
        pages cm
    Includes bibliographical references and index.
    ISBN 978-0-8010-4935-4 (pbk.)
        1. Ethics in the Bible. 2. Bible. Old Testament—Criticism, interpretation, etc. 3. Christian ethics—Biblical teaching. I. Green, Joel B., 1956– II. Lapsley, Jacqueline E., 1965–
    BS1199.E8O43 2013
    241.5—dc23   2013024422

13   14   15   16   17   18   19   7   6   5   4   3   2   1

CONTENTS

4. Wisdom and Psalms

5. Prophets

6. Deuterocanonical/Apocryphal Books

CONTRIBUTORS

Adams, Samuel L. PhD, Yale University. Assistant Professor of Biblical Studies, Union Presbyterian Seminary.

Birch, Bruce C. PhD, Yale University. Professor of Old Testament, Emeritus, Wesley Theological Seminary.

Boda, Mark J. PhD, Cambridge University. Professor of Old Testament, McMaster Divinity College. Professor, Faculty of Theology, McMaster University.

Brown, William P. PhD, Emory University. Professor of Old Testament, Columbia Theological Seminary.

Carroll R. (Rodas), M. Daniel. PhD, University of Sheffield. Distinguished Professor of Old Testament, Denver Seminary. Adjunct Professor, Seminario Teológico Centroamericano, Guatemala.

Chapman, Stephen B. PhD, Yale University. Associate Professor of Old Testament, Duke Divinity School.

Day, Linda. PhD, Princeton Theological Seminary. Assistant Professor, Chaplain, Hiram College.

deSilva, David A. PhD, Emory University. Trustees' Distinguished Professor of New Testament and Greek, Ashland Theological Seminary.

Dobbs-Allsopp, Chip. PhD, Johns Hopkins University. Associate Professor of Old Testament, Princeton Theological Seminary.

Duggan, Michael W. PhD, The Catholic University of America. Associate Professor of Theology and Religious Studies, St. Mary's University College.

Green, Barbara. PhD, University of California at Berkeley and Graduate Theological Union. Professor of Biblical Studies, Dominican School of Philosophy and Theology, Graduate Theological Union.

Green, Joel B. PhD, University of Aberdeen. Professor of New Testament Interpretation, Associate Dean for the Center for Advanced Theological Studies, Fuller Theological Seminary.

Harrington, Daniel J. PhD, Harvard University. Professor of New Testament, Boston College School of Theology and Ministry.

Hawk, L. Daniel. PhD, Emory University. Professor of Old Testament and Hebrew, Ashland Theological Seminary.

Holt, Else K. PhD, Faculty of Theology, University of Aarhus. Associate Professor, Faculty of Theology, University of Aarhus.

Kelle, Brad E. PhD, Emory University. Associate Professor of Old Testament, Point Loma Nazarene University.

Kiel, Micah D. PhD, Princeton Theological Seminary. Associate Professor of Theology, St. Ambrose University.

Klein, Ralph W. ThD, Harvard Divinity School. Professor of Old Testament Emeritus, Lutheran School of Theology at Chicago.

Lapsley, Jacqueline E. PhD, Emory University. Associate Professor of Old Testament, Princeton Theological Seminary.

Lee, Eunny P. PhD, Princeton Theological Seminary.

LeMon, Joel M. PhD, Emory University. Assistant Professor of Old Testament, Candler School of Theology, Emory University.

McCall, Robin C. PhD, Princeton Theological Seminary.

Mein, Andrew. DPhil, Oxford University. Tutor in Old Testament, Westcott House, Cambridge.

Olson, Dennis T. PhD, Yale University. Charles T. Haley Professor of Old Testament Theology, Princeton Theological Seminary.

Perdue, Leo G. PhD, Vanderbilt University. Professor of Hebrew Bible, Brite Divinity School.

Portier-Young, Anathea. PhD, Duke University. Associate Professor of Old Testament, Duke Divinity School.

Premnath, D. N. ThD, Graduate Theological Union, Berkeley. Academic Dean and Associate Professor of Hebrew Bible, St. Bernard's School of Theology and Ministry.

Sandoval, Timothy J. PhD, Emory University. Associate Professor of Hebrew Bible, Brite Divinity School.

Seow, Choon-Leong. PhD, Harvard University. Professor of Old Testament Language and Literature, Princeton Theological Seminary.

Smith-Christopher, Daniel. DPhil, Oxford University. Professor of Theological Studies, Loyola Marymount University.

Verhey, Allen. PhD, Yale University. Professor of Theological Ethics, Duke University Divinity School.

Vondergeest, Craig. PhD, Union Theological Seminary, Virginia. Assistant Professor of Religion, Presbyterian College.

Willis, Amy C. Merrill. PhD, Emory University. Assistant Professor of Religious Studies, Gonzaga University.

ABBREVIATIONS

General

ca.	circa
chap(s).	chapter(s)
Gk.	Greek
Heb.	Hebrew
Lat.	Latin
LXX	Septuagint
MT	Masoretic Text
NET	New English Translation
NRSV	New Revised Standard Version
NT	New Testament
OT	Old Testament
RSV	Revised Standard Version
v(v).	verse(s)

Old Testament

Gen.	Genesis
Exod.	Exodus
Lev.	Leviticus
Num.	Numbers
Deut.	Deuteronomy
Josh.	Joshua
Judg.	Judges
Ruth	Ruth
1–2 Sam.	1–2 Samuel
1–2 Kgs.	1–2 Kings
1–2 Chr.	1–2 Chronicles
Ezra	Ezra
Neh.	Nehemiah
Esth.	Esther
Job	Job
Ps./Pss.	Psalms
Prov.	Proverbs
Eccl.	Ecclesiastes
Song	Song of Songs
Isa.	Isaiah
Jer.	Jeremiah
Lam.	Lamentations
Ezek.	Ezekiel
Dan.	Daniel
Hos.	Hosea
Joel	Joel
Amos	Amos
Obad.	Obadiah
Jon.	Jonah
Mic.	Micah
Nah.	Nahum
Hab.	Habakkuk
Zeph.	Zephaniah
Hag.	Haggai
Zech.	Zechariah
Mal.	Malachi

New Testament

Matt.	Matthew
Mark	Mark
Luke	Luke
John	John

Acts	Acts
Rom.	Romans
1–2 Cor.	1–2 Corinthians
Gal.	Galatians
Eph.	Ephesians
Phil.	Philippians
Col.	Colossians
1–2 Thess.	1–2 Thessalonians
1–2 Tim.	1–2 Timothy
Titus	Titus
Phlm.	Philemon
Heb.	Hebrews
Jas.	James
1–2 Pet.	1–2 Peter
1–3 John	1–3 John
Jude	Jude
Rev.	Revelation

Apocrypha and Septuagint

Add. Esth.	Additions to Esther
Bar.	Baruch
Jdt.	Judith
1–2 Esd.	1–2 Esdras
1–4 Macc.	1–4 Maccabees
Sg. Three	Song of the Three Young Men
Sir.	Sirach
Sus.	Susanna

Tob.	Tobit
Wis.	Wisdom of Solomon

Dead Sea Scrolls

CD-A	*Damascus Document*[a]
1QS	*Rule of the Community*

Other Rabbinic Works

Rab.   *Rabbah (+ biblical book)*

Greek and Latin Works

Aristotle

Eth. nic.   *Ethica nichomachea (Nico-machean Ethics)*

Augustine

Ep.   *Epistulae (Letters)*

Other Authors

Thomas Aquinas

ST   *Summa theologiae*

Secondary Sources

AB	Anchor Bible
AOTC	Abingdon Old Testament Commentaries
BibSem	Biblical Seminar
BIS	Biblical Interpretation Series
BZAW	Beihefte zur Zeitschrift für die alttestamentliche Wissenschaft
CBET	Contributions to Biblical Exegesis and Theology
CBQ	*Catholic Biblical Quarterly*
CBQMS	Catholic Biblical Quarterly Monograph Series
CC	Continental Commentaries
CEJL	Commentaries on Early Jewish Literature
CSHJ	Chicago Studies in the History of Judaism
EUS	European University Studies
EvQ	*Evangelical Quarterly*
ExAud	*Ex Auditu*

FAT   Forschungen zum Alten Testament
FOTL   Forms of Old Testament Literature
GAP   Guides to Apocrypha and Pseudepigrapha
HBT   *Horizons in Biblical Theology*
HSM   Harvard Semitic Monographs
IBC   Interpretation: A Bible Commentary for Teaching and Preaching
Int   *Interpretation*
IRSC   Interpretation: Resources for the Use of Scripture in the Church
JBL   *Journal of Biblical Literature*
JHS   *Journal of Hebrew Scriptures*
JJS   *Journal of Jewish Studies*
JLR   *Journal of Law and Religion*
JPSTC   JPS Torah Commentary
JPsyC   *Journal of Psychology and Christianity*
JSJSup   Supplements to the Journal for the Study of Judaism
JSOT   *Journal for the Study of the Old Testament*
JSOTSup   Journal for the Study of the Old Testament: Supplement Series
LBS   Library of Biblical Studies
LHBOTS   Library of Hebrew Bible/Old Testament Studies
LTE   Library of Theological Ethics
NAC   New American Commentary
NCamBC   New Cambridge Bible Commentary
NIBC   New International Bible Commentary
NICOT   New International Commentary on the Old Testament
NIVAC   NIV Application Commentary
OBT   Overtures to Biblical Theology
OTG   Old Testament Guides
OTL   Old Testament Library
OThM   Oxford Theological Monographs
OTR   Old Testament Readings
OTS   Old Testament Studies
PBM   Paternoster Biblical Monographs
PSB   *Princeton Seminary Bulletin*
SBL   Studies in Biblical Literature
SBLAB   Society of Biblical Literature Academia Biblica
SBLDS   Society of Biblical Literature Dissertation Series
SBLEJL   Society of Biblical Literature Early Judaism and Its Literature
SBLSymS   Society of Biblical Literature Symposium Series
SHBC   Smith & Helwys Bible Commentary
SHS   Scripture and Hermeneutics Series
STR   Studies in Theology and Religion
TCrS   Text-Critical Studies
ThTo   *Theology Today*
TW   *Theologische Wissenschaft*
VT   *Vetus Testamentum*
VTSup   Supplements to Vetus Testamentum
WBC   Word Biblical Commentary
WestBC   Westminster Bible Companion

INTRODUCTION

Joel B. Green

For a long time, study of the Bible and study of Christian ethics (or moral theology) were regarded as separate enterprises. This is true to such a degree that those of us who want to study the two together, Scripture *and* Christian ethics, face a series of important questions. These questions cannot forestall our work, though, because of the importance of the Old and New Testaments for Christian ethics. The church that turns to the Bible as Christian Scripture does so on account of its belief that the Bible is authoritative for faith and life, for what we believe and what we do. Working out the shape of faithful life before God, then, necessarily involves interacting with, learning from, and sometimes struggling with the church's Scriptures.

Affirming the nonnegotiable relationship of the Bible to faithful life is only the beginning, however. A cascade of issues immediately follows as we seek to flesh out how the Bible might function authoritatively in theology and ethics. Indeed, the church's history serves as a warning in this regard. This is because the Bible has been used to support immorality and injustices of many kinds—for example, the marginalization and abuse of women, the institution of slavery, a constellation of racist practices, and the persecution of the Jewish people. The Bible has been badly used and misappropriated—sometimes scandalously through its being commandeered to serve the aims of those in power and sometimes simply through unskilled reading. In such cases as these, it seems that we need protection from the Bible, or at least from its interpreters. It is easy enough, then, to recognize the importance of raising and addressing some methodological issues.

What questions require our attention? Some are obvious, others more subtle. Among the more pressing would be the following:

- What of the historical rootedness of the biblical materials? These texts come from another time and place, and work with some commonly held assumptions and social realities that we no longer share. Jesus directs his followers to wash each other's feet, for example. Here we find as straightforward a command as Jesus' directive at the Last Supper that his followers eat the bread and drink the cup in his remembrance. Yet most Christian traditions ignore it, or they transform it into an abstract principle, like "serve each other." But why should we convert the practice of foot-washing into an abstraction while making the Lord's Supper central to Christian worship? Expanding our horizons, other questions arise. What of concubinage, household duty codes, or inheritance laws, for example, and other such matters firmly rooted in the ancient soil in which the biblical books were written?

- What of the many, sometimes competing, voices we hear in the Bible? Written over hundreds of years and in response to evolving situations, the biblical materials do not always speak with a common voice on the questions they address. When, if at all, is divorce an allowable option, and for whom? Should we, or should we not, eat meat sacrificed to idols?

- What of the fact that the biblical materials have their ethical concerns, we have ours, and these two do not always coincide? For most us in the West, eating meat sacrificed to idols is not a pressing concern, but it attracted its share of attention from Paul and the writers of Acts and Revelation. Nor do many of us think much about gleaning rights or other forms of economic sharing, even if Old Testament instruction on such practices begs for renewed attention. (Few preachers talk as much about poverty and the poor as the Bible does!) Conversely, the biblical writers could hardly have anticipated the swirl of ethical worries arising from technological advances that today allow us to contemplate and, at least in initial ways, to foster transhumanism. And many of us find ourselves far more concerned than the biblical materials, at least at an explicit level, with environmental ethics.

- What of those biblical texts that seem morally repugnant to us? What are we to make of biblical texts that authorize in God's name the decimation of a people or the stoning of wrongdoers?

To these questions we can add a few others that identify more specifically some methodological conundrums.

- How do we work with and between the Old and New Testaments? Do we give each its own discrete voice? Do we understand the ethics of the New Testament in continuity with or as a disruption of the moral witness of the Old Testament?

- Do we want to know what the biblical writers *taught* their first readers about faithful life, or do we want to know what the biblical books *teach* us about faithful life? That is, is our task a *descriptive* one, or are we interested in how Scripture might *prescribe* morality?

- Do we learn from the biblical writers the *content* of Christian ethics, or do we learn from them *how to engage in reflection* on Christian ethics? Another way to ask this is to distinguish between what the Old and New Testaments teach about morality and how the Old and New Testament writers go about their ethical reflection. Those whose concern is with the former approach are often interested in setting out the boundaries of appropriate ethical comportment. Those interested in the latter often think that we need to learn from the Bible an approach to ethical reflection that may take us beyond what the biblical materials teach.

- Are we concerned with describing what biblical books teach about right living, or are we concerned with how engagement with the books of the Bible might have the effect of sculpting our character, our dispositions, our commitments, for ethical lives? When we turn to Scripture with a concern for ethics, are we focused first and foremost on "ethics" as moral *decision-making* or as moral *formation*? Do we come to the Scriptures asking, "What should we do?" or do we come asking, "What kind of people ought we to be?"

Undoubtedly, many will want to respond at least to some of the questions with a resounding "both-and" rather than "either-or." Sketching the terms of the conversation like this can help to identify the poles of the discussion, but does not prohibit a range of responses along a continuum.

Even on this sampling of questions, the state of today's discussion about Scripture and ethics supports very little by way of consensus. Naming these issues serves rather to map the terrain, so to speak, or to identify the fault lines in the conversation. Readers of the essays collected here will find that contributors have not been asked to adopt a certain perspective or approach. They have been given the more general task of focusing on the ethics of each of the books of the Old Testament, major Old Testament traditions, and the Apocrypha, and on the possible significance of each for contemporary Christian ethics. They sketch some of the moral issues explicitly addressed in the book and some of the patterns of moral reasoning displayed in the book. As such, they supplement and extend the conversation begun in the introductory essays on "Ethics in Scripture" and "Old Testament Ethics."

Students will find here a needed introduction to the larger conversation concerned with the Bible and ethics, not its final word. Students of the Bible, whether in introductory classes or in more advanced courses concerned with the theology of Scripture, will find a reminder that more is going on with these documents than questions of history or theological debate. Students in Christian ethics will find here an introduction to the ethical witness of the Scriptures, including a reminder of the ways in which moral formation and instruction are always theologically and contextually grounded. A central question for God's people in every time and place was and remains what it means to be faithful to God in the midst of these challenges, these historical exigencies, these options for faith and life. Whether cast as reflecting the divine image, as loyalty to the covenant, as faithful response to God's liberating initiative, or as imitating Jesus, these texts broadcast as their central concern the identity and ethics of a faithful people. The call to faithful life is not only for people within the biblical stories, or only for the people to whom the biblical materials were first addressed. It remains our call too, and these reflections on the ethical witness of Scripture help to shape the itinerary of the journey ahead.

The essays that follow are selected from the *Dictionary of Scripture and Ethics*, published in 2011 by Baker Academic, and are made available here in order to make them more readily available for use in classroom and personal study. The *Dictionary of Scripture and Ethics* is a major reference tool with over five hundred articles treating not only the biblical books, but a wide array of topics concerned with issues in Christian ethics (like gambling, bioethics, the seven deadly sins, terrorism, and animals) and different approaches to ethics and Scripture (like cross-cultural ethics, Reformed ethics, narrative ethics, Latino/Latina ethics, and virtue ethics). In other words, the conversation begun in the present volume is continued, and expanded, in the dictionary itself.

1

OVERVIEW

♦ Ethics in Scripture ♦

Allen Verhey

Ethics may be defined as disciplined reflection concerning moral conduct and character. In Scripture, such reflection is always disciplined by convictions about God's will and way and by commitments to be faithful to God. Biblical ethics is inalienably theological. To sunder biblical ethics from the convictions about God that surround it and sustain it is to distort it. The fundamental unity of biblical ethics is simply this: there is one God in Scripture, and it is that one God who calls forth the creative reflection and faithful response of those who would be God's people.

That unity, however, is joined to an astonishing diversity. The Bible contains many books and more traditions, each addressed first to a particular community of God's people facing concrete questions of conduct in specific cultural and social contexts. Its reflections on the moral life, moreover, come in diverse modes of discourse. They come sometimes in statute, sometimes in story. They come sometimes in proverb, sometimes in prophetic promises (or threats). They come sometimes in remembering the past, sometimes in envisioning the future. The one God of Scripture assures the unity of biblical ethics, but there is no simple unitive understanding even of that one God or

1

of that one God's will. To force biblical ethics into a timeless and systematic unity is to impoverish it. Still, there is but one God, to whom loyalty is due and to whom God's people respond in all of their responses to changing moral contexts.

Ethics in the Old Testament

Ethics in Torah

The one God formed a people by deliverance and covenant. The story was told in countless recitals of Israel's faith. The God of Abraham heard their cries when they were slaves, rescued them from Pharaoh's oppression, and made them a people with a covenant (e.g., Deut. 6:20–25; 26:5–9; Josh. 24:2–13). The covenant, like an ancient suzerainty treaty, acknowledged and confirmed that God was the great king of Israel and that Israel was God's people. (George E. Mendenhall provided the classic description of ancient treaties in relation to Torah.) And like those ancient treaties, Israel's covenant began by identifying God as the great king and by reciting God's kindness to Israel (e.g., Exod. 20:2). It continued with stipulations forbidding loyalty to any other god as sovereign and requiring justice and peace in the land (e.g., Exod. 20:3–17). And it ended with provisions for the periodic renewal of covenant and with assurances of God's blessing on faithfulness to covenant and the threat of punishment for violation of the covenant (e.g., Exod. 23:22–33).

The remembered story and the covenant formed a community and its common life. And if Gerhard von Rad is right, they also provided a framework for the gathering of stories and stipulations into larger narrative and legal traditions (J, E, D, and P; various codes), and finally, for the gathering of those traditions into the Torah.

Much of the Torah (usually translated "law") is legal material. Various collections (e.g., the Decalogue [Exod. 20:1–17; Deut. 5:6–21]; the Covenant Code [Exod. 20:22–23:19]; the Holiness Code [Lev. 17–26]; the Deuteronomic Code [Deut. 4:44–28:46]) can be identified and correlated with particular periods of Israel's history. The later collections sometimes revised earlier legislation. It was evidently not the case that the whole law was given at once as a timeless code. Rather, the lawmakers displayed both fidelity to the earlier legal traditions and creativity with them as they responded both to new situations and to God.

Although the Torah contains no tidy distinction between ceremonial, civil, and moral laws, the traditional rubrics do identify significant functions of the legal material. As "ceremonial," the legal materials in Torah struggled against temptations offered by foreign cults to covenant infidelity and nurtured a communal memory and commitment to covenant. As "civil," the Torah had a fundamentally theocratic vision. In this theocratic vision, the rulers were ruled too; they were subjects, not creators, of the law. Such a conviction, by its warnings against royal despotism, had a democratizing effect. As "moral," the statutes protected the family and its economic participation in God's gift of the land. They protected persons and their property. They required fairness in disputes and economic transactions. And they provided for the care and protection of vulnerable members of the society, such as widows, orphans, resident aliens, and the poor.

The legal materials never escaped the story or the covenant. Set in the context of narrative and covenant, the legal traditions were construed as grateful response to God's works and ways. Moreover, the story formed and informed the statutes. The story of the one God who heard the cries of slaves in Egypt stood behind the legal protections for the vulnerable (e.g., Exod. 22:21–23; Lev. 19:33–34).

The narratives of the Torah were morally significant in their own right. Artfully told, they rendered the work and the will of the God to whom loyalty was due. They put on display something of God's cause and character, the cause and character to be shared by the faithful people of God. Noteworthy among such narratives were the stories of creation. They affirmed that the one God of covenant is the God of creation too. This is no tribal deity; this is the one God of the universe. In the beginning there is a narrative prohibition of idolatry as compelling as any statute; nothing that God made is god. In the beginning there is a celebration of the material world and a narrative prohibition of anything like Platonic or gnostic dualism; all that God made is good. It was, in the beginning, an orderly and peaceable world. There is a narrative invitation to a common life of gratitude for the blessings of God. When the curse fell heavy on God's good creation, the one God would not let human sin or the curse have the last word in God's world. God came again to covenant and to bless, blessing Abraham with the promise that in him "all the families of the earth shall be blessed" (Gen. 12:1–3). The Yahwist's stories of the patriarchs not only trace the blessing of David's empire to that promise but also form political dispositions to use the technical and administrative skills of empire to bless the subject nations (Gen. 18–19; 26; 30:27–28; 39–41) (see Wolff).

Ethics in the Prophets

The one God who created the world, who rescued slaves from Pharaoh and made covenant with a people, spoke to those people through the prophets. The prophets came as messengers of the great king. They came with a particular word for a particular time, but they always reminded the people of the story and the covenant and called the people to respond faithfully.

Frequently, in resistance to unfaithfulness, they brought a word of judgment. The sum of their indictment was always the same: the people have violated the covenant (e.g., 1 Kgs. 19:10, 14; Hos. 8:1). Concretely—and the message of the prophet was always concrete—some specific idolatry or injustice was condemned as infidelity to the covenant. The infidelity of idolatry was never merely a cultic matter. The claims of Baal, for example, involved the fertility of wombs and land and an account of ownership. The prophetic announcement of God's greater power freed the people to farm a land stripped of claims to divinity but acknowledged as God's gift, and it required them to share the produce of that land with the poor. The infidelity of injustice was never merely a moral matter, for the one God of covenant demanded justice, and the welfare of the poor and powerless was the best index of covenant fidelity. So the prophets denounced unjust rulers, greedy merchants, corrupt judges, and the complacent rich. Their harshest criticisms, however, were aimed at those who celebrated covenant in ritual and ceremony but violated it by failing to protect the poor and powerless (e.g., Amos 5:21–24).

On the other side of God's judgment the prophets saw and announced the good future of God. God will reign and establish both peace and justice, not only in Israel but also among the nations, and not only among the nations but also in the whole creation. That future was not contingent on human striving, but it already made claims on the present, affecting human vision and dispositions and actions. The prophets and the faithful were to be ready to suffer for the sake of God's cause in the world.

Ethics in Wisdom

The will and way of the one God could be known not only in the great events of liberation and covenant, not only in the oracles of the prophets, but also in the regularities of nature and experience. When the sages of Israel gave moral counsel, they seldom appealed directly to Torah or to covenant. Their advice concerning moral character and conduct was, rather, disciplined and tested by experience.

Carefully attending to nature and experience, the wise comprehended the basic principles operative in the world. To conform to these principles was at once a matter of piety, prudence, and morality. The one God who created the world has established and secured the order and stability of ordinary life. So the sage could give advice about eating and drinking, about sleeping and working, about the way to handle money and anger, about relating to friends and enemies and women and fools, about when to speak and when to be silent—in short, about almost anything that is a part of human experience.

The ethics of the sage tended to be conservative, for the experience of the community over time provided a fund of wisdom, but the immediacy of experience kept the tradition open to challenge and revision. The ethics of the sage tended to be prudential, but experience sometimes could teach that the righteous may suffer, and that there is no tidy fit between piety, prudence, and morality (Job). The ethics of the sage tended to delight both in the simple things of life, such as the love between a man and a woman (Song of Songs), and in the quest for wisdom itself. Experience itself, however, could teach that wisdom has its limits in the inscrutable (Job 28), and that the way things seem to work in the world cannot simply be identified with the ways of God (Ecclesiastes).

Wisdom reflected about conduct and character quite differently than did the Torah and the prophets, but, like "the beginning of wisdom" (Prov. 1:7; 9:10), "the end of the matter" was a reminder of covenant: "Fear God and keep his commandments; for that is the whole duty of every one" (Eccl. 12:13). The beginning and end of wisdom kept wisdom in touch with Torah, struggling to keep Torah in touch with experience, and covenant in touch with creation.

Ethics in the New Testament

The one God of creation and covenant, of Abraham and Israel, of Moses and David, of prophet and sage raised the crucified Jesus of Nazareth from the dead. That good news was celebrated among his followers as the vindication of Jesus and his message, as the disclosure of God's power and purpose, and as the guarantee of God's good future. The resurrection was a cause for great joy; it was also the basis for NT ethics and its exhortations to live in memory and in hope, to see moral conduct and character in the light of Jesus' story, and to discern a life and a common life "worthy of the gospel of Christ" (Phil. 1:27).

Jesus and the Gospels

The resurrection was the vindication of Jesus of Nazareth as the Christ. He had come announcing that "the kingdom of God has come near" (Mark 1:15), that the coming cosmic sovereignty of God, the good future of God, was at hand. And he had made that future present; he had made its power felt already in his words of blessing and in his works of healing. He called the people to repent, to form their conduct and character in response to the good news of that coming future. He called his followers to "watch" for it and to pray for it, to welcome its presence, and to form community and character in ways that anticipated that future and responded to the ways that future was already making its power felt in him.

Such was the eschatological shape of Jesus' ethic. He announced the future in axioms such as "Many who are first will be last, and the last will be first" (Mark 10:31; Matt. 19:30; Luke 13:30). He made that future present by his presence among the disciples "as one who serves" (Luke 22:27; cf. Matt. 20:28; Mark 10:45; John 13:2–17). And he called the people to welcome such a future and to follow him in commands such as "Whoever wants to be first must be last of all and servant of all" (Mark 9:35; cf. 10:44). To delight already in a coming kingdom in which the poor are blessed was even now to be carefree about wealth (Matt. 6:25, 31, 34; Luke 12:22) and to give generously to help the poor (Mark 10:21; Luke 12:33). To welcome even now a kingdom that belongs to children (Mark 10:14) was to welcome and to bless them (Mark 9:37). To respond faithfully to a future that was signaled by Jesus' open conversation with women (e.g., Mark 7:24–30; John 4:1–26) was already to treat women as equals. To celebrate God's forgiveness that made its power felt in Jesus' fellowship with sinners (e.g., Mark 2:5; Luke 7:48) was to welcome sinners and to forgive one's enemies.

Because Jesus announced and already unveiled the coming reign of God, he spoke "as one having authority" (Mark 1:22), not simply on the basis of the law or the tradition or the regularities of experience. And because the coming reign of God demanded a response of the whole person and not merely external observance of the law, Jesus consistently made radical demands. So Jesus' radical demand for truthfulness replaced (and fulfilled) legal casuistry about oaths. The radical demand to forgive and to be reconciled set aside (and fulfilled) legal limitations on revenge. The demand to love even enemies put aside legal debates about the meaning of "neighbor." His moral instructions were based neither on the precepts of law nor on the regularities of experience, but he did not discard them either; law and wisdom were qualified and fulfilled in this ethic of response to the future reign of the one God of Scripture.

This Jesus was put to death on a Roman cross, but the resurrection vindicated both Jesus and God's own faithfulness. This one who died in solidarity with the least, with sinners and the oppressed, and with all who suffer was delivered by God. This Jesus, humble in his life, humiliated by religious and political authorities in his death, was exalted by God. When the powers of death and doom had done their damnedest, God raised up this Jesus and established forever the good future he had announced.

The Gospels used the church's memories of Jesus' words and deeds to tell his story faithfully and creatively. So they shaped the character and conduct of the communities that they addressed. Each Gospel provided a distinctive account both of Jesus and of the meaning of discipleship. In Mark, Jesus was the Christ as the one who suffered, and he called for a heroic discipleship. Mark's account of the ministry of Jesus opened with the call to discipleship (1:16–20). The central section of Mark's Gospel, with its three predictions of the passion, made it clear how heroic and dangerous an adventure discipleship could be. "If any want to become my followers, let them deny themselves and take up their cross and follow me" (8:34 [and note the allusions to martyrdom in 8:35; 10:38–39]).

Hard on the heels of that saying Mark set the story of the transfiguration (9:2–8), in which a voice from heaven declared, "This is my Son, the Beloved; listen to him!" It is striking that the voice did not say, "Look at him, all dazzling white." The voice said, "Listen to him." Silent during the transfiguration, Jesus ordered the disciples to say nothing of what they had seen until the resurrection, and then he told them once again that he, the Son of Man, "is to go through many sufferings and be treated with contempt" (9:12). Mark proceeded to tell the story of the passion, the story of a Christ who was rejected, betrayed, denied, deserted, condemned, handed over, mocked, and crucified, but still was the Son of God, the Beloved, and finally vindicated by God. The implications are as clear as they are shocking: Jesus is the Christ not by displaying some tyrannical power, not by lording it over others, but rather by his readiness to suffer for the sake of God's cause in the world and by his readiness to serve others humbly in self-giving love (cf. 10:42–44). And to be his disciple in this world is to share that readiness to suffer for the sake of God's cause and that readiness to serve others humbly in self-giving love.

The call to heroic discipleship was sustained by the call to watchfulness to which it was joined (13:33–37), by the expectation that, in spite of the apparent power of religious leaders and Roman rulers, God's good future was sure to be.

Mark's call to watchful and heroic discipleship touched topics besides the readiness to suffer for the sake of God's cause, and it illumined even the most mundane of them with the same freedom and daring. Discipleship was not to be reduced to obedience to any law or code. Rules about fasting (2:18–22), Sabbath observance (2:23–3:6), and the distinction between "clean" and "unclean" (7:1–23) belonged to the past, not to the community marked by freedom and watchfulness. The final norm was no longer the precepts of Moses, but rather the Lord and his words (8:38). In chapter 10 Mark gathered the words of Jesus concerning marriage and divorce, children, possessions, and political power. The issues were dealt with not on the basis of the law or conventional righteousness, but rather on the basis of the Lord's words, which appealed in turn to God's intention at creation (10:6), the coming kingdom of God (10:14–15), the cost of discipleship (10:21), and identification with Christ (10:39, 43–45). Mark's Gospel provided no moral code, but it did nurture a moral posture at once less rigid and more demanding than any code.

Matthew's Gospel utilized most of Mark, but by subtle changes and significant additions Matthew provided an account of Jesus as the one who fulfills the law, as the one in whom God's covenant promises are fulfilled. And the call to discipleship became a call to a surpassing righteousness.

Matthew, in contrast to Mark, insisted that the law of Moses remained normative. Jesus came not to "abolish" the law but to "fulfill" it (Matt. 5:17). The least commandment ought still to be taught and still to be obeyed (5:18–19; 23:23). Matthew warned against "false prophets" who dismissed the law and sponsored lawlessness (7:15–27). To the controversies about Sabbath observance Matthew added legal arguments to show that Jesus did what was "lawful" (12:1–14; cf. Mark 2:23–3:6). From the controversy about ritual cleanliness Matthew omitted Mark's interpretation that Jesus "declared all foods clean" (Mark 7:19; cf. Matt. 15:17); evidently, even kosher regulations remained normative. In Matthew's Gospel the law held, and Jesus was its best interpreter (see also 9:9–13; 19:3–12; 22:34–40).

The law, however, was not sufficient. Matthew accused the teachers of the law of being "blind guides" (23:16, 17, 19, 24, 26). They were blind to the real will of God in the law, and their pettifogging legalism hid it. Jesus, however, made God's will known, especially in the Sermon on the Mount. There, he called for a righteousness that "exceeds that of the scribes and Pharisees" (5:20). The Beatitudes (5:3–11) described the character traits that belong to such righteousness. The "antitheses" (5:21–47) contrasted such righteousness to mere external observance of laws that left dispositions of anger, lust, deceit, revenge, and selfishness unchanged. This was no calculating "works-righteousness"; rather, it was a self-forgetting response to Jesus' announcement of the kingdom (4:12–25).

Matthew called the community to play a role in moral discernment and discipline. The church was charged with the task of interpreting the law, vested with the authority to "bind" and "loose" (18:18), to make legal rulings and judgments. These responsibilities for mutual admonition and communal discernment were set in the context of concern for the "little ones" (18:1–14) and forgiveness (18:21–35), and they were to be undertaken with prayer (18:19). Jesus was still among them (18:20), still calling for a surpassing righteousness.

In Luke's Gospel, the emphasis fell on Jesus as the one "anointed . . . to bring good news to the poor" (4:18). Mary's song, the Magnificat (1:46–55), sounded the theme early on as she celebrated God's action on behalf of the humiliated and hungry and poor. In Luke, the infant Jesus was visited by shepherds in a manger, not by magi in a house (2:8–16; cf. Matt. 2:11–12). Again and again—in the Beatitudes and woes (6:20–26), for example, and in numerous parables (e.g., 12:13–21; 14:12–24; 16:19–31)—Jesus proclaimed good news to the poor and announced judgment on the anxious and ungenerous rich. Luke did not legislate in any of this; he gave no social program, but he insisted that a faithful response to this Jesus as the Christ, as the "anointed," included care for the poor and powerless. The story of Zacchaeus (19:1–10), for example, made it clear that to welcome Jesus "gladly" was to do justice and to practice kindness. Luke's story of the early church in Acts celebrated the friendship and the covenant fidelity that were displayed when "everything they owned was held in common" so that "there was not a needy person among them" (Acts 4:32–34; cf. 2:44–45; cf. also Deut. 15). Character and community were, and were to be, fitting to "good news to the poor."

The "poor" included not just those in poverty, but all those who did not count for much by the world's way of counting. The gospel was good news, for example, also for women. By additional stories and sayings (e.g., 1:28–30; 2:36–38; 4:25–27; 7:11–17; 10:38–42; 11:27–28; 13:10–17; 15:8–10; 18:1–8), Luke displayed a Jesus remarkably free from the chauvinism of patriarchal culture. He rejected the reduction of women to their reproductive and domestic roles. Women such as Mary of Bethany, who would learn from Jesus and follow him, were welcomed as equals in the circle of his disciples (10:38–42).

And the gospel was good news to "sinners" too, to those judged unworthy of God's blessing. It was a gospel, after all, of "repentance and the forgiveness of sins" (24:47), and in a series of parables Jesus insisted that there is "joy in heaven over one sinner who repents" (15:7; cf. 15:10, 23–24). That gospel of the forgiveness of sins was to be proclaimed "to all nations" (24:47); it was to be proclaimed even to the gentiles, who surely were counted among the "sinners." That story was told, of course, in Acts, but already early in Luke's Gospel the devout old Simeon recognized in the infant Jesus God's salvation "of all peoples" (2:31; cf., e.g., 3:6). The story of the gentile mission may await Acts, but already in the Gospel it was clear that to welcome this Jesus, this universal savior, was to welcome "sinners." And already in the Gospel it was clear that a faithful response to Jesus meant relations of mutual respect and love between Jew and gentile. In the remarkable story of Jesus' healing of the centurion's servant (7:1–10), the centurion provided a paradigm for gentiles, not despising but loving the Jews, acknowledging that his access to God's salvation was through the Jews; and the Jewish elders provided a model for Jews, not condemning this gentile but instead interceding on his behalf. In

Acts 15, the Christian community included the gentiles without requiring that they become Jews; the church was to be an inclusive community, a welcoming community, a community of peaceable difference.

John's Gospel told the story in ways quite different from the Synoptic Gospels, and its account of the moral life was also quite distinctive. It was written that the readers might have "life in [Jesus'] name" (20:31), and that life was inalienably a life formed and informed by love. Christ was the great revelation of God's love for the world (3:16). As the Father loves the Son (e.g., 3:35; 5:20), so the Son loves his own (13:1). As the Son "abides" in the Father's love and does his commandments, so the disciples are to abide in Christ's love (15:9–10) and keep his commandments. And his commandment was simply that they should love one another as he had loved them (15:12; cf. 15:17). This "new commandment" (13:34) was, of course, hardly novel, but it rested now on a new reality: the love of God in Christ and the love of Christ in his own.

That reality was on display in the cross, uniquely and stunningly rendered by John as Christ's "glory." The Son of Man was "lifted up" on the cross (3:14; 12:32–34). His glory did not come after that humiliating death; it was revealed precisely in the self-giving love of the cross. And that glory, the glory of humble service and love, was the glory that Jesus shared with the disciples (17:22). They too were "lifted up" to be servants, exalted in self-giving love.

The commandment in John was to love "one another" (e.g., 15:12) rather than the "neighbor" or the "enemy." John's emphasis surely fell on mutual love, on relations within the community. But an emphasis was not a restriction, and the horizon of God's love was the whole world (3:16). And as God so loved the world that he sent his Son, so Jesus sent his followers "into the world" (17:18; cf. 20:21). The mission of the Father's love seeks a response, an answering love; it seeks mutual love, and where it finds it, there is "life in Christ's name."

Paul and His Gospel

Before the Gospels were written, Paul had addressed pastoral letters to the churches. He always wrote as an apostle (e.g., Rom. 1:1) rather than as a philosopher or a code-maker. And he always wrote to particular communities facing specific problems. In his letters he proclaimed the gospel of the crucified and risen Christ and called for the response of faith and faithfulness.

The proclamation of the gospel was always the announcement that God had acted in Christ's cross and resurrection to end the reign of sin and death and to establish the coming age of God's own cosmic sovereignty. That proclamation was sometimes in the indicative mood and sometimes in the imperative mood. In the indicative mood, Paul described the power of God to provide the eschatological salvation of which the Spirit was the "first fruits" (Rom. 8:23) and the "guarantee" (2 Cor. 5:5). But the present evil age continued; the powers of sin and death still asserted their doomed reign. The imperative mood acknowledged that Christians were still under threat from these powers and called them to hold fast to the salvation given them in Christ. "If we live by the Spirit, let us also be guided by the Spirit" (Gal. 5:25).

Reflection about the moral life was disciplined by the gospel. Paul called the Romans, for example, to exercise a new discernment, not conformed to this present evil age but instead "transformed by the renewing of your minds" (Rom. 12:2). There is no Pauline recipe for such discernment, no checklist or wooden scheme, but certain features of it are clear enough. It involved a new self-understanding, formed by the Spirit and conformed to Christ (e.g., Rom. 6:11; Gal. 2:20). It involved a new perspective on the moral situation, an eschatological perspective, attentive both to the ways in which the power of God was already effective in the world and to the continuing assertiveness of sin and death. It invoked some fundamental values, gifts of the gospel and of the Spirit, notably freedom (e.g., 2 Cor. 3:17; Gal. 5:1) and love (e.g., 1 Cor. 13; Phil. 1:9). And it involved participation in a community of mutual instruction (e.g., Rom. 15:14). Discernment was not simply a spontaneous intuition granted by the Spirit, nor did it create rules and guidelines *ex nihilo*. Existing moral traditions, whether Jewish or Greek, could be utilized, but they were always to be tested and qualified by the gospel.

This new discernment was brought to bear on a wide range of concrete issues faced by the churches: the relations of Jew and gentile in the churches, slave and free, male and female, rich and poor. Paul's advice was provided not as timeless moral truths but rather as timely applications of the gospel to specific problems in particular contexts.

The Later New Testament

The diversity of ethics in Scripture is only confirmed by other NT writings. The Pastoral Epistles encouraged a "quiet and peaceable life in all godliness and dignity" (1 Tim. 2:2). It was an ethic of moderation and sober good sense, avoiding the enthusiastic foolishness of others who might claim the Pauline tradition, whether ascetic or libertine.

The subtle theological arguments of the book of Hebrews did not exist for their own sake; they supported and sustained this "word of exhortation" (13:22). The theological basis was the covenant that was "new" (8:8, 13; 9:15; 12:24) and "better" (7:22; 8:6), and the fitting response to that covenant was to "give thanks" and to "offer to God an acceptable worship with reverence and awe" (12:28). Such worship, however, was not a matter of cultic observances. It involved "sacrifice," to be sure, and that "continually," but the sacrifice that is pleasing to God is "to do good and to share what you have" (13:15–16). Hebrews 13 collected a variety of moral instructions, including, for example, exhortations to mutual love, hospitality to strangers, consideration for the imprisoned and oppressed, respect for marriage, and freedom from the love of money.

The Letter of James too was a collection of moral instructions, and a somewhat eclectic collection at that. There was no single theme in James, but there was an unmistakable solidarity with the poor (1:9–11; 2:1–7, 15–16; 4:13–5:6) and a consistent concern about the use of that recalcitrant little piece of flesh, the tongue (1:19, 26; 3:1–12; 4:11; 5:9, 12). James contains, of course, the famous polemic against a "faith without works" (2:14–26), and it seems likely that he had in mind a perverted form of Paulinism, but James and Paul perhaps are not so far apart. When James called for an active faith (2:22), readers of Paul might be reminded of Paul's call for a "faith working through love" (Gal. 5:6).

The ethic of 1 Peter was fundamentally a call to live with integrity the identity and community formed in baptism. The "new birth into a living hope through the resurrection of Jesus Christ from the dead" (1:3; cf. 1:23) was a cause for great joy (1:6, 8), but it was also reason to "prepare your minds for action" and to "discipline yourselves" (1:13). In 1 Peter the author made extensive use of what seem to have been moral traditions associated with instructions for baptism (and which are also echoed in other NT texts [see Selwyn]). The mundane duties of this world in which Christians are "aliens and exiles" (2:11) were not disowned, but they were subtly and constantly reformed by being brought into association with the Christian's new moral identity and community.

The Letters of 2 Peter and Jude defended sound doctrine and morality against the heretics who "promise them freedom" (2 Pet. 2:19). In 2 Peter is a carefully wrought catalog of virtues, beginning with "faith," ending with "love," and including in the middle a number of traditional Hellenistic virtues (1:5–8).

The Johannine Epistles, like the Pastoral Epistles and 2 Peter, defended sound doctrine and morality, but these epistles made their defense in ways clearly oriented to the Johannine perspective. To believe in Jesus—in the embodied, crucified Jesus—is to stand under the obligation to love. In Jesus' death on the cross we know what love is (1 John 3:16). And to know that love is to be called to mutual love within the community (e.g., 1 John 2:9–11; 3:11, 14–18, 23; 4:7–12, 16–21; 2 John 5–6).

The book of Revelation, like most other apocalyptic literature, was motivated by a group's experience of alienation and oppression. In the case of Revelation, the churches of Asia Minor suffered the vicious injustice and petty persecution of the Roman emperor. Revelation encouraged and exhorted those churches by constructing a symbolic universe that made intelligible both their faith that Jesus is Lord and their daily experience of injustice and suffering. The rock on which that universe was built was the risen and exalted Christ. He is "the firstborn of the dead, and the ruler of the kings of the earth" (1:5). He is the Lamb that was slain and is worthy "to receive power and wealth and wisdom and might" (5:12). The victory had been won, but there were still sovereignties in conflict. On the one side were God, his Christ, and those who worship them; on the other side were Satan, his regents, the beasts, and "the kings of the earth," and all those who think to find security with them. The bestiality of empire was on display, and it called for "patient endurance" (1:9; 2:2–3, 10, 13, 19; 3:10; 13:10; 14:12).

The conflict is not a cosmic drama that one may watch as if it were some spectator sport; it is an eschatological battle for which one must enlist. Revelation called for courage, not calculation, for watchfulness, not computation. And "patient endurance" was not passivity. To be sure, Christians in this resistance movement against the bestiality of empire did not take arms to achieve a power like the emperor's. But they resisted. And in their resistance, even in the style of it, they gave testimony to the victory of the Lamb that was slain. They were to live courageously and faithfully, resisting the pollution of empire, its cult surely and its lie that Caesar is Lord, but also its murder, fornication, sorcery, and idolatry (cf. the vice lists in 21:8; 22:15; see also 9:20–21). They were to be the voice of all creation, until "those who destroy the earth" would be destroyed (11:18), until the Lord makes "all things new" (21:5).

Ethics in Scripture are diverse, not monolithic. Yet, the one God of Scripture still calls in it and through it for a faithful response, still forms and reforms conduct and character and community until they are something "new," something "worthy of the gospel of Christ."

Bibliography

Barton, J. *Ethics and the Old Testament.* 2nd ed. SCM, 2002.

Birch, B. *Let Justice Roll Down: The Old Testament, Ethics, and the Christian Life.* Westminster John Knox, 1991.

Burridge, R. *Imitating Jesus: An Inclusive Approach to New Testament Ethics.* Eerdmans, 2007.

Hays, R. *The Moral Vision of the New Testament: Community, Cross, and New Creation; A Contemporary Introduction to New Testament Ethics.* HarperSanFrancisco, 1996.

Mendenhall, G. *Law and Covenant in Israel and the Ancient Near East*. Biblical Colloquium, 1955.

Selwyn, E. *The First Epistle of St. Peter*. 2nd ed. Macmillan, 1947.

Verhey, A. *Remembering Jesus: Christian Community, Scripture, and the Moral Life*. Eerdmans, 2002.

von Rad, G. *The Problem of the Hexateuch and Other Essays*. Trans. E. Trueman Dicken. Oliver & Boyd, 1966, 1–78.

Wolff, H. "The Kerygma of the Yahwist." Pages 41–66 in W. Brueggemann and H. Wolff, *The Vitality of Old Testament Traditions*. John Knox, 1975.

Wright, C. *Old Testament Ethics for the People of God*. InterVarsity, 2004.

✦ Scripture in Ethics: Methodological Issues ✦

Bruce C. Birch

All traditions that regard the text of the Bible as Scripture would agree that these texts should be important resources for Christian ethics. Yet there is little agreement on, and often little attention paid to, how Scripture and ethics relate. Although the literature on this relationship has grown significantly in the last two decades, the tendency in practice in the Christian life is to leave this relationship unexamined. Texts are only casually or haphazardly brought into conversation with formative or normative concerns for Christian ethics. This essay seeks to raise some issues of perspective, foundational understandings, and methodological practice that might be helpful in constructing a more self-conscious relating of Scripture to the moral life in Christian practice. The views reflected here in brief draw on and are consistent with longer treatments of this subject in previous publications (Birch and Rasmussen; Birch, *Let Justice Roll Down*).

Perspectives on Biblical Ethics

It is helpful to think of different arenas within which questions of the relationship between the Bible and ethics can be raised. Each of these arenas poses different challenges and offers differing insights, but it is important not to confuse them or assume only one to be significant.

The World behind the Text

Some treatments of biblical ethics have focused on recovering, understanding, and critically assessing the morality of the biblical communities out of which the biblical texts were produced. Since these texts represent the witness of Israel and the early church stretching over more than fifteen centuries, the ethical systems of differing times, places, and groups reflected in the biblical text are diverse and complex.

Naturally, there has been considerable interest in recovering the morality of Jesus as the central figure in Christian faith, understood by most Christian traditions as God incarnate in human history. How Jesus lived, who he understood himself to be, and how his death and resurrection became the confessional foundation for the formation of the church make Jesus' own understanding of ethics crucially important. The popular slogan "What would Jesus do?" reflects this concern to use the ethics of Jesus as a model for moral conduct.

By the same token, entire denominational traditions have placed a high value on discovering and emulating the pattern of moral life practiced in the earliest church, especially as reflected in the book of Acts and the writings of Paul and other early church leaders in the NT Epistles. These NT writings often are treated as manuals of conduct for contemporary Christian life.

Efforts to discern and understand the ethics of Jesus or the early church may help to deepen our knowledge of the biblical communities that produced the witnesses of the biblical text. However, these communities were diverse and complex, and their testimonies in the biblical texts do not produce a single, unified ethic that can be emulated. There are four canonical Gospels, and each has a unique portrait of Jesus. There have been many notable efforts to recover the actual words and teachings of Jesus in a historical sense, and these have produced no uniform result. The writings of Paul and other NT authors reflect the unique circumstances of early congregations in differing time periods, and although all contribute to the resources for Christian ethics, there is once again no singular unified Christian ethic to be recovered and emulated.

With respect to the OT, the witness of Israel to its life lived in covenant with God is even more diverse and stretched over a longer period of time and historical circumstances. Efforts to find unifying themes throughout the OT texts or developmental patterns of moral conduct have been notably unsuccessful. We cannot produce a typical or complete history of ancient Israelite ethics. Different texts reflect different social strata and historical settings. Many recent studies have helped us to understand these glimpses of ancient Israel more fully in their own contexts, but there is no singular code of moral conduct to be emulated here. Instead, there is a richness of testimony of life lived in relation to God, both in obedience and disobedience. We may learn from these and be informed from them in our own moral efforts, and this methodology is addressed later in this essay.

The Text as Canon

Another way to understand biblical ethics is to see it as the moral conversation contained within the texts collected, edited, recognized, and passed on as a canon of Scripture. For Christians, the canons of the OT and the NT (and, for Roman Catholic and Orthodox Christians, the Apocrypha) have been collectively passed on through the generations as foundational for Christian faith and practice, theology and ethics. As soon as these texts have been gathered into the collections of Law, Prophets, Writings, Gospels, and Epistles and given authority as scriptural canon throughout historical processes of collection and recognition, a new context is created for assessing the biblical resources for Christian ethics. Individual books and at times divergent voices within a single book may be studied for their moral witness, but also subject to study and reflection are the moral conversations that take place between books and texts within the canon. Tensions, agreements, convergences, continuities, and contradictions are now handed on from one generation to the next. One concern of biblical ethics is to listen carefully and critically to the moral witness of the entire canon.

The character of the moral conversation created by the formation of canon is to some degree an artificial construct that transcends the witness to any particular historical context in biblical times. Biblical ethics at this canonical level can be informed by what we can critically discover about the particularities of the world behind the text, but the canon itself forms a new context within which texts make their moral witness in a larger conversation. This canonical moral witness may or may not be capable of connection to concrete moral worlds behind the text (e.g., the entire book of Job reveals little about the world out of which its witness came).

The nature of the moral conversation may differ greatly within the canon. Sometimes continuities of moral witness may be observed, such as the consistent concern for the welfare of the poor and the dispossessed. New juxtapositions raise new issues for moral conversation. Why do we have four Gospel portraits of Jesus, and what does each contribute, singly and in juxtaposition, to the moral vision grounded in the life and witness of Jesus of Nazareth? What are the moral implications of encountering the universal God of creation before beginning the particular story of God's promise to Abraham? How is this altered further by Paul's extension of God's people to include gentiles as well as Jews? Sometimes the canon forces us to deal with moral tensions. For example, what is the proper role of faith to public civil authority? We must read both the story of Daniel and Rom. 13.

Biblical authority will be discussed more fully below, but here it should be said that a proper understanding of canon emphasizes that canon is not a definitive collection of timeless, divinely revealed truths. Canon is a collection of witnesses to an ongoing encounter with the presence of God in the lives of persons and communities. The canon is witness to a process of experiencing, witnessing, preserving, and passing on testimony to the experience of divine reality in a wide range of human contexts. Thus, the canon functions not as a static deposit of timeless truth, but rather as a partner in conversation with our own experience of God's presence in our lives. "The canon functions not in isolation from our own experience of God but precisely in the process of letting our own story be intersected by the biblical story and reflecting critically and acting faithfully in the church out of those intersections. The end result toward which we should strive is a deabsolutized canon which allows for the honoring of ancient witness to the degree that it reveals to us the basic truths of our faith while at the same time honoring the power and authority of our own experience of God" (Birch and Rasmussen 156–57).

The Text as Scripture in the Present

The canon of Scripture, both OT and NT, originated in ancient times, but these collections of texts and their voices have been passed on through the generations to the present as authoritative in some fundamental way for the moral character and conduct of contemporary communities of faith. Thus, biblical ethics can refer to critical reflection on these texts and the way in which they inform the moral life of contemporary Christians. Some of the issues and dynamics of this will be discussed below, but here we should note that studies focused on Scripture as a resource for contemporary ethics will not find there some uniform system or pattern of moral identity and behavior that can simply be adopted or imposed. Nor is it productive to force upon the canon some moral system formed outside the text.

It may well be that the canon invites readers into a process of moral conversation and discernment with a diversity of witnesses that communities of faith have passed on as valued dialogue partners. These texts do not invite us into a ready-made set of moral rules, norms, and conclusions. The process of conversation and discernment will yield diverse results: illumination and insight in one instance, but dialogic struggle and tension in another. In reading of Jesus' life and ministry, we may find models to emulate in practice and thought. But in reading of Israel's experience as God's people, we will encounter testimony to both obedient and disobedient life lived before God. The faithful moral alternative in one biblical context may not be the faithful choice in another. Differences between the biblical world and our own must be faced honestly, and the use of Scripture as an ethical resource cannot be a simple pattern of emulating ancient ways, nor will we find a single, unified moral code to merely adopt. What the canon represents is the judgment of generations of faithful communities that have found these texts worthy of moral contemplation and ethical reflection. They witness to the experience of relationship to God and the challenge of life as God's people in diverse contexts and circumstances. The moral authority of these texts is foundational for the moral character and conduct of contemporary communities of faith, but only in dialogue with the traditions that passed on these texts and with the best critical understanding of our own experience of God and the world we live in now.

Foundational Understandings

The relationship between Scripture and ethics is dynamic and multifaceted. The Bible is certainly no simple prescriptive manual, nor is it just distant historical background for the Christian life. The church's claim that the Bible is a living resource for the life of faith is a serious one, but to understand that relationship requires clarity about some foundational matters. The sections below discuss some of these, related to community, moral agency, biblical authority, and divine reality.

The Centrality of Community

The canon of Scripture is the product of community. Whatever the diverse origins of particular texts or books of the Bible, the communities of ancient Israel and the early church collected, preserved, debated, and passed on the particular collection of ancient faith witnesses that we know as the OT and the NT. As a resource for Christian ethics, the witness of these texts is fully available only in the context of contemporary faith communities.

The Bible is the story of a community of those who understood themselves to be God's people, both ancient Israel as God's covenant people and the early church as the body of Christ. For those communities, the moral life was never a matter of individual character and conduct alone. The moral life is lived in the midst of and held accountable by the faith community. Individual moral life is lived in the context of a community that understands itself to be called into being by the gracious activity of God, seeks together to discern the nature of the moral life, and holds its members accountable to one another. Israel, the early church, generations of the faithful, and the contemporary church in its diverse forms all serve as interpretive communities within which the Bible is both a witness to the experience of God's grace and a testimony with the power to mediate that divine grace to transform new generations.

The Bible is the church's book. The church is shaped by the story and testimony of the canon of Scripture. Both the church's identity and its ongoing activity are shaped in dialogue with the Bible as a foundational resource. This relationship between ecclesial community, the Bible, and the moral life has multiple dimensions.

The church acts as the shaper of moral identity. In the life of faith communities the stories of Israel, Jesus, and the early church are encountered in worship, teaching, and testimony. Here others are invited to make the biblical story a part of their own identity.

The church acts as the bearer of moral tradition. Differing ecclesial traditions give testimony to the power of the text of Scripture to shape Christian life and mission. We do not begin anew each time we open the pages of the Bible seeking resources for the moral life; others have gone before us, and we stand in rich streams of moral tradition as we seek to be faithful moral agents in our own time.

The church is the community of moral deliberations. Christians are not isolated readers of the text trying to discern the witness of Scripture to moral life. The life of faith communities provides contexts and forums for sharing both insights and challenges in claiming the biblical witness as central to moral life in our own world. Discernment happens not by heroic individual reflection but rather by sharing our deliberations with others in the effort to see how biblical witness to God's grace can help us discern that grace in the pathways of our own lives.

The church is the agent of moral action. There is always a place for the faithful ethical action of a committed individual, but those actions are a part of a larger active witness by ongoing historical communities. The power of even an individual act of moral witness is magnified by awareness of the larger church community of moral action to make God's grace visible in the world. And actions joined in systems of active witness can have remarkable transformative power.

The text of Scripture is where the originating and the ongoing interpretive communities meet. It is out of those intersections that the Bible has moral influence mediated through faith communities, both ancient and modern.

Moral Agency and Aspects of Christian Ethics

The Bible assumes that we, as humans created by God, are capable of moral responsibility. In the language of Christian ethics, we are created as moral agents, capable of being shaped by relationships to God and neighbor and capable of making moral decisions that affect those relationships. As such, the Bible also assumes that we can be held morally accountable for our lives as moral agents in the world, accountable for who we are and what we do as individuals and as communities. Moral agency encompasses both character and conduct, both our being and our doing. Here we will look at three aspects: (1) decision-making and action; (2) character formation; and (3) virtue, value, obligation, and vision.

For many, Christian ethics automatically suggests decision-making and action. In this dimension of Christian ethics the central question is: What are we to do? This can be applied to any of the many moral issues that face ancient or modern persons and communities. How is the Bible a resource for questions of moral conduct?

Over the centuries there have always been some tempted to make the Bible into a prescriptive code of conduct. This has never been very successful. At best, the result has been a picking and choosing of biblical texts that seem more usable in this way—for example, the Ten Commandments or the teachings of Jesus. But the simple truth is that the Bible never makes moral decisions for us, nor do biblical texts lay out strategies or courses of action. And biblical texts do not speak with a single voice. The commandment says, "Do not kill," but other laws in the Pentateuch allow capital punishment and waging of war. The teachings of Jesus include those often called his "hard sayings," radical demands of the kingdom that few can meet.

Many of our modern issues requiring moral discernment and action simply could not be anticipated by the biblical communities (e.g., issues of bioethics). Others appear in such radically altered modern contexts that moral response seems complex and unclear. The early church dealt with issues of economic disparity by owning and sharing everything in common, but this does not translate immediately into morally responsible decisions in a complex global economy where economic disparities are intertwined with complex sociopolitical systems.

Still, the Bible is an important resource for the ethics of doing as long as we do not expect the text to do our decision-making for us. The texts of Scripture do make clear broad moral imperatives that frame our moral decisions—for example, the constant concern for those marginalized in human community: the poor, the weak, the hungry, the outcast. Scripture offers images that challenge our moral imagination and consideration of moral alternatives (e.g., Jesus with the woman taken in adultery). The Bible supplies important principles, norms, and standards that can guide our decisions in particular contexts: justice, love, compassion, righteousness. We should note, however, that this does not let us off the hook in deciding what the most just or loving action might be in a given context. The Bible also makes clear that faithful life as moral agents is never lived in isolation; we are a part of God's people, called to hold one another accountable for our actions in the world and to regard the failure to act at all as a moral failure.

Christian ethics, however, involves more than what we do. It involves who we are to be. Alongside moral decision-making and action we must consider character formation, questions of identity, of "our basic moral perception." "Character formation is the learning and internalizing of a way of life formative of our own moral identity. It is our moral 'being,' the expression of who we are. . . . Character includes our basic moral perception—how we see and understand things—as well as our fundamental dispositions, intentions, and motives" (Birch and Rasmussen 190).

Moral character and identity are shaped by many elements: family, culture, relationships, particular experiences. But Christian moral character must have a fundamental relationship to the Bible. Christian moral agents are nurtured by relationship to the stories, hymns, visions, commandments, and teachings of the entire Scripture handed on and reflected upon by generations of God's people. In the life of Christian congregations we are exposed to the entire range of materials in Scripture, and this helps to shape our identity as people of faith and moral agents. This material shapes us in different ways both by the diversity of the texts themselves and by the way they are read, taught, and used in the lives of congregations and individuals.

While moral character and conduct, being and doing, provide a broad framework for the moral life and the Bible as a resource for Christian ethics, there are many other useful categories that provide nuance, perspective, and insight into the full complexity of moral agency. A full discussion of the Christian moral life would want to discuss categories such as virtue, value, obligation, and vision. Virtue focuses on qualities that mark us as Christian moral persons and communities (kindness, courage, humility, love, righteous anger, and others). Value tends to focus on qualities that mark the social embodiment of morality (justice, love, equality, peace). Scripture helps to name and form virtues and values, and these overlap in actual human experience. Obligation has to do with duties, commitments, and responsibilities that arise out of the decision to live our lives in the context of Christian community and the Scripture that foundationally defines its life. Some obligations are a part of the common frameworks that we share with others in our social contexts (e.g., family, citizenship, culture). Christian obligation arises out of our decision to be a part of the church, and then the Bible becomes a part of the resources that the church uses to shape its character and conduct in the world. Moral vision is the large picture of the moral drama that Scripture invites us into as partners with God in the redemptive activity of God's people. Moral vision is

the category that suggests a framework anchored in the character and conduct
of God that encompasses our being and our doing as Christian moral agents.

The Nature of Biblical Authority

The nature of biblical authority and how it functions in the life of Christian
traditions and communities have been the subjects of considerable diversity
of opinion, and this is one reason why Christian faith has such a variety of
expressions. The Bible, understood as Scripture, is acknowledged by all Christian traditions as normative for the understanding and living of the Christian
life. It shapes Christian identity and practice, as referenced in the preceding
section. But how does the normative character of the Bible express itself? What
is its relation to other authorities that also shape human moral life?

"Authority is not a property inherent in the Bible itself. It is the recognition
of the Christian community over centuries of experience that the Scripture is a
source of empowerment for its life in the world" (Birch and Rasmussen 142).
To function in this way, however, the Bible must be understood as pointing
beyond itself to the experience of the biblical communities with the character
and activity of God. Authority rests not in the pages of the text, but rather in
its function as a mediating witness to God, who called biblical communities
of covenant and church into being and is still graciously active in our present
experience.

Human moral life is shaped by many sources of authority. We become moral
agents because we have been given identity and have been guided in our actions
by a complex matrix of authoritative influences that are then shaped by us as
individuals and members of various communities. These influences include
family, nationality, ethnic identity, cultural context, formal and informal education, gender experience, signal life events, influential individuals in varied
roles, and professed religious belief. The Christian moral life must include the
Bible and its interpretive traditions as authoritative in some manner; otherwise, there is no basis on which to label our ethics as Christian. However, in
Christian ethics the Bible, though always primary, is never self-sufficient. The
Bible cannot be the sole source of authoritative influence, and thus it is never
the exclusive authority for the moral life. Nevertheless, the Bible is indispensable for ethics to be labeled as Christian because it places us in a common
tradition with other varieties of Christian experience throughout history and
in today's world.

The Bible's primary and central role finds expression in a variety of ways
because the Bible itself is an entire library of diverse texts. First and foremost, the Bible tells the story of who we are as the people of God connected

historically to the communities responsible for the witness and preservation of the biblical texts. Centrally important within this entire biblical story is the story of Jesus, told in the diverse voices of the Gospels. But Jesus' story is connected both to Israel's story and to the early church's story. That story can model for the church both faithful and unfaithful moral life. To reflect on the biblical story is to aid us in discerning God's presence and activity in our own stories. For those who choose to be part of the Christian community, the Bible becomes an active dialogue partner in assessing and drawing on the other sources of moral influence in our lives. It is a matter of both content and process.

The authority of Scripture resides partly in its witness to a process of discerning and responding to the character and action of God in the life of the biblical witnesses. This in turn invites us to a similar process of discernment in our own time, guided by the way in which Scripture sensitizes us to the presence and activity of God here and now. But,

> attention to biblical authority as it mediates a process does not mean there is no continuity of biblical content to be claimed. . . . Our identity as the church is obviously shaped by images, concepts, and metaphors that are part of the Bible's content and not just witness to a process. But these cannot be regarded as revelatory deposits functioning as divinely sanctioned doctrine. The content must be constantly tested by the process. Which stories and images continue to manifest the redeeming power of God? Some matters of content are reassessed by the church, e.g., the biblical acceptance of slavery, Paul's admonition for women to keep silent in the church. Some matters of content are reasserted, e.g., God's preferential option for the poor and oppressed. Some matters of content remain central although our interactions with them may change, e.g., the gospel story of the life, death, and resurrection of Jesus. (Birch and Rasmussen 157)

Already implied in this brief discussion of biblical authority for Christian ethics is the recognition that the broad diversity of biblical material suggests various ways in which these materials are used and are experienced as authoritative. "Different types of biblical material must be appropriated in different ways. . . . The problem with most discussions of biblical authority is that they seem to imply a monolithic view of the Bible and its use. There is no single way in which the Bible is authoritative in ethical matters" (Birch, *Let Justice Roll Down*, 157). A constant moral imperative to care for the poor and dispossessed will carry authority in a contemporary ethical discussion in response to poverty. At the same time, diverse witnesses to the attitude of the faithful toward the power of the state will range as widely as the story of Daniel and the admonitions of Paul in Rom. 13. The authority of Scripture here is not to prescribe a course of action or even a line of response. It operates more to define a framework within which moral options in relating to the power of the state must be considered and weighed. Stories and hymns have authority in shaping the character of our lives as persons and communities that read and sing them and respond to the character of God revealed in them.

The Bible as the Scripture of the church forms the necessary authoritative framework within which ethical reflection must take place if it is to be Christian. Within that framework other moral influence can be engaged in dialogue and discernment. The God of the biblical text is still active in our own lives, our own faith communities, and our own religious experience. Hence, we must discuss the importance of witness to divine reality both in the biblical text and in our own time as a focus for Christian moral claims.

Divine Reality

For those who regard the Bible as Scripture, the texts that have been collected and passed on in the OT and the NT are witnesses to divine reality. They are the gathered testimonies of Israel and the early church to their experience of God in the life of Israel as God's covenant people; in the testimonies to the life, death, and resurrection of Jesus; in the formation and spread of the early church. Hence, Scripture as a resource for the Christian moral life mediates a divine reality that is assumed to be still present and active in the lives of contemporary confessing communities. Understanding who God is and how God has been active, what God wills and what God models, is essential to the Bible's role in Christian ethics.

The common popular view of the Bible's use in Christian ethics focuses on morality as obedience to God's revealed will. In its unexamined form this finds expression in those who think of the Bible as a prescriptive handbook for moral behavior. On closer examination, this always proves to be a highly selective sample of biblical texts. In more sophisticated forms the stress on revealed divine will has tended to identify a canon within the canon of texts regarded as serious expressions of God's will for how we are to conduct ourselves, guides to moral behavior and God's intention for us. The result has been emphasis on important texts such as the Decalogue, the preaching of the prophets, the teachings of Jesus, and the moral admonitions of Paul and other early church voices. Such texts are indeed centrally important, for the Bible does call us to live a life obedient to God's purposes for us, and for Christians, the teachings of Jesus in particular are important guides to moral conduct in lives that express love of God and neighbor.

However, God is much more than a lawgiver or a moral teacher in the Bible, and earlier we noted the limitations of the Bible in giving us moral instruction on what we are to do. It is more faithful to the range and diversity of biblical materials to focus on the character of God as well as the will of God, especially as revealed in divine activity related to the biblical communities of faith.

In addition to the roles of lawgiver and teacher, associated with the will of God as seen in, for example, the Decalogue and the teachings of Jesus, God plays many other roles in Scripture. These include creator, promise giver, deliverer, judge, redeemer, sovereign, and covenant partner. These roles do not appear in systematic discursive treatments in the biblical texts. They appear in stories of God's encounters and relationships with key biblical figures and ongoing biblical communities. They appear in relationships that the biblical stories tell us God has risked in divine presence within human history and divine encounters with individuals and communities that have given testimony in the biblical texts to these encounters.

Some scholars have appropriately highlighted the imitation of God (*imitatio Dei*) or of Christ (*imitatio Christi*) as a basis for ethics in the use of Scripture. Texts such as Lev. 19:2, "You shall be holy, for I the LORD your God am holy," or the entire emphasis of 1 John on loving as God has loved, make this moral imitation of God explicit. Many other texts name qualities of God's character that model moral character for God's people: love, righteousness, justice, compassion, faithfulness, service.

The Practice of Using Scripture as a Moral Resource

Beyond the scope of this essay lies the complex set of practices that persons and communities must cultivate in light of the methodological perspectives discussed above. It is an ongoing process that stretches and matures through the Christian life. These practices include:

- *The development of critical skill in reading and understanding the biblical texts as fully as possible.* This is more than exegesis of individual and isolated texts; it is the development of patterns of reading that allows conversation between texts within the canon while honoring the full witness of each text. Fortunately, many useful tools are available to aid our reading, such as study Bibles, commentaries, concordances, dictionaries, computer programs, and Internet resources.
- *The practice of "reading in communion"* (see Fowl and Jones). Christian ethics is not informed by isolated individual reading of biblical texts so much as the reading together in community that takes place in the

ongoing use of Scripture in the life of congregations. This is not simply the obvious practice of formal study of the Bible in various programs within the church; it also involves exposure to the Scripture in liturgy, preaching, hymns, and devotion. When this exposure to the biblical story is rich, the ongoing conversation in Christian community about the issues that challenge us will be informed by the implicit and explicit shaping of lives and decisions that comprise our identity as Christian moral agents in the world.

Clearly, the relating of Scripture to Christian ethics is a rich and complex conversation that is both historical and global. We are invited into the conversation not for the discovery of fixed moral truths, but rather to experience the moral power of life lived in the presence of God and as a part of God's people.

Bibliography

Barton, J. "Approaches to Ethics in the Old Testament." Pages 113–30 in *Beginning Old Testament Study*, ed. J. Rogerson. Westminster, 1982.

―――. "The Basis of Ethics in the Hebrew Bible." *Semeia* 66 (1996): 11–22.

―――. *Ethics and the Old Testament*. Trinity Press International, 1998.

―――. "Understanding Old Testament Ethics." *JSOT* 9 (1978): 44–64.

―――. *Understanding Old Testament Ethics: Approaches and Explorations*. Westminster John Knox, 2003.

Birch, B. "Divine Character and the Formation of Moral Community in the Book of Exodus." Pages 119–35 in *The Bible in Ethics: The Second Sheffield Colloquium*, ed. J. Rogerson, M. Davies, and M. D. Carroll R. JSOTSup 207. Sheffield Academic, 1995.

―――. *Let Justice Roll Down: The Old Testament, Ethics, and Christian Life*. Westminster John Knox, 1991.

―――. "Moral Agency, Community, and the Character of God in the Hebrew Bible." *Semeia* 66 (1994): 23–41.

―――. "Old Testament Narrative and Moral Address." Pages 75–91 in *Canon, Theology, and Old Testament Interpretation: Essays in Honor of Brevard S. Childs*, ed. G. Tucker, D. Petersen, and R. Wilson. Fortress, 1988;

Birch, B., and L. Rasmussen. *Bible and Ethics in the Christian Life*. Rev. ed. Augsburg, 1989.

Blount, B. *Then the Whisper Put on Flesh: New Testament Ethics in an African American Context*. Abingdon, 2001.

Cahill, L. "The New Testament and Ethics: Communities of Social Change." *Int* 44 (1990): 383–95.

Childs, B. *Biblical Theology of the Old and New Testaments: Theological Reflections on the Christian Bible*. Fortress, 1993.

———. *Old Testament Theology in Canonical Context*. Fortress, 1985.

Clements, R. *Loving One's Neighbor: Old Testament Ethics in Context*. University of London Press, 1992.

Eichrodt, W. "The Effect of Piety on Conduct (Old Testament Morality)." Pages 316–79 in vol. 2 of *Theology of the Old Testament*, trans. J. Baker. OTL. Westminster, 1967.

Fowl, S., and L. Jones, *Reading in Communion: Scripture and Ethics in Christian Life*. Eerdmans, 1991.

Hauerwas, S. *A Community of Character: Toward a Constructive Christian Ethic*. University of Notre Dame Press, 1981.

———. *The Peaceable Kingdom: A Primer in Christian Ethics*. University of Notre Dame Press, 1983.

Hays, R. *The Moral Vision of the New Testament: Community, Cross, and New Creation; A Contemporary Introduction to New Testament Ethics*. HarperSanFrancisco, 1996.

Hempel, J. *Das Ethos des Alten Testaments*. BZAW 67. Töpelmann, 1938.

Janzen, W. *Old Testament Ethics: A Paradigmatic Approach*. Westminster John Knox, 1994.

Knight, D. "Political Rights and Powers in Monarchic Israel." *Semeia* 66 (1994): 93–118.

Matera, F. *New Testament Ethics: The Legacies of Jesus and Paul*. Westminster John Knox, 1996.

Nasuti, H. "Identity, Identification, and Imitation: The Narrative Hermeneutics of Israelite Law." *JLR* 4 (1986): 9–23.

Ogletree, T. *The Use of the Bible in Christian Ethics: A Constructive Essay*. Fortress, 1983.

Otto, E. *Theologische Ethik des Alten Testaments*. TW. Kohlhammer, 1994.

Rodd, C. *Glimpses of a Strange Land: Studies in Old Testament Ethics*. T&T Clark, 2001.

Verhey, A. *The Great Reversal: Ethics and the New Testament*. Eerdmans, 1984.

Wenham, G. "The Gap between Law and Ethics in the Bible." *JJS* 48 (1997): 17–29.

———. *Story as Torah: Reading the Old Testament Ethically*. OTS. T&T Clark, 2000.

Wilson, R. "Approaches to Old Testament Ethics." Pages 62–74 in *Canon, Theology, and Old Testament Interpretation: Essays in Honor of Brevard S. Childs*, ed. G. Tucker, D. Petersen, and R. Wilson. Fortress, 1988.

———. "Sources and Methods in the Study of Ancient Israelite Ethics." *Semeia* 66 (1994): 55–63.

Wright, C. *An Eye for an Eye: The Place of Old Testament Ethics Today*. InterVarsity, 1983.

———. *Old Testament Ethics for the People of God*. InterVarsity, 2004.

♦ Old Testament Ethics ♦

M. Daniel Carroll R.

The Meaning of "Old Testament Ethics"

There are two fundamental ways to understand the phrase "Old Testament ethics." One is to focus on the descriptive task of identifying what might have been the moral beliefs and behavior of the people of God as a whole, or of various groups within Israel, at any one historical period or across OT times. From this perspective, the study of OT ethics consists of those efforts to reconstruct the ethics of ancient Israel by certain textual methods and through historical, sociological, anthropological, and comparative studies. The emphasis is on the multiplicity of ethical perspectives within the text and on the social settings, theological sources (such as covenant, the law, wisdom), and ideologies of those who may have produced this material. There is disagreement over whether a largely coherent ethical framework undergirds the OT's various appreciations of moral matters, and scholars have offered different hypotheses regarding the possible development of Israel's ethical views.

The second way to understand the phrase "Old Testament ethics" is to focus on the normative task of discerning what the OT can contribute to moral life today as part of Christian Scripture. The NT certainly invites such considerations (note, e.g., 1 Cor. 10:11; 2 Tim. 3:16–17; Heb. 11). The goal is to bring the OT to bear on the modern world. While the research interests of descriptive approaches may be utilized (if and how this is done will depend on the individual author), the purpose is to offer ways in which the text can demonstrate its contemporary relevance to believing communities and to the world. The OT is embraced in some measure as a trustworthy guide and a foundational authority for the practice of the Christian faith. The significance of its authority, however, is a topic of debate.

The Authority of the Old Testament

Historically, the authority of the OT was assumed by the Christian church. There were occasional exceptions to this consensus, the most famous being the stance of Marcion of Sinope (c. 85–160 CE), who rejected the entire OT and those sections of the NT that he thought reflected Jewish influence. In contrast, the generalized confidence in the OT's authority was grounded in the conviction that it was the word of God. In spite of theological disagreements about its teaching and how it should be interpreted, the consensus was that the OT was divine revelation and thus indispensable and supremely relevant to believers, the church, and the greater society. Those of more conservative persuasions continue to articulate the inspiration of the OT in similar ways.

Recently, some have reformulated the concept of the authority of the Bible (and of the OT). Instead of the traditional view of the OT's authority as being an ontological quality—that is, a property inherent in the text—biblical authority is explained as a functional reality. From this perspective, the Bible is taken as a unique collection of witnesses to the presence and work of God that the church authorizes as the primary resource for its moral life. Faith communities recognize its enduring value in shaping Christian character and conduct. An ontological stance may accept this view as complementary to its own, but many see it as an alternative to those classic conceptions. The concern is that this different focus on the concept of biblical authority can open the way for more significant input from sources other than the Bible, such as philosophy and the social sciences. It also allows for weighing what parts of the Bible may no longer manifest the redeeming designs of God and need not be accepted as binding.

There also are those who are strongly suspicious of the ethical authority of the OT. Its positions on ethical dilemmas are said to be dated and overly constrained by the worldview and mores of its cultural settings. This historical argument can be accompanied by a range of ideological critiques, which include disparaging the OT as politically nationalistic, hopelessly misogynistic, ethnically exclusive, problematic in its portrayal of the violence of its characters and of God, and insensitive to the plight of the disabled, animals, and the created order (Rodd; O'Brien). These perceptions reflect a hermeneutics of suspicion that often reads "against the grain" of textual meaning to question the unspoken agendas and embedded prejudices that lie hidden beneath the surface.

These kinds of doubts have generated several types of responses. One has been to revisit the OT and to begin to recover or rehabilitate pertinent ethical voices within the text that have been ignored (e.g., women's stories, the impulses toward peace). Another outcome has been to reinterpret texts that have been misunderstood and thus misused in ethical discourse to support harmful positions, whether consciously or not (e.g., gender issues, racial apartheid, the disregard of ecology). A third result has been to reassess problematic passages and concepts within the scope of the larger canon, where they can find development or complementary perspectives. We will return to this point below. All of these efforts ascribe authority to the OT and value its ethical lessons in whole or in part.

The most extreme option is to reject the OT's teachings and, in some cases, the God who is revealed therein. The goal of various scholars is to resist vigorously what it presents about life and the deity. Those who accept the OT as Scripture cannot endorse this overly critical judgment. This does not mean that none of the negative observations has any merit. A thoughtful position on the authority of the OT must be able to respond to legitimate concerns about its ethical content with the necessary complexity and erudition. These challenges have spurred reflection on the nature and role of language (especially of metaphor), the history of interpretive practices, and the complexity of the theological world of the OT—all of which have led to richer and more nuanced conceptions of its authority as Scripture.

Another key topic related to the authority of the OT is the characterization of its relationship to the NT within the Christian canon. This is fundamental to articulating how the OT can and should speak to the church as Scripture. These theological and hermeneutical issues have occupied theologians for two millennia. Some of the more important questions are these: What kind of continuity exists between the people of God of each Testament, and is it of such a degree that the OT moral demands have abiding value (the Israel-church question within Christian theological systems)? How is OT law to be understood as an ethical resource in light of the coming of Jesus, the implications of the cross for salvation and life, and the inauguration of the kingdom of God (the "third use of the law" debate and the law/gospel tension)? Can the OT be used as a discrete and separate ethical resource with direct application to contemporary moral discourse, or must its teaching and insights be run through a NT or Christian theological grid? Is there development of ethical perspectives as one moves from the OT into the NT? If so, does that mean that NT teaching qualifies, complements, and/or supersedes the OT perspective on a given subject? Does the NT itself offer any guidelines for the appropriation of the OT, and if so, should they have normative status? A full-orbed biblical ethics will incorporate decisions on these and other foundational matters into its methodological framework.

Approaches to Old Testament Ethics

If the OT is accepted as a suitable ethical resource, then it is incumbent to sort out the way(s) it is utilized for the moral life of faith communities today. Approaches to appropriating the text can be divided into three broad categories. These categories are not mutually exclusive classifications, and some approaches do not fit neatly into a single grouping, but this taxonomy can serve as a heuristic tool for sorting out the use of the OT for ethics. Because of the biblical focus of this volume, this survey emphasizes contemporary formulations by biblical scholars instead of those of theologians, both past and present, whose appropriation of the Bible for ethics has been quite sophisticated (e.g., Augustine, Luther, Barth, Bonhoeffer, O'Donovan).

Focusing on what is "behind the text." To say that certain approaches concentrate on what is "behind the text" means that they are less interested in what appears in the final, or canonical, form of the OT and more interested in uncovering background matters pertinent to the ethics of ancient Israel. These can be of two kinds, both of which essentially are efforts at reconstruction. Some investigate the historical and culture setting, others the hypothetical editorial history of the text.

Studies that locate the ethics of the OT within the moral world of its day compare its moral worldview and demands with those of surrounding cultures (Weinfeld). This has been done especially in regard to OT law, in particular legislation related to slavery, the poor, and issues concerning women (e.g., marriage, sexuality, and inheritance). Depending on the topic at hand, the OT is perceived as mirroring the limitations of its time or as humanizing the treatment of the vulnerable and eliminating the privileging of certain social hierarchies before the law. Positive assessments of the OT vis-à-vis the ancient Near East point to the enduring significance of the underlying principles of its ethics.

Another comparative approach, which moves beyond these synchronic juxtapositions and evaluations, suggests the possibility of an engagement with the "natural morality," or commonly accepted mores, of Israel's context (Rogerson). The ethical commitments of the people of God would have had points of both agreement and disagreement with these widely shared values. At the same time, Israel's ethics were grounded in its particular "imperatives of redemption"—that is, those demands based on God's unique gracious acts on their behalf, like the exodus (e.g., Exod. 22:21 [22:22 MT]; 23:9). These imperatives, in turn, found concrete expression in Israel's laws through "structures of grace," those social and economic measures intended to incarnate that redemption in their society; that is, there would have been overlap with surrounding cultures as well as distinctiveness in the ethical values and arrangements of Israel. For the church, the cross of Christ is the redemptive act that makes claims on how Christians are to act toward others and configure their lives. The concomitant structures of grace on behalf of the needy within faith communities obviously will look different in the twenty-first century than they did millennia ago in ancient Israel. The "natural morality" model can encourage Christians to work with those of other persuasions, who hold similar moral commitments, to seek to pass legislation and establish social structures and organizations in modern society that might approximate God's ideals. In other words, the OT law in many ways is largely context-specific; it is not to be imitated, although the processes of engagement with the broader context can be instructive. The peculiar ethics of the people of God in any time and place can connect at some level in constructive ways with the broader world, even as it follows its own narrative.

Other studies try to better comprehend the socioeconomic situation and dynamics of ancient Israel within which the ethics recorded in the OT functioned. The social sciences have been a primary tool to analyze the text and archaeological evidence and propose explanatory models. Several of the more prominent include the theories of rent capitalism and the tributary mode of production, both of which are based on the claim that the monarchy triggered the rise of latifundia (landed estates controlled by economic and political elites). A recent suggestion is that Israel essentially functioned as a peasant economy, even as its political structure changed. Society functioned according to kinship and patronage, with their culturally accepted mutual expectations and obligations between the various social strata. Even though that world of patronage is quite different from most contemporary societies, what is constant across the OT and what carries over the centuries is the divine demand for justice. This moral value will be worked out differently than it was in ancient times, but it remains the calling of the people of God (Houston).

A second kind of "behind the text" research concentrates on ascertaining the stages of the literary production of the OT. These critical textual efforts can be combined with sociological work on the plausible sociohistorical contexts of the authors and tradents of each step in that process. The OT, it is claimed, is an anthology of the ethical agendas of multiple social forces from different time periods as well as of competing points of view from the same settings. The implications that are drawn from these textual and historical reconstructions vary. Some believe that the original textual layers represent a higher ethical commitment to the vulnerable, which was neutralized to some degree by the later additions (Gottwald). Others find a different lesson in the incongruities and possible contradictions: awareness of this mixture of views makes it impossible to assign a consistent ethical point of view to the text. Its very complexity is a witness to the struggles of the moral discourse within Israel. The pluralism of the OT's ethics fits nicely with the ethos of postmodern culture (Pleins).

At least three comments are in order. First, these efforts at historical, social, and textual reconstruction can be of great value, but sometimes the intricacy of the argumentation and the level of scholarship required to comprehend the given model can make this work inaccessible to the broader Christian public. Their possible contribution to the ethical thinking of the church is diminished, if not negated. Second, the viability of these hypotheses is heavily dependent on the success of the particular reconstruction proposed, which is only as convincing as the quality of the data and their interpretation or the suitability of the applied social theory and the skill with which it is used. New developments and discoveries can impact what may have once been confident conclusions. Third, background studies need not serve the kinds of reconstruction programs cited here. Some provide information about sociocultural, economic, and political contexts to final form or canonical approaches, which use this material to provide a realistic historical backdrop to their work instead of a detailed critical reconstruction of the world of Israel or of the OT text.

Systems approaches. Several types of approaches fall under this rubric. One is to privilege a part of the OT. It is not uncommon to hear, for instance, of a "prophetic voice" in reference to a powerful reformer such as Martin Luther King Jr., or of a "prophetic church" or movement, also in connection with social issues. These people and organizations are identified with the posture of the prophetic literature, its denunciation of the oppression of the vulnerable, and the scathing critique of the powerful. Most often appeal is made to the eighth-century BCE prophets Isaiah, Micah, and Amos.

Historically, prominence has been given to the law (especially the Ten Commandments). This has been true especially in the Reformed tradition and is in part a legacy of John Calvin's Geneva and his *Institutes of the Christian Religion*. Emphasis on the law regularly is combined with the notion of the "cultural mandate," based on Gen. 1:26–28, that champions bringing all aspects of human life under the sovereign rule of God and his Christ. Examples that follow this trend include Oliver Cromwell's commonwealth in Britain and the Puritan experiment of the seventeenth century, and Abraham Kuyper's "sphere sovereignty" construct in the Netherlands in the late nineteenth and early twentieth centuries and his theological heirs who share a transformationalist view of Christian culture. A strain within Reformed circles that achieved some notoriety in the 1980s was a movement called "theonomy," which sought to apply OT law and its penalties to secular society (Bahnsen). This stress on the law as the substratum of OT ethical teaching also finds expression of a different sort in the work of Walter Kaiser. Grounded in exegesis of the Hebrew text and not in dogmatic theology, Kaiser believes that universal ethical principles can be extracted from individual laws through the "ladder of abstraction" and then applied today.

Christopher Wright also accentuates the law through a paradigm approach. A paradigm, on this view, is a transcendent set of beliefs and values that are the basis of a worldview and the organization of society. Wright postulates that there are three components of the OT's paradigm for ethics, and that these can be expressed in triangular fashion. The three angles are the theological (God), the social (Israel), and the economic (the land). This arrangement explains Israel's ethical lens for arranging and evaluating its socioeconomic life, but it can also be projected paradigmatically to encompass humanity and creation, typologically to NT parallels within the church, and eschatologically to the promise of a redeemed world at the end of time. The premier example of his method is the Jubilee (Lev. 25), which finds its echoes, respectively, in sinful humanity's life in rebellion against God in a fallen creation, in the generous sharing within the Christian community, and eventually in the restoration of all things in the new heavens and earth.

This approach makes several helpful contributions. First, Wright takes seriously the tangible realities dealt with by OT legislation, as well as the details of the laws themselves—their rationale and pragmatic impact. Those laws express God's lasting ethical demands in a way appropriate to that ancient society. Those demands necessarily would take a different shape in the legislation and socioeconomic structures suitable to other circumstances and eras. The law was a concrete paradigm that could not be duplicated, even as it was instructive to non-Israelite peoples (Deut. 4:5–8). Second, the paradigm concept and the interconnected triangles demonstrate a continuity of God's moral will across time. Third, Wright's proposal considers how the NT takes up and develops OT material. Thus, he is able to offer a comprehensive ethics that encompasses all of Scripture.

Literary and canonical approaches. These studies pay special attention to the final form, or canonical shape, of the OT. They often appeal to literary theory to probe the power of texts—that is, how texts impact the moral imagination of readers. Good literature, when engaged properly, can shape ethical views through plot, the depiction of scenes, the portrayal of characters, and by stirring emotions. Readers witness, and can vicariously enter into, the ethical decision-making taking place within a text and at some level participate in its motivations, struggles, and consequences. Literature also can attune readers to the darker side of reality within their own lives and societies, as well as present a world of possibilities for change. It can become a training ground, in other words, in ethical discernment and the nurturing of the virtues. Although these studies may employ research on backgrounds, the primary concern is the text itself.

The fact that the OT is both literature and Scripture adds immeasurable weight to this potentially powerful process of reading. Because it is literature with divine authority, reading of this text carries greater urgency. That Scripture is the text of a community adds further impetus to a virtue ethics orientation, because ideally the Christian church should provide the context for the requisite ethical growth and the presence of exemplars, who would echo and reinforce that reading. Literary approaches have been used with much profit in OT narratives (Perry) and the prophets (Brueggemann)—indeed, in the breadth of OT genres (Brown; Carroll R. and Lapsley).

Interest in the canon and its significance for theological interpretation and ethics has increased in the last few decades. The issues concerning the canon are many and diverse (Bartholomew et al.), but there are several ramifications for ethics that deserve mention. To begin with, the multiple ethical voices within the canon can be handled in several ways within moral discourse. Some trace trajectories in ethical views across the Scripture from the OT to the NT and see changes from restrictive formulations to more life-affirming possibilities. This tack has been applied to various topics, such as the institution of slavery, the role of women, and war (Swartley). The breadth and diversity of the canon also provide a comprehensive appreciation of moral issues. For instance, there are several dimensions of the OT's awareness and treatment of the problems of poverty: the law demonstrates the need for legislation related to debt, the provision of food, and fairness in legal proceedings; narratives depict the painful plight of the needy; the wisdom literature points out that some of the poor have only themselves to blame, while at the same time declaring their worth before God and encouraging the wise person to be charitable; the prophets rail against systemic injustice that perpetuates poverty and proclaim the hope of a future of plenty when poverty will be no more. Each slice of the canon contributes to a fuller ethical perspective, which would be diminished by concentrating on only one or a few of the pieces.

Second, emphasis on the canon reconnects ethics with Christian communities. This is a pragmatic observation in that this is the only text that the vast majority of Christians will ever read or know for moral discourse. A canonical focus has ecclesiastical importance as well. It places ethics within the long history of interpretation of the Scripture for ethics, and that history becomes a resource of ethical reflection. It also allows for ethics to be linked, as it was very emphatically in the OT, with liturgy, because the centrality of moral thinking within the canon can be incorporated into the worship of the church. Finally, a canonical approach to ethics will benefit greatly from its relationship to the resurgence of theological interpretation of Scripture. These creative studies are recovering readings of Scripture that have much to teach the church, discovering new insights from which OT ethics has much to gain.

Conclusion

The field of OT ethics is as fascinating as it is complex. Debates concerning its moral authority and about how best to appropriate it for ethics will continue,

even as they have for centuries. The fact that these discussions persist is proof
of the OT's enduring value for ethics.

Bibliography

Bahnsen, G. *Theonomy in Christian Ethics*. Rev. ed. P&R, 1984.

Bartholomew, C., et al. *Canon and Biblical Interpretation*. SHS 7. Zondervan, 2006.

Barton, J. *Understanding Old Testament Ethics*. Westminster John Knox, 2003.

Birch, B. *Let Justice Roll Down: The Old Testament, Ethics, and Christian Life*. Westminster John Knox, 1991.

Brown, W. *Character and Scripture: Moral Formation, Community, and Biblical Interpretation*. Eerdmans, 2002.

Brueggemann, W. *The Prophetic Imagination*. 2nd ed. Fortress, 2001.

Carroll R., M. D., and J. Lapsley, eds. *Character Ethics and the Old Testament: Moral Dimensions of Scripture*. Westminster John Knox, 2007.

Gottwald, N. "Theological Education as a Theory-Praxis Loop: Situating the Book of Joshua in a Cultural, Social Ethical, and Theological Matrix." Pages 107–18 in *The Bible in Ethics: The Second Sheffield Colloquium*, ed. J. Rogerson, M. Davies, and M. D. Carroll R. JSOTSup 207. Sheffield Academic Press, 1995.

Houston, W. *Contending for Justice: Ideologies and Theologies of Social Justice in the Old Testament*. LHBOTS 428. T&T Clark, 2006.

Kaiser, W., Jr. *Toward Old Testament Ethics*. Zondervan, 1983.

O'Brien, J. *Challenging Prophetic Metaphor: Theology and Ideology in the Prophets*. Westminster John Knox, 2008.

Perry, R. *Old Testament Story and Christian Ethics: The Rape of Dinah as a Case Study*. PBM. Paternoster, 2004.

Pleins, J. *The Social Visions of the Hebrew Bible: A Theological Introduction*. Westminster John Knox, 2001.

Rodd, C. *Glimpses of a Strange Land: Studies in Old Testament Ethics*. OTS. T&T Clark, 2001.

Rogerson, J. *Theory and Practice in Old Testament Ethics*. Ed. M. D. Carroll R. JSOTSup 405. T&T Clark, 2004.

Swartley, W. *Slavery, Sabbath, War, and Women: Case Issues in Biblical Interpretation*. Herald Press, 1983.

Weinfeld, M. *Social Justice in Ancient Israel and in the Ancient Near East*. Fortress, 1995.

Wright, C. *Old Testament Ethics for the People of God*. InterVarsity, 2004.

2

||||||||||||||||||||||||||||||||||||||||||||||||||||||||||||||||||||||||||||||||||||||||

PENTATEUCH

◆ Ethics of Torah ◆

Dennis T. Olson

The ethics of Torah is a predominantly Jewish ethical perspective shaped by obedience to biblical laws and commandments as an expression of Israel's covenant relationship with God. Torah ethics encompasses not only the biblical commandments but also the subsequent interpretations and clarifications of the biblical commandments and teachings in the writings of ancient and medieval rabbinic Judaism.

The Meaning of Torah

Understanding the ethics of Torah begins with a survey of the varied meanings of the Hebrew term *tôrâ* in the Bible and subsequent Jewish and Christian traditions. The term *tôrâ* often is translated as "law," but it may better be understood more broadly as "teaching" or "instruction." The word is used in the Bible and subsequent religious traditions to mean a variety of things. It can refer to specific priestly instructions concerning rituals ("This is the *tôrâ* [NRSV: "ritual"] of the burnt offering [Lev. 6:9]; "This is the *tôrâ* [NRSV: "law"] in cases of jealousy" [Num. 5:29–30]). More generally, *tôrâ* can refer to the whole body of instruction taught by priests (Ezek. 22:26; Mal. 2:6–9). Leviticus 10:11 uses the Hebrew verb *yārâ* ("teach"), which lies at the root of the noun *tôrâ*, to describe the teaching function of priests (see also Jer. 18:18; Ezek. 7:26). Also, *tôrâ* can designate the story or "teaching of the LORD" concerning God's deliverance of Israel from Egypt that is to be remembered in every generation in association with the Festival of Unleavened Bread and Passover (Exod. 13:9).

Torah is used most frequently in the Bible alongside other terms that signify the commandments and laws that Israel is to obey as an expression of its covenant relationship and obligations before God (Exod. 24:12; Lev. 26:46; Neh. 9:13–14; Ps. 78:10; Jer. 44:10). Priests are not the only teachers of *tôrâ*. The prophet Isaiah associates *tôrâ* with the words of the prophets and the servant of God (Isa. 8:16, 20; 42:4, 21; 51:4). The wisdom and instructions of the sages in biblical books such as Proverbs and Ecclesiastes that were derived as much from human observation and experience as divine revelation can also be called *tôrâ* (Prov. 1:8; 3:1; 4:2; 6:20, 23; 28:9; 31:26). This facilitated the blending of biblical laws and commandments with wisdom sayings and proverbs into a broad category of *tôrâ* as inclusive of the divine will and all normative traditions that ancient Israelites were called to follow or obey (Pss. 1:2; 19:7–10; 119:1).

Torah, Deuteronomy, and the Pentateuch

Another variation in the meaning of *tôrâ* arose with its use in the book of Deuteronomy, which is the only book of the Bible that refers to itself as *tôrâ* (1:5; 4:8, 44; 17:18–19; 27:3, 8, 26; 28:58, 61; 29:28; 31:9, 11, 12, 24; 32:46) and as "this book of the *tôrâ*" (29:20; 30:10; 31:26). Some have associated the meaning of *tôrâ* in this context with a law code in connection with the book's common name, "Deuteronomy." The name "Deuteronomy" comes from the Greek (Septuagint) translation of the Hebrew phrase in Deut. 17:18 that commands every king of Israel to study "a copy of this *tôrâ*." The Greek translates this phrase as *deuteronomion touto*, "this second [or 'repeated'] law," with the Hebrew *tôrâ* translated by the Greek word *nomos*, meaning "law." This Greek rendering of *tôrâ* as *nomos* and the subsequent Latin translation *lex* ("law") led to Christian misunderstandings that the Torah meant legalism.

Although *tôrâ* likely referred at some earlier stage in the composition of the book of Deuteronomy primarily to its central law code of Deut. 12–26, the term *tôrâ* came to be applied to the many different sections and genres included in the whole book of Deuteronomy (law codes, narratives, exhortations, poetry, blessings). The term *tôrâ* thus encompassed the whole set of diverse catechetical or formational literature within Deuteronomy that Moses is portrayed as writing down in "the book of the *tôrâ*" of Moses. This "book of the *tôrâ*" was to be regularly read out loud to the people, studied, and obeyed (Deut. 17:18; 31:9–13, 24–29). As the book of Deuteronomy was joined with the books of Genesis through Numbers, the term *tôrâ* was extended to include all five books of Genesis through Deuteronomy (the Pentateuch) as the central revelation of God to God's people Israel (Ezra 3:2; 7:6; Neh. 8:1–18; Mal. 4:22; Sirach, prologue; Matt. 5:17; Luke 24:44; Rom. 3:21).

Oral and Written Torah

The written Torah is portrayed in Scripture as mediated from God to Moses on Mount Sinai (Exod. 20:18–21; Deut. 5:22–33) and written down in the "book of the *tôrâ*" (Exod. 24:4; Deut. 31:9, 24–26). Rabbinic Judaism claimed that a second, orally transmitted Torah was given by God to Moses, which was transmitted orally from generation to generation alongside the written Torah. This oral Torah comprised an authoritative collection of rabbinic interpretations (legal halakah and mid-rashic haggadah) on biblical laws and texts that was not written down until after the destruction of the second temple, beginning with the Mishnah in the second century CE. Additional rabbinic commentaries known as the Gemara elaborated on the Mishnah and eventually were gathered together with the Mishnah into the Talmud by the sixth century CE. The Talmud itself exists in two versions: the Jerusalem Talmud and the more comprehensive Babylonian Talmud. The oral Torah involves a massive legal and ethical commentary tradition that is approximately fifty times larger than the biblical Torah of the Pentateuch.

The oral Torah fulfilled two functions. First, it addressed what seemed to be contradictory elements in the several diverse law codes and narratives of the Bible and sought to harmonize them. Second, the oral Torah filled in perceived gaps left by sometimes sparse biblical laws in order to facilitate the practical implementation of biblical commandments in everyday life and ritual practice. The need for ongoing interpretation of biblical law is suggested internally within the OT itself in the story of the daughters of Zelophehad when, far from Sinai, Moses consults with God about a legal quandary involving daughters inheriting their father's land (Num. 27:1–11). Law always required ongoing interpretation. Thus, "Torah" came to be used in various ways to designate the Pentateuch, the whole OT or Tanakh, the Bible and the

Talmud together, and, most broadly, the entire body of authoritative Jewish traditions and interpretations taken as a whole.

The written and oral Torah are the source for what Jewish tradition (most notably, the medieval Jewish interpreter Rambam) had specified as a definitive list of 613 commandments (*mitzvot*) that are rooted in Scripture and that form the primary obligations for people of Jewish faith. These commandments touch upon all facets of a person's life, including religious obligations, relationships with others, Sabbath observance, Jewish festivals, marriage and sexuality, judicial and financial matters, practices of ritual purity, and the like. Obedience to these many commandments, however, is animated overall by the spirit of the central Jewish confession of the Shema, which commands the people of God to "love the LORD your God with all your heart, and with all your soul, and with all your might" (Deut. 6:4–6). One of the most important obligations of Torah ethics and one of the most important expressions of the love of God is the recitation, study, and ongoing interpretation of the Torah itself as commanded in Deut. 6:6–9.

Before Creation: The Preexistent Torah and Israel's Holiness

Some Second Temple Jewish traditions (Sir. 24:23; Bar. 3:9–4:4) merged the concept of Torah with the image of personified "Woman Wisdom," which was the first of God's created works (Prov. 8:22–23, 29–31). In their view, the Torah was the architectural blueprint from which God constructed the world (*Gen. Rab.* 1:1). The wisdom of Torah was woven into the fabric of all creation with all of its blessings available to those who studied, discerned, and obeyed the teachings of Torah. Theoretically, Torah was available for all to obey. But practically, it was only with God's giving of the Torah to Moses and the chosen people at Mount Sinai that the Torah was revealed in all its fullness. Israel thereby took on the responsibility as God's chosen people to actualize the blessings of Torah through intentional obedience to God's precepts and teaching revealed at Mount Sinai. Israel was God's "priestly kingdom and holy nation" whose obedience to Torah mediated the blessings of God to the whole of God's world (Exod. 19:5–6).

The Sabbath

This view of the Torah as an embedded potentiality in creation that only became fully actualized through Israel's obedience of God's revealed Torah at Sinai was well illustrated in the rabbinic tradition with the Sabbath commandment. God rested on the seventh day of creation (Gen. 2:2–3) and thereby made the Sabbath holy long before the commandment to obey the Sabbath is given at Sinai (Exod. 20:8–11). No human observed the Sabbath rest until God gave the command to Israel in the manna story in Exod. 16 and in the Ten Commandments in Exod. 20:8–11. Only then did the Torah's law to observe Sabbath rest become actualized into the world of human activity and obedience.

Observance of the Sabbath became an especially important element of Jewish identity during and after the Babylonian exile with the destruction of the Jerusalem temple. Thus, the Priestly creation story in Gen. 1, often dated to the exilic or postexilic period in Israel's history (post–587 BCE), placed the Sabbath as the high point of its creation story on the last or seventh day of creation. Other ancient Near Eastern creation stories often concluded their accounts with the climactic building of a palace for the appointed king of the nation. In Gen. 1, the Sabbath becomes "a palace in time" that in some way replaced the physical temple and palace that had existed in space within the walls of Jerusalem (Heschel).

Along with the commanded observance of a Sabbath day of rest, the Torah contains a large number of commands to observe and celebrate numerous festivals throughout the year that commemorate events and stories essential to Jewish identity and remembrance. For example, detailed instructions for how each generation is to observe the Passover meal every year are woven into the narrative account of the rescue of the Israelite slaves from their bondage in Egypt (Exod. 12–13). All Israelites were also to attend three pilgrimage festivals in Jerusalem every year, according to Deut. 16:16 (the Festival of Unleavened Bread, the Festival of Weeks, the Festival of Booths). These festivals had roots in the agricultural calendar of harvest. The alignment of one's life and use of time with God's prescribed calendar is a means to become attuned to the sacred rhythms built into God's creational order (Fishbane).

Holiness and Purity, Justice and Righteousness

The theme of the holiness of Israel as specially set apart from the other nations was grounded in the holiness of Israel's God (Lev. 19:2). Israel's law was also unique and set apart, unique in its justice and wisdom in comparison to all the other laws of other nations (Deut. 4:5–8). The Priestly tradition in the Torah, especially the book of Leviticus, prescribes an extensive symbolic system of boundaries within creation intended to separate one kind from another. Whenever such boundaries were crossed, ritual impurity resulted. God and anything associated with God were holy and had to be kept away from the profane. For humans, a serious contamination arose when the boundary between death and life was crossed or blurred: a living person who touched a corpse became unclean (Lev. 22:4; Num. 5:2). Many other conditions involving food or bodily secretions or other improper mixtures could render a person impure. Uncleanness was a condition that every person encountered at numerous times in life, sometimes unavoidably so. For example, attending a parent's funeral is an obligation, and yet doing so made the mourner ritually impure by virtue of being in the same room as a corpse. Certain prescribed rituals could restore an impure person to a ritually pure state over time.

Intermingled among the laws of purity and impurity in the Torah are laws involving a whole range of human activities, realms, and endeavors, from business and commerce to marriage and sexuality, to care of the land, to kindness to one's neighbor, to punishment of sinners. Particularly in the Holiness Code of Lev. 19–26, the concern for holiness extends not just to priests but to all God's people and to the land of Israel as well. The Torah or Pentateuch of Genesis through Deuteronomy is a complex anthology of diverse narratives, multiple law codes, and other diverse traditions, all of which are understood in an ethics of Torah as resources for teaching and guiding the reader in the wide range of relationships, both human and divine.

Promise and Obedience

Christians have sometimes mistakenly characterized Jewish law or Torah observance as legalism. However, strong voices within the OT portray the obedience of the Torah as a joyful gift that offers freedom, delight, mercy, joy, and blessing to those who follow the ways of Torah (Ps. 119). At the definitive event of the giving of the Torah at Mount Sinai, the Ten Commandments make clear that Israel is already God's chosen and rescued people simply because God graciously loved Israel and selected Israel as God's "firstborn son" before the law was ever given (Exod. 4:22–23). God rescued Israel from Egyptian slavery before the first of the Ten Commandments was revealed (Exod. 20:2). Reaching back to Abraham and Sarah, God had promised to make of them a great nation, and God was committed to that covenantal promise (Gen. 12:1–3; 15:1–21; Exod. 3:7–10). The commandments of Sinai thus express the rules of the household of God to which Israel already belongs by the mercy and love of God, who chose Israel as a heritage (Deut. 32:8–9) from among all the other nations (Deut. 9:4–7). For the OT and Jewish Torah ethics, the promises of God and obedience to Torah exist in a synergistic bond of mutuality: "Promise leads to obedience, but obedience renews the promise" (Levenson 152).

Another dialectic emerges in the affirmation of the ability of God's people to obey the commandments of the Torah, on one hand, and the seeming inability of God's people to obey God's law, on the other. Thus, the commandments are "not too hard for you," and "the word is very near to you" (Deut. 30:11–14). At the same time, Moses says to Israel, "For I know well how rebellious and stubborn you are" (Deut. 31:26–29 [cf. Deut. 9:6–9; Josh. 24:19–22]). Israel is able to obey the law, and yet Israel often seems unable to be obedient. Therein lies one of the mysterious complexities of the divine-human relationship.

Bibliography

Fishbane, M. *Sacred Attunement: A Jewish Theology*. University of Chicago Press, 2008.

Harvey, W. "Torah." Pages 160–72 in *The Blackwell Reader in Judaism*, ed. J. Neusner and A. Avery-Peck. Blackwell, 2001.

Heschel, A. *The Sabbath: Its Meaning for Modern Man*. Farrar, Straus & Giroux, 1979.

Levenson, J. *Creation and the Persistence of Evil: The Jewish Drama of Divine Omnipotence*. Princeton University Press, 1994.

Neusner, J. *The Theology of the Oral Torah: Revealing the Justice of God*. McGill-Queen's University Press, 1999.

Ratheiser, G. *Mitzvoth Ethics and the Jewish Bible: The End of Old Testament Theology*. T&T Clark, 2007.

Silver, D. *Judaism and Ethics*. Ktav, 1970.

Sweeney, M. *Reading the Hebrew Bible after the Shoah: Engaging Holocaust Theology*. Fortress, 2008.

◆ Genesis ◆

Dennis T. Olson

The book of Genesis recounts stories of God's creation of the world and the beginning of human civilization (chaps. 1–11) as well as the stories of the first generations of the ancestors of ancient Israel as they interacted with other nations, beginning with Abraham and Sarah (chaps. 12–50). God elects the line of Abraham and Sarah as God's special people in order to bless them and so that they might be a blessing to "all the families of the earth" (12:1–3).

Human Community, the Image of God, and Human Vocation

In contrast to the polytheism of surrounding cultures, ancient Israel's story of origins portrays their one God as responsible for all creation (1:1). God creates humans as social beings in community, "male and female" (1:27). God

creates the humans "in the image of God" with a vocation to "have dominion" over the earth's creatures (1:26–28; 5:1–2), a royal dominion like Israel's
kings, who were obligated to care for the most vulnerable members of their
society (Ps. 72; Ezek. 34).

The "Goodness" of Creation and the Persistence of Evil

In the book of Genesis, God repeatedly pronounces the creation "good" and
"very good" (1:4, 10, 12, 18, 21, 25, 30), affirming the value of the material world.
The "goodness" of creation includes the gifts of Sabbath rest every seventh day
(2:1–3; cf. Exod. 20:8–11), sexuality and procreation among God's creatures
(1:22, 28; 2:21–25), and the provision of abundant food (1:30; 2:9, 16; 9:1–4).

To call the creation "good," however, does not indicate idealized perfection.
The primeval and watery forces of chaos and evil (1:2) are not eliminated in
creation but rather pushed to the margins though still present (1:6–7; 7:11).
Similarly, the serpent that tempts the humans (Eve and Adam, "who was with
her" [3:6]) to eat the forbidden fruit was a "wild animal that the LORD God
had made" (Gen. 3:1), not an evil or satanic deity invading God's creation
from the outside.

Moral Ambiguity in the Human Characters of Genesis

As with the creation generally, the main characters in Genesis are good but
also flawed. Adam and Eve are innocent and without shame (2:25), but eventually they disobey God (3:1–19). Noah is "righteous" before the flood (6:9),
but after the flood things go awry (9:20–27). Abraham passes God's dramatic
"test" of trust and obedience (22:1, 12), but he also endangers others in order
to protect his own safety (12:10–20; 20:1–18). Jacob was favored and blessed
by God (25:23; 28:13–15), yet he deceives, swindles, and cons his way to success and wealth (25:29–34; 27:1–40). Joseph graciously forgives his brothers
(45:4–15; 50:15–21), but he also enslaves starving Egyptians and confiscates
their land (47:13–26; see also 15:13; 16:3–6). Joseph's actions suggest that
the Hebrews are as morally capable of enslaving and oppressing others as the
Egyptians are (Exod. 1:8–14).

Violence and Glimpses of Reconciliation in Genesis

The use or threat of human violence spurred by jealousy or revenge is a constant
motif present throughout Genesis. Cain murders his brother, Abel (4:8–16).

Lamech threatens excessive revenge (4:23–24). Human violence is a primary reason for God sending the worldwide flood (6:11). After the flood, Nimrod arises as the world's first warrior (10:9). Abraham defends against the military attacks of four kings (14:1–24). The inhabitants of the city of Sodom threaten Lot and his visitors with rape and violence (19:1–11). Abraham nearly kills his own son Isaac (22:1–19). Esau resolves to kill his twin brother, Jacob, for stealing his birthright (27:41; 32:6–7). A "man" wrestles and injures Jacob (32:22–32). Jacob's sons kill all the male inhabitants of Shechem in retaliation for the rape of their sister Dinah (34:25–31). Joseph's jealous brothers conspire to kill him before changing their minds and selling him as a slave (37:18–19). Years later the brothers fear that the now-powerful Joseph will inflict violent revenge against them (45:3; 50:15–21). In the midst of these ongoing threats and acts of violence, Genesis also offers important glimpses of reconciliation and peacemaking amid conflict (12:10–20; 13:5–13; 20:1–18; 21:22–34; 26:1–11, 17–33; 30:1–21; 31:43–55; 33:4–11; 38:24–36; 45:1–15; 50:15–21).

Ethical Topics in Genesis

Numerous important and often controversial ethical issues arising from the Genesis narratives include the question of gender equality or inequality (1:27; 3:16; cf. Gal. 3:28; 1 Tim. 2:11–15), capital punishment in the case of human murder (4:8–16; 9:5–7), the historical use of Noah's curse of Ham and Canaan as justification for African American slavery (9:24–27), the debate over whether the cultural and linguistic diversity at the end of the Babel story was a gift or punishment (11:1–9), the question of whether the sin of Sodom was homosexuality or inhospitality and violence (19:1–11), and the justification of using violence in response to the rape of Dinah (34:1–31). Interpreters have long wrestled with the question of how a loving God could command a father, Abraham, to kill his own son, Isaac, as a test of faith and obedience (22:1–19). In light of the urgency of current ecological concerns and global warming, the creation narratives of chapters 1–2 provide an important resource for ongoing ethical and religious reflection on the care of the earth and the relationships of God, humans, and the environment.

Bibliography

Fretheim, T. "Genesis." Pages 317–674 in vol. 1 of *The New Interpreter's Bible*, ed. Leander Keck. Abingdon, 1994.

Habel, N., and S. Wurst, eds. *The Earth Story in Genesis*. Pilgrim Press, 2000.

Levenson, J. *Creation and the Persistence of Evil: The Jewish Drama of Divine Omnipotence*. Princeton University Press, 1994.

———. *The Death and Resurrection of the Beloved Son: The Transformation of Child Sacrifice in Judaism and Christianity*. Yale University Press, 1993.

Olson, D. "Untying the Knot? Masculinity, Violence, and the Creation-Fall Story of Genesis 2–4." Pages 73–86 in *Engaging the Bible in a Gendered World: Essays in Honor of Katharine Doob Sakenfeld*, ed. C. Pressler and L. Day. Westminster John Knox, 2006.

Trible, P. *God and the Rhetoric of Sexuality*. OBT. Fortress, 1978.

♦ Exodus ♦

Dennis T. Olson

The book of Exodus recounts God's liberation of the Israelites from slavery and their departure from Egypt (chaps. 1–15), the challenges of the journey through the wilderness (chaps. 16–18), the establishment of a special covenant relationship between God and Israel at Mount Sinai (chaps. 19–24), the breaking and restoring of the covenant in the incident of the golden calf (chaps. 32–34), and the building of the tabernacle as a visible sign of God's holy presence in the midst of the Israelite community (chaps. 25–31; 35–40).

Ethical Issues in Exodus 1–15

Women and Civil Disobedience

Exodus begins with the Bible's first instance of peaceful civil disobedience against an oppressive empire. The two Hebrew midwives refuse to carry out Pharaoh's orders to kill the male babies of the enslaved Hebrew minority community (1:8–22). Women—including Pharaoh's daughter, who disobeys her own father's decrees (2:1–10)—also figure prominently in rescuing the baby Moses.

The Use of Violence for the Sake of Social Justice?

Moses secretly kills an Egyptian supervisor who was beating a Hebrew slave (2:11–15). Was Moses justified in this act of violence for the sake of social justice? Both Jewish and Christian interpreters have differed widely in answering that question. The biblical text itself does not render a clear verdict one way or the other, inviting readers to contemplate the complex ethical issues involved.

The Ten Plagues: Justice and Ecology

God sends a series of ten plagues upon the Egyptians in an effort to persuade Pharaoh to let the Israelites go (chaps. 7–13). These anticreational plagues that disturb the natural order and balance of nature may be understood as ecological disasters that are the consequences of Pharaoh's human injustice, which disturbs the moral order of the cosmos (Fretheim 105–11).

The Hardening of Pharaoh's Heart: Human Freedom and Divine Determinism

Exodus brings the theme of God's "hardening Pharaoh's heart" (9:12; 10:1, 20, 27; 11:10; 14:4, 8) together with other texts that speak of Pharaoh's "hardening" his own heart (7:22; 8:32; 9:34). The motif of the hardening of the heart appears to hold human free will and divine determinism together in complex interplay. But at some point later in the plague sequence, Pharaoh's sin becomes so engrained that he reaches a point of no return. It is then that God hardens Pharaoh's heart.

God's Liberation of the Poor or of Israel?

The story of God's liberation of slaves living under oppressive conditions in Egypt has been a defining narrative for many exponents of liberation theology and postcolonial criticism of the Bible. The exodus story, they argue, reflects the dynamics of oppressive empires and God's preferential option for the poor. Others argue that the biblical form of the exodus story is primarily not about God's preference for the poor in general but rather for the people of Israel in particular. Yet Israel's laws do refer to Israel's experience in Egypt as a motivation for justice and generosity to slaves, the poor, resident aliens, and other marginalized members of the society (22:21; 23:9; Deut. 15:12–15).

The Ten Commandments—Exodus 20:1–17

The centerpiece of the covenant on Mount Sinai is the Decalogue, or Ten Commandments. The first and most important commandment demands singular loyalty: "You shall have no other gods before me" (20:3). This is followed by a ban on all graven images or idols (20:4–6), which Israel would soon disobey in the incident of the golden calf (32:1–24). Other commandments prohibit the misuse of God's name, require the observance of a Sabbath day of rest every seven days, and obligate children to honor their parents. The commandments conclude by prohibiting murder, adultery, stealing, bearing false witness against a neighbor, and coveting what belongs to a neighbor (20:7–17). The commandments hold together obligations to God with obligations to humans and also to nonhuman creation (20:10).

The Covenant Code—Exodus 20:22–23:19

Most scholars argue that these laws are some of the oldest laws of the Bible. They resemble other law codes of the ancient Near East in their form of case law with conditional statements followed by consequences or penalties. These laws cover a wide range of quite specific circumstances within an ancient society. Since they follow immediately after the more generalized Ten Commandments, the Covenant Code functions as an illustrative exposition of how the Ten Commandments might be applied in specific rulings. The juxtaposition of the Decalogue and the Covenant Code signals the need for ongoing legal and ethical interpretation and application to specific contexts.

The Golden Calf—Exodus 32–34

Israel's first great sin is to make and worship a golden calf while Moses is away on top of Mount Sinai with God. The disobedience is so severe that God initially plans to destroy all Israel (32:10). However, Moses successfully intercedes with God so that God does not completely destroy the Israelites (32:11–14). Moses also convinces God to reveal something deeper about the divine character and goodness that has not been seen before. In the process, God reveals his name and character, shown to be grounded much more in his love, faithfulness, mercy, and forgiveness (34:6–7) than previous presentations of God's name and character in Exodus indicate (see 3:13–16; 20:5–6; 23:20–21). However, obedience to God's newly reformulated laws continues to be required, and consequences remain in effect for acts of disobedience (34:7, 10–28).

Bibliography

Fretheim, T. *Exodus*. IBC. Westminster John Knox, 1991.

Levenson, J. "Exodus and Liberation." *HBT* 13 (1991): 134–74.

Meyers, C. *Exodus*. NCamBC. Cambridge University Press, 2005.

Olson, D. "The Jagged Cliffs of Mount Sinai: A Theological Reading of the Book of the Covenant (Exod. 20:22–23:19)." *Int* 50 (1996): 251–63.

———. "Violence for the Sake of Social Justice? Narrative, Ethics, and Indeterminacy in Exodus 2:11–15." Pages 138–48 in *The Meanings We Choose: Hermeneutical*

Ethics, Indeterminacy and the Conflict of Interpretations, ed. C. Cosgrove. JSOTSup 411. T&T Clark International, 2004.

Pixley, G., and C. Boff. "A Latin American Perspective: The Option for the Poor in the Old Testament." Pages 207–16 in *Voices from the Margin: Interpreting the Bible in the Third World*, ed. R. Sugirtharajah. Orbis, 2006.

◆ Leviticus ◆

Robin C. McCall

The third book of the Pentateuch, Leviticus, is comprised of two major sections. The first section (chaps. 1–16) is largely concerned with ritual instructions and laws having to do with ancient Israel's cultic practices, and as such, it clearly reflects the influence of writers and redactors affiliated with the Priestly (P) tradition. The second section (chaps. 17–26) is concerned less with ritual than with moral and ethical behavior in the community of Israel. This block of texts is collectively known as the Holiness Code, and it seems to reflect a later Priestly perspective than that found in the first section of Leviticus. Because the Holiness Code's focus is explicitly on ethics in ancient Israel, it is treated in a separate entry in this dictionary. Leviticus 27 is included by many scholars as a part of the Holiness Code, whereas others see it as a separate, concluding chapter to the book.

The P material in Lev. 1–16 does not share the Holiness Code's concern that holiness be "democratized" to the whole community of Israel. Indeed, James Watts has recently suggested that Leviticus was preserved in Israel primarily as an apology for the hegemony of the Aaronide priesthood. In the P material, the maintenance of distinctions between holy and common, clean and unclean, as well as the teaching of Torah, are the purview of Israel's priests (Lev. 10:10–11). Ethics in the P material (and often in the Holiness Code) is not explicit, but rather implicit in the worldview of the Israelite cult.

Ritual Ethics

William Brown has suggested that in ancient Israel, morality and ethics were inseparable from cosmology. We can discern some key aspects of the priestly worldview inherent in Leviticus from other P texts in the Pentateuch. Genesis 1 makes it clear that the maintenance of proper boundaries within the created order is paramount for the priests: God creates, as it were, biospheres on days 1–3, and days 4–6 parallel them as the biospheres are filled with appropriate entities (the ruling lights, plants, animals, humans). Rhythmic cycles of times and seasons are established as integral to the proper functioning of the cosmos. Space too was sacred, as the detailed instructions for the building of the tabernacle (Exod. 25–27) illustrate. Breaches of the created order and its rhythms risk allowing the ingress of the "formless void" (*tōhû wābōhû* [Gen. 1:2]) of chaos that God bounded and organized at creation. Leviticus encodes this "ethos of the cosmos" in a kind of ritual ethics, wherein the regular practice of rituals allows the practitioner to literally embody the priestly worldview by understanding one's own body and life as a microcosm of the created order.

It was the job of the Israelite priesthood to recognize and maintain the proper boundaries of the created order so that Yahweh might continually reside in Israel's midst, enthroned within the holy of holies, the most sacred sector of the sanctuary (Lev. 16:2). The departure of Yahweh would mean the breakdown of the created order, so the maintenance of the sanctuary's holiness was of supreme importance. In the priestly worldview, people, places, things, and times could be either holy or common and either ritually clean or unclean, and these statuses were "contagious" to each other. That which was holy must be kept separate from that which was either common or ritually unclean, lest they pollute each other in catastrophic ways (see Lev. 10:1–2; Num. 16:35; 1 Chr. 13:9–10).

Yet the living of everyday life necessitates that people and things move back and forth between cleanness and uncleanness, holiness and commonness. Ordained priests (see Lev. 8–9) mediated between God and the people by employing rituals to facilitate the safe transition between the states of holy/common and clean/unclean. Jacob Milgrom has suggested that "life versus death" is the governing paradigm whereby the priests determined cleanness versus uncleanness. Thus, Leviticus attempts to delineate clearly when one is in danger of proximity to death, such as the loss of life force (e.g., menses [Lev. 12], semen [Lev. 15]), or contact with corruption (e.g., corpses [Lev. 22:4], leprosy [Lev. 13:1–46], or rot in fibers or walls [Lev. 13:47–59; 14:33–38]), and then to provide a ritual pathway back to the safety of life. The dietary laws in Lev. 11 are an effort to restrict humans' killing for food to a small selection of species and give the necessary death a ritualized context intended to show reverence for the animal's life—that is, its blood (Lev. 17:11, 14)—which belongs to God. Some rituals were designed to cleanse an impure person or thing (e.g., Lev. 4:1–5:13) or provide a means by which one could make reparation to God for sin (e.g., Lev. 5:14–6:7 [MT 5:14–26]). The ritual for Yom Kippur (Lev. 16) provides a means by which accreted sins within the community can be removed from the sanctuary, ensuring that it remains habitable for Yahweh.

Still other rituals mark the recognition of sacred times and seasons (Lev. 23), and some seem intended solely for positive interaction between an individual and Yahweh (e.g., Lev. 3).

Leviticus in the Present Day

The ethical significance of Leviticus today necessitates an understanding of the book's motivations more than rote observation of its laws and rituals. In practical terms, it is impossible today to live by many of the laws and rituals found in Leviticus. The sanctuary that Leviticus presupposes as God's earthly dwelling place is no longer extant. The blood sacrifice was done in the service of maintaining a harmonious world order, whereas to us, the two concepts stand in direct conflict. The Israelite priests' tasks of maintaining people and things within strict categories may lead to isolation or prejudice in today's world. Yet the often arcane laws and rituals of Leviticus were intended to provide guidelines for the care of the natural world, to strengthen interpersonal relationships within the Israelite community, and to allow for regular interaction with God. We humans need rituals to help us frame our lives in meaningful ways: bar/bat mitzvahs, baptisms, weddings, and funerals are our versions of Leviticus's rites of passage. There is much of value, even for those who do not follow a strict kosher diet, in the mindfulness of our fellow creatures' lives inherent in the laws of *kashrut*. The priests' goal of keeping the world as closely aligned as possible with God's "very good" creation (Gen. 1:31) is still a worthy one, especially in light of present-day concern for our beleaguered environment. A constant awareness of God's presence in Israel's midst is the ontological foundation of Leviticus's ritual and ethical views; people of faith today can share this foundation, even if our praxis is modified.

Bibliography

Balentine, S. *Leviticus*. IBC. John Knox, 2002.

Brown, W. *The Ethos of the Cosmos*. Eerdmans, 1999.

Grabbe, L. *Leviticus*. OTG. Sheffield Academic Press, 1993.

Milgrom, J. *Leviticus*. 3 vols. AB 3, 3A, 3B. Doubleday, 1991–2001.

———. *Leviticus: A Book of Ritual and Ethics*. CC. Fortress, 2004.

Nelson, R. *Raising Up a Faithful Priest: Community and Priesthood in Biblical Theology*. Westminster John Knox, 1993.

Watts, J. *Ritual and Rhetoric in Leviticus: From Sacrifice to Scripture*. Cambridge University Press, 2007.

◆ Holiness Code ◆

Robin C. McCall

"Holiness Code" is a designation for the collection of laws in Lev. 17–26. These laws are the most definitive texts of the "Holiness School," which, while clearly related to the material of the Pentateuch associated with the Israelite priesthood (called "P"), are now widely agreed to postdate and supplement the P material. Despite this general agreement, the precise dating of the Holiness Code remains disputed. Many scholars argue that it comes from a period prior to the Babylonian exile (586 BCE), while others contend that the Holiness School material is exilic or even, in part, postexilic.

The Holiness Code's Relevance to Contemporary Issues

The rigid laws found in the Holiness Code often strike contemporary readers as pedantic and arcane. A closer reading, however, reveals that its laws touch on some of the biggest social and ethical issues of our time. In the context of ongoing debates about marriage and adoption rights for gay and lesbian couples, the code's injunction against male homosexuality (Lev. 18:22; cf. 20:13) may be its most oft-cited law. Agricultural laws (e.g., Lev. 19:23; 25:2–7) and the code's strong interest in the effects of human sinfulness on the land (Lev. 18:28; 20:22; 25:18–19) invite reflection on the ethics of how we treat the earth. Laws designed to provide for the poor and disenfranchised (e.g., Lev. 23:22; 25) have direct implications for the ever-growing problems associated with socioeconomic disparity around the world today. And the establishment of the Year of Jubilee—that is, every fiftieth year, in which God specifies that Israel's fields are to lie fallow, land that has been sold is to revert to its hereditary owner, and enslaved Israelites are to be granted manumission (cf. Lev. 25:10–55)—has given rise to contemporary social efforts such as the ONE campaign, an organization devoted to debt relief, healthcare, and the alleviation of extreme poverty in developing nations.

Democratized and Relational Holiness

The name "Holiness Code" derives from Lev. 19:2, which serves as the ontological motivation for the laws therein: "Speak to all the congregation of the people of Israel and say to them: 'You shall be holy, for I the LORD your God am holy.'" Although it is never explicitly defined by the biblical text, holiness has its source in Yahweh, and Yahweh bestows it upon people (Lev. 21:8), space, time, and things (e.g., Lev. 21:23; 22:15–16). Baruch Levine has suggested that holiness is not so much Yahweh's nature as it is a description of the ways Yahweh acts, in justice and righteousness. Also, because God is holy, God is set apart from that which is common. Israel's priests are expected to imitate God's holiness. This view of holiness is common to both the P material of the Pentateuch and the Holiness School.

The Holiness Code makes clear by the nature of its laws that holiness is realized in active terms, through one's ethics and behavior. In this way, the very name of the collection implies that ethics—specifically, the establishment of a community-wide ethic based on the unique worldview of the Holiness School—is the Holiness Code's central concern. The instructions given by God in these laws relate to the holiness of Israel in all aspects of life: in its interactions with God, within the community, with other nations, with the land itself, and even with objects, times, and spaces. The fundamental goal of the laws is the establishment of a community that is holy, even more than the sanctification of individuals, but neither can exist apart from the other.

The Holiness Code departs from the earlier Priestly material of Leviticus and the rest of the Pentateuch by requiring the aforementioned combination of ethical behavior and distinctness not merely of Israel's priests, but of all the people of Israel. Robert Kugler has referred to this trend within the texts of the Holiness School as the "democratization" of holiness, and nowhere is it more evident than in the Holiness Code. The Israelites' emulation of God's holiness is intended to mark them as uniquely God's own. The Holiness Code goes further than P too by suggesting that Israel's actions have, in turn, a consecrating effect on God (Lev. 22:32); in other words, there is a reciprocal quality to holiness. Moreover, in imitating God's holiness, Israel is to serve as an example for its neighbors to follow, even as it maintains the careful boundaries that delineate holy from common. In these ways, "holiness" must be understood as a relational concept.

The confluence of ritual and moral law in the Holiness Code is one of its most distinctive qualities. The P material of Leviticus is almost wholly concerned with the proper practice of ritual requirements in Israel. Failure to follow proper ritual procedures results in a person or thing becoming ritually impure—a state that may be contagious to other people or things, and that renders the impure person or thing dangerously unfit to be in the presence of holiness. In the Holiness Code, though, a person may also contract impurity for transgressing a moral injunction. But the resulting impurity is also moral as well as ritual; it carries with it a stigma of sinfulness that is absent in ritual impurity. Moreover, whereas ritual impurity can be removed by ritual means, such as washing (e.g., Lev. 15:5–8), moral impurity can be removed only by punishment (e.g., Lev. 20:2–5) or by acts of atonement (e.g., Lev. 19:20–22).

Exclusivism and the Threat of Exile

The steady buildup of moral impurity in the community defiles not only the people but also the sanctuary (Lev. 20:3) and the land (Lev. 18:28). At the time of the Holiness Code's inception, Israel was keenly aware of the real threat of exile. Israel had experienced it at the hands of Assyria, and, depending on the dating of the code to which one subscribes, the same threat was either imminent or fully present from Babylon. It is hardly surprising that the code's most severe punishment for breaking many of its laws is not death, but *karet*: exile from the community (the punishment occurs thirteen times [e.g., Lev. 17:10; 18:29; 20:3]). To be "cut off" (Heb. *kārat*) from the community threatens not just the offender's life but also the extinction of his or her whole family line, so that the offender's existence will not even be remembered once he or she is dead. Therefore, the implied punishment of national exile in Lev. 20:22 ("You shall keep all my statutes and all my ordinances, and observe them, so that the land to which I bring you to settle in may not vomit you out" [cf. Lev. 18:26–28]) carries with it the very real threat of national extinction. The establishment and preservation of a clear national identity for Israel in the face of that threat, then, is also a principal aim of the Holiness Code. Israel's social and historical circumstances demanded that a definition of holiness include a strong measure of exclusivism. This does not mean that Israel was isolated from its ancient Near Eastern neighbors; they interacted with their neighbors and shared many aspects of culture with the nations around them. But the Holiness Code seeks to develop and codify Israel's theology and ethics in ways that are uniquely Israelite, distinctively different from those of their neighbors.

For most (though not all) modern-day readers, the threat of community dissolution is not as immediate as it was for Israel at the time the Holiness Code was established. Indeed, maintaining the goal of strict distinctness may well pose problems for communities of faith that seek instead to reach out to their neighbors. In part because so many of the Holiness Code's laws are presented in incontrovertible terms, there is a temptation to treat them, or at least some of them, as simple moral absolutes. But to separate the injunctions of the Holiness Code from, first, the culture and circumstances that birthed them and, second, the unique theological worldview that undergirds them is to strip them of their meaning and purpose. It is true that some of the Holiness Code's laws, such as the laws prohibiting incest in Lev. 18, dovetail with the social mores of our time. But others do not. For instance, the injunction in Lev. 19:19 against wearing clothing made out of two different materials is not widely practiced, and may even seem absurd, in the modern era. And yet the principles underlying both these types of laws are identical. Recognizing and practicing careful divisions in everyday life is necessary, in the Holiness worldview, in order to maintain safe distinctions between holy and common, and between Israel and its environs. Today, however, while the first distinction is laudable, the second may be problematic. The Holiness Code invites contemporary readers to reflect on the meaning of holiness and how it is to be manifested, ethically and morally, within their own communities of faith. When dealing with the specific laws of the Holiness Code today, we must consider the extent to which an ethic of exclusivism figures into our community's definition of holiness.

Bibliography

Bono [Paul David Hewson]. Keynote address at the 54th National Prayer Breakfast, February 2, 2006: http://www.americanrhetoric.com/speeches/bononationalprayer breakfast.htm.

Joostens, J. *People and Land in the Holiness Code: An Exegetical Study of the Ideational Framework of the Law in Leviticus 17–26.* VTSup 67. Brill, 1996.

Klawans, J. *Impurity and Sin in Ancient Judaism.* Oxford University Press, 2000.

Knohl, I. *The Sanctuary of Silence: The Priestly Torah and the Holiness School.* Fortress, 1995.

Kugler, R. "Holiness, Purity, the Body, and Society: The Evidence for Theological Conflict in Leviticus." *JSOT* 76 (1997): 3–27.

Levine, B. *Leviticus.* JPSTC. Jewish Publication Society, 1989.

Milgrom, J. *Leviticus.* 3 vols. AB 3, 3A, 3B. Doubleday, 1991–2001.

———. *Leviticus: A Book of Ritual and Ethics.* CC. Fortress, 2004.

Wright, D. "Holiness in Leviticus and Beyond: Differing Perspectives." *Int* 53 (1999): 351–64.

◆ Numbers ◆

Dennis T. Olson

The book of Numbers, the fourth book of the OT, derives its name from the two census lists that number the people in each of the twelve tribes of Israel during their wilderness journey to the promised land of Canaan (chaps. 1; 26). These two census lists mark two different generations of Israelites, one old and rebellious and the other new and hopeful. Numbers moves from Israel's obedient preparations for the march from Mount Sinai to Canaan (chaps. 1–10), to an abrupt series of increasingly serious rebellions against God and Moses by the old generation (chaps. 11–20), to glimpses of hope in the midst of the dying out of the old generation (chaps. 21–25), to the rise of a new generation standing with hope on the edge of the promised land (chaps. 26–36).

Israel's Second Great Sin: Refusing God's Gift of the Land

Israel's idolatrous worship of the golden calf in Exod. 32 was its first great sin in its wilderness journey from Egypt to Canaan. Israel's second great sin is presented in the spy story in Num. 13–14. The Israelites refuse to accept God's gift of the land of Canaan because they fear the power and size of the Canaanite enemy. God's reaction is initially a plan to destroy all the Israelites, but then God relents in response to Moses' intercession and appeal to God's merciful character (14:10–19).

However, severe consequences also result from Israel's lack of trust in God. God resolves that the old wilderness generation will have to wander in the wilderness for an additional thirty-eight years until they all die out in the wilderness. Only their children as a new generation of Israelites will be allowed to enter into the land of Canaan (14:20–35).

Challenging Ethical Issues in Numbers

The book of Numbers contains one of the most blatant examples of patriarchy and gender inequality in the Bible: the legal case of a wife suspected of adultery (5:11–31). The law allows a husband who suspects his wife of adultery to bring that charge against her even though he has no evidence. The wife is subjected to a humiliating public ritual involving a trial of ordeal. The wife, however, has no right to bring a similar charge against her husband.

Another ethically challenging text in Numbers is the story of the priest Phinehas, who kills a Midianite woman and Israelite man as punishment for Israel's entanglement with Midianite women and the worship of their foreign gods (25:1–18). Later in Numbers, God commands Israel to engage in a holy war against the Midianites because they tempted Israel away from the worship of Israel's God (31:1–54). These texts have been used in the history of biblical interpretation to legitimate the use of violence and holy war as a weapon of religious intolerance.

Positive Ethical Resources in Numbers

The book of Numbers also provides some positive ethical resources for the community of faith. God's ultimate will for his people is expressed by the benediction or blessing that God commands the priests to place upon the people of Israel (6:22–27).

The two narratives of chapter 11 and chapter 12 affirm the wisdom of the wide distribution of authority and leadership among many parts of the community (see 11:16–30) and, at the same time, the importance of maintaining Moses' authority as a central leader. The two stories together suggest the wisdom of a dialogical balance between distributed and centralized authority in the structure of community governance.

The story of the foreign prophet Balaam in chapters 22–24 affirms God's ability to work through and accomplish his purposes through a foreign religious leader such as Balaam. God's sovereignty is clear as he unravels the plans of the Moabite king to curse Israel and instead ensures the blessing of Israel by the prophet Balaam.

The case of the five daughters of Zelophehad in chapters 27 and 36 illustrates the need for ongoing reinterpretation of earlier laws and traditions in the face of new contexts and circumstances.

Bibliography

Bach, A. "Good to the Last Drop: Viewing the Sotah (Num. 5.11–31) as the Glass Half Empty and Wondering How to View It Half Full." Pages 26–54 in *The New Literary Criticism and the Hebrew Bible*, ed. J. Exum and D. Clines. JSOTSup 143. JSOT Press, 1993.

Collins, J. "The Zeal of Phinehas: The Bible and the Legitimation of Violence." *JBL* 122 (2003): 3–21.

Olson, D. *Numbers*. IBC. Westminster John Knox, 1996.

Sakenfeld, K. "In the Wilderness, Awaiting the Promised Land: The Daughters of Zelophehad and Feminist Interpretation." *PSB* 9 (1988): 179–96.

♦ Deuteronomy ♦

Dennis T. Olson

The book of Deuteronomy (meaning "a copy of the law" or "second law," from the Greek translation of 17:18) is presented as the last set of instructional sermons from ancient Israel's elderly leader Moses to a new generation

of Israelites who are at the border preparing to enter the promised land of
Canaan.

Core Ethical Assumptions in Deuteronomy

Many parts of Deuteronomy repeat or reinterpret earlier laws and narratives in
the Pentateuch, especially the laws of the Covenant Code in Exod. 20:22–23:19.
About 50 percent of the Covenant Code laws in Exodus are repeated with
small but significant variations in Deuteronomy. The book of Deuteronomy
often adds its unique theological stamp to this material, shaped especially by
Deuteronomy's emphasis on "oneness": (1) Israel's relational loyalty to one
God alone; (2) the identity of Israel as one people set apart from the nations;
(3) the requirement of one centralized place of worship to which all Israel
gathers in festivals; (4) adherence to one Torah, which all Israel is called to obey.

Deuteronomy's central confession is the Shema (from the first word of the
Hebrew text, meaning "hear"): "Hear, O Israel: the LORD is our God, the
LORD alone," followed by the command "You shall love the LORD your God
with all your heart, and with all your soul, and with all your might" (Deut.
6:4–5). Jesus coupled this verse with Lev. 19:18 to describe the Great Commandments, which summarize all the law of Moses (Matt. 22:36–40; Mark
12:28–34; Luke 10:25–28).

Scholars have associated Deuteronomy's requirement for the centralization
of worship in ancient Israel with the reforms of King Hezekiah and King
Josiah, who cleansed the Jerusalem temple and destroyed worship sites and
altars outside Jerusalem (2 Kgs. 18:3–6, 22; 22–23). These royal reforms seem
to coincide with Deuteronomy's decree that all offerings of grain and animal
sacrifices and all celebrations of holy festivals are to be held in the one "place
which the LORD your God will choose" (Deut. 12:5, 13, 18, 26; 14:23; 15:20;
16:6, 11, 15–16; 17:10; 31:11). Although Deuteronomy centralizes sacrifice
and worship in one place, it maintains that God's sovereignty and concern for
holiness extend to the whole land and to every family within Israel.

Deuteronomy refers to itself frequently as "the book of the *tôrâ*" (1:5; 4:8,
44; 17:18–19; 27:3, 8, 26; 28:58, 61; 29:20, 28; 30:10; 31:9, 11–12, 24; 32:46).
Some have translated *tôrâ* for Deuteronomy as referring to the polity or constitution of the people of Israel. Its emphasis on law, obedience, and allegiance
to God alone suggests its role as a core legal foundation for the identity and
organization of Israel as the people of God. Others have also noted the strong
educational or instructional meaning associated with the Hebrew term *tôrâ*
along with the frequent references in Deuteronomy to members of an older

generation teaching a new generation (4:1, 5, 10, 14; 5:31; 6:1; 11:19; 31:19; 32:2; 33:10). Thus, Deuteronomy as *tôrâ* may be understood as a program of ethical, political, and theological catechesis achieved through a variety of formational strategies: narratives (chaps. 1; 9), laws (6:1; 12–26), rituals (chaps. 16; 26), poetic song (31:19; 32), oral recitation (31:9–13), and exemplary models of character (Moses in chap. 34).

Deuteronomy and the Sabbath

The Sabbath commandment in 5:12–15 and its further explication in the sabbath laws of 14:22–16:17 underscore the strong connection between the worship of God and concern for care and justice for the vulnerable members of the community. Regular worship of God on weekly Sabbaths and annual festivals is combined with the sharing of offerings with the most vulnerable members of the community (the poor, widows, orphans, landless Levites). The Sabbath laws also include the cancellation of all debts every seven years and the required freeing of slaves after seven years of service (15:1–6, 12–18). The Sabbath laws also hold in creative tension the ideal that there will "be no one in need among you" (15:4) with the realism that "there will never cease to be some in need on the earth" (15:11). This tension creates the need for structural provisions for the periodic cancellation of debts as well as more spontaneous and voluntary acts of charity and support to the poor (15:7–11).

Other Ethical Resources

Deuteronomy's laws also set in motion creative tensions between proper respect for authority (5:16) and provisions that ensure that those in leadership remain worthy of respect and authority (16:18–18:22). These same laws also prescribe a delicate balance between centralized leadership and distributed authority (see also 1:9–18). Ecological concern for the care of animals and vegetative life is evident in several laws (5:14; 20:19–20; 22:1–4, 6–7). Deuteronomy uses the metaphor of "circumcising the foreskin of the heart" to hold together the need for humans to strive to be obedient (10:16) and the promise that God will work within humans to create obedience (30:6).

One of the most ethically challenging texts in Deuteronomy is the law of holy war in 20:1–20, which commands the Israelites to kill "everything that breathes" (v. 16) when they enter the land of Canaan (see Josh. 6:21). In the end, however, Israel was unable or unwilling to carry out the law, as Israel allowed some Canaanites to remain alive in the land (Rahab [Josh. 2; 6]; the

Gibeonites [Josh. 9; Judg. 1:21, 27–36]). Thus, God abandoned the strategy of holy war and allowed the Canaanites to remain in the land as a perpetual test of Israel's obedience in the face of the ongoing temptation to worship other gods (Judg. 2:19–23; 3:1–5).

Bibliography

Hamilton, J. *Social Justice and Deuteronomy: The Case of Deuteronomy 15*. SBLDS 136. Scholars Press, 1992.

Levinson, B. *Deuteronomy and the Hermeneutics of Legal Innovation*. Oxford University Press, 1997.

McDonald, N. *Deuteronomy and the Meaning of "Monotheism."* FAT 2/1. Mohr Siebeck, 2003.

Millar, J. *Now Choose Life: Theology and Ethics in Deuteronomy*. Eerdmans, 1998.

Miller, P. *Deuteronomy*. IBC. Westminster John Knox, 1990.

Olson, D. *Deuteronomy and the Death of Moses: A Theological Reading*. Fortress, 1994.

Vogt, P. *Deuteronomic Theology and the Significance of Torah: A Reappraisal*. Eisenbrauns, 2006.

3

⥾⥾⥾

HISTORICAL BOOKS

◆ Ethics of Deuteronomistic History ◆

Stephen B. Chapman

The books of the Former Prophets (Joshua, Judges, 1–2 Samuel, 1–2 Kings) have become known by this title in accordance with an influential theory proposed by German OT scholar Martin Noth. Noth viewed the Former Prophets, together with Deuteronomy, as composing a unified, large-scale literary corpus whose primary purpose was to provide an explanation for Israel's sixth-century defeat and exile. With this goal in mind, a single editor-like exilic author had combined numerous preexistent traditions. The author, commonly referred to as the Deuteronomist, had creatively shaped the telling of this history (DtrH), highlighting certain aspects and glossing over others, dividing it into discrete periods and inserting into its continuous narrative a number of salvation-historical speeches by various characters or the narrator himself (Josh. 1:1–9; 12:1–6; 23:1–16; Judg. 2:11–3:6; 1 Sam. 12:1–15; 1 Kgs. 8:14–53; 2 Kgs. 17:7–23). These speeches cumulatively tracked the action of the overarching story and reinforced the author's theological perspective.

Despite some objections, subsequent scholarship at first upheld Noth's thesis strongly, although gradually with the proviso that the DtrH had instead been created in stages and by more than one hand. Building on the work of Rudolf

Smend, many German scholars argued that the original exilic edition of the DtrH had been supplemented by two further layers of material, one focusing on the activity of prophets (DtrP) and another, later, layer exhibiting a characteristic emphasis on nomistic/Torah piety (DtrN). Following Frank Moore Cross, US scholars tended to adopt a two-stage view in which the first edition of the DtrH (DtrH[1]) was produced in the preexilic period as Josianic propaganda, then modified after Josiah's death and Judah's downfall in order to conform to these newly disastrous circumstances (DtrH[2]). However, the entire notion of a DtrH is now being criticized, with a new generation of scholars stressing the untidiness of the material, the presence of pluriform perspectives, the substantial differences between the individual books, and the possibility of even later postexilic dates for these books' composition and literary development. Yet, there is still no gainsaying the presence of Deuteronomy-like elements in each of the books, especially the motif of "other gods" (e.g., Deut. 6:14) and the repeated references to an approaching exile (e.g., Deut. 28:63–64).

The primary literary effect of the complex's disastrous conclusion is to create irony at the intersection between individual narratives and the wider story. For example, the stirring exploits of local heroes nevertheless fail to achieve permanent change (Judg. 2:16–23). Some episodes that might at first appear commendable are eventually revealed to be examples of Israel's sinful decline (Judg. 11:29–40; 19). So too praise of certain kings and the institution of the kingship itself (2 Sam. 7; 1 Kgs. 8) now occur within a broader literary frame in which monarchy is viewed as a primary reason for Israel's downfall (Deut. 17:14–20; 1 Sam. 12:12–15; 2 Kgs. 17:8; 21:10–15). While not quite as bleak as Noth envisioned (as Gerhard von Rad pointed out, God's promise to Israel is "forever"; the exiles will survive), the DtrH does indeed justify the righteousness of God by laying the blame for Israel's destruction squarely with Israel.

Israel, Land, and the Nations

The book of Joshua begins with Israel's armed occupation of Canaan at God's direction. The narrative gives an initial impression of a speedy, violent, and total conquest (Josh. 10; 21:43–45). God not only sanctions this warfare but also participates in it (Josh. 5:13–15; 10:6–11; 11:6–9). Disturbing is not only the lack of greater sympathy for the land's inhabitants but also the way that this portion of the Bible has provided ideological cover for numerous land grabs in history (e.g., the United States' takeover of Native American land, the Afrikaners in South Africa, the Ulster Scots in Northern Ireland). The litany of "utter destruction" in Josh. 10–11 reads almost like a celebration of genocide. Here again, however, Israel's violent loss of the land at the conclusion of the DtrH later casts doubt on Israel's earlier manner of occupying it. The effectiveness of the conquest is in fact subverted in the course of the narrative through passing references to its gradualism (Josh. 11:18–20; see also Deut. 7:22: "little by little"; cf. Exod. 23:30) and incompleteness (Josh. 13:1–13; 15:63; 16:10; 17:12–13; Judg. 1). Moreover, the narrative's only extended episode of urban conquest depicts a style of warfare more liturgical than actual: Jericho's walls are brought down by a priestly parade rather than siege works (Josh. 6). In the end, although violence in God's name is never rejected, a distancing is evident. Various battles have their outcomes reported without the details of the engagements being specified. By associating the "conquest" so closely with Israel's unique territorial inheritance, the narrative makes this primal instance of dispossession unrepeatable (i.e., there is only one "promised land"). Even more suggestively, Israel's ultimate loss of the land reinforces a conditional message of responsibility (Deut. 29; Josh. 23:6–13), even a sense of futility (Josh. 23:15–16; but cf. Deut. 30), with respect to Israel's privileged hold on its geographic claim.

The other peoples within the land and in the nations outside Israel are often portrayed as threats and enemies. Yet beginning with Rahab (Josh. 2; 6) and continuing in figures such as the queen of Sheba (1 Kgs. 10), the widow of Zarephath (1 Kgs. 17), and Naaman (2 Kgs. 5), the DtrH also depicts non-Israelites who come to know God through their interactions with Israel—a theme further emphasized by the placement of Ruth between Judges and 1 Samuel in the Christian canon. Additionally, the DtrH subverts Israel's ethnic distinctiveness by portraying Israelites who are more similar to foreigners than different, even if that similarity is interpreted as a mark of unfaithfulness (e.g., Samson, Solomon). In this way, the DtrH also illustrates and extends the Genesis account of how God is using Israel to bring blessing to "all the families of the earth" (Gen. 12:1–3; cf. 1 Kgs. 8:41–43). Or in a saying attributed to Rabbi Hizkiyah in the Zohar, a medieval Jewish text, "The blessed Holy One cast Israel into exile among the nations only so that the other nations would be blessed because of them, for they draw blessings from above to below every day."

Responsible Leadership

The book of Joshua also makes clear from the outset that Israel's leaders must submit to the rule of law (Josh. 1:7–9; cf. Deut. 17:14–20). Human authority can change within a spiritual succession (e.g., Moses to Joshua, the judges, Saul to David, Elijah to Elisha), but biological succession is viewed with intense suspicion (Judg. 8:22–23; 1 Sam. 2; 8:1–3). "Absolute monarchy" is not found in the DtrH. Instead, God is considered Israel's true king (Judg. 8:23; 1 Sam. 7; cf. Isa. 6:5), and human leadership is treated as fundamentally derivative of divine authority (God is supposed to "choose" those in leadership). Furthermore, kings and other leaders are held accountable within a variety of wider social contexts and interactions, such as Israel's tribal structure, moral tradition, legal system, priestly customs—and even outsider figures possessing specialized knowledge (e.g., the wise woman of Tekoa [2 Sam. 14]) or ability to communicate directly with God (e.g., the prophet Elijah [1 Kgs. 17–19; 2 Kgs. 1–2]). Still, the quality of leaders and the character of their leadership matter greatly to the health of the nation and to the furtherance of God's purposes in the world. God's leaders can be outnumbered (1 Sam. 14:6–15) and physically unprepossessing (1 Sam. 17) because they draw their true strength from ruling justly (2 Sam. 23:3). "Power politics" and coercive policies (1 Kgs. 5:13–18) are rejected in favor of a pious openness ("heart" [Josh. 24:23; 1 Sam. 16:7]) to the prophetic word (Josh. 24:2; 1 Sam. 15:22–23).

Indeed, prophetic figures begin to predominate in the course of the DtrH until Israel's destiny becomes almost a tug-of-war between righteous prophets and unrighteous kings. Only two kings receive unqualified praise (Hezekiah [2 Kgs. 18:5–6]; Josiah [2 Kgs. 23:25]), and both have reigns featuring a reform of Israelite worship in which prophets play a leading role (Isaiah [2 Kgs. 19–20]; Huldah [2 Kgs. 22:14–20]). The DtrH sponsors a view of history in which Israel's prophets all finally offer a common message (2 Kgs. 17:13) and stand within a succession begun by Moses (Deut. 18:15–22). In this perspective, law and prophecy are complementary rather than competitive authorities, particularly in the constraint that both provide to royal power. The Latter Prophets are significantly less inclined to ground moral imperatives in legal warrants (they instead usually emphasize spiritual/moral values such as "righteousness" and "covenant faithfulness"). The theological unity of law and prophecy is therefore a crucial Deuteronomistic insight and one that lies at the origin of the eventual shape of the OT canon (i.e., "the law and the prophets").

Human Dignity

Particularly striking throughout the DtrH is the richness of its individual characters, especially since their literary characterization typically is handled with great economy of means (e.g., little physical description, infrequent use of affective/

emotional terms). Yet figures such as Delilah, Hannah, Jonathan, Abigail, Joab, Bathsheba, Jehu, and Jezebel are fascinating for their complexity and lifelikeness. Although the DtrH operates with a strong sense of divine involvement in history, human nature is depicted as varied, human choice as real, and human freedom as precious. Even the catastrophe at the end of the DtrH underscores the value God places on human freedom; otherwise, given the stakes, why give Israel any choice? God is correspondingly portrayed as having the capacity for direct action (1 Sam. 25:38) but more customarily acting through human judgments (2 Sam. 17:14). Even though human figures are shown to be embedded within social groups and contexts, each individual has access to God and therefore a concomitant dignity. In a classic story about the abuse of royal power (1 Kgs. 21), the rights of Naboth, an ordinary Israelite, are upheld against Ahab's covetousness. Jezebel's plot against Naboth turns on the bearing of false witness—in other words, the suppression of Naboth's ability to function as a trustworthy moral agent. The irreducible worth and complexity of individual moral character explain why the DtrH does not demonize its villains and presents its heroes unvarnished.

Women are often the victims of horrible mistreatment in the DtrH's narratives (Judg. 1:12–15; 11:29–40; 19; 21; 1 Sam. 1; 2 Sam. 13; 2 Kgs. 15:16), yet they can be simultaneously portrayed as fully realized human agents possessing a personal dignity equivalent to that of men (Judg. 1:14–15; 11:36–40; 1 Sam. 1:12–18). Women are not completely restricted to the domestic sphere, and occasionally they become leaders in warfare (e.g., Deborah, Jael), politics (e.g., Abigail, Michal, Bathsheba), and government (e.g., Jezebel, Athaliah, the queen of Sheba). Although Israelite women are for the most part apparently excluded from central positions of political power, the DtrH's overall perspective is surprisingly egalitarian rather than misogynistic. Ironically, even episodes of victimization can reinforce this egalitarian perspective by calling attention to the unfairness of the social structures in which women's moral agency and spiritual freedom are eclipsed (1 Sam. 1; 2 Sam. 3:12–16).

Even so, Israel is finally depicted as more than the sum of its individuals. At the heart of the DtrH is the challenge facing the people of Israel to *be* a people. That they are exiled *as* a people (2 Kgs. 24:14–16; 25:11) is a feature of the story pointing beyond itself to Israel's continuing communal future on the other side of divine judgment.

Bibliography

Ellul, J. *The Politics of God and the Politics of Man.* Eerdmans, 1972.

Klein, L. *The Triumph of Irony in the Book of Judges.* JSOTSup 68. Almond, 1988.

Noth, M. *The Deuteronomistic History.* 2nd ed. JSOTSup 15. JSOT Press, 1991.

Pleins, J. *The Social Visions of the Hebrew Bible: A Theological Introduction.* Westminster John Knox, 2001.

Römer, T. *The So-Called Deuteronomistic History: A Sociological, Historical and Literary Introduction.* T&T Clark, 2005.

von Rad, G. *Old Testament Theology.* 2 vols. Harper & Row, 1962–65.

Wenham, G. *Story as Torah: Reading Old Testament Narrative Ethically.* Baker Academic, 2000.

♦ Joshua ♦
L. Daniel Hawk

Few biblical books present readers with challenges as varied and vexing as does the book of Joshua. The overall structure seems simple enough: a theological prologue (1:1–18); an account of Israel's conquest of the land (2:1–12:24); an overview of the allotment, delineation, and occupation of tribal territories (13:1–21:45); and a closing collection of miscellaneous materials (22:1–24:33). The content of the book, however, raises multiple perspectives on what happened and how the events are to be understood. Chief among these is the clash between materials that present Israel's occupation as a conquest of the entire land through victories over helpless Canaanites (e.g., 10:28–12:24; 21:43–45), and others that describe vast tracts of land outside Israel's possession and a more robust resistance from the indigenous peoples (e.g., 13:2–6; 17:14–18; 19:47–48).

The book's disparate perspectives are the result of a long and complex process of composition that was not completed probably until Israel's return from exile in Babylon. Joshua, in short, bears the traces of Israel's theological reflection on its traditions of violent origins and of the nation's thinking through and recasting the traditions in light of its experience with God. Remarkably, conflicting perspectives and memories have not been harmonized but rather have been allowed to stand in tension with each other in the canonical text.

Theological and Moral Tensions

Joshua presents Israel's occupation of Canaan as a campaign of invasion, conquest, and extermination initiated by God and prosecuted in obedience to divine commandments. The Lord is prominent in the book as the divine warrior, one of the most ancient and ubiquitous images of God in the OT. In this role, the Lord confirms his faithfulness and demonstrates his power to fulfill his promises to Israel's ancestors. The Lord's victories over the opposing forces give him claim to the land by right of conquest. This claim in turn establishes the foundation for the affirmation that the Lord gives the land to Israel and determines what areas each of its tribes and clans will settle. For its part, Israel achieves success as it responds to God's initiative, acts in unity with God and within itself, and strictly observes the words of Moses. The conquest of the land, therefore, combines militant triumphalism with doxology, particularly in the Deuteronomistic speeches that open the book (1:1–18) and the accounts of victories over cities and kings (6:1–27; 8:1–29; 10:6–12:24).

Other texts, however, display uneasiness with the ostensive triumphalism of the conquest narrative and subtly undercut its claims. Three anecdotes precede each of the first three battle accounts at Jericho, Ai, and Gibeon (2:1–24; 7:1–26; 9:1–27). The three stories follow a parallel structure that centers thematically on exposing what is hidden. The first and third present encounters with indigenous peoples who praise Israel's God and display exemplary Israelite virtues (Rahab and the Gibeonite emissaries), while the second relates a sacrilege committed by a pedigreed Israelite (Achan). Read together, the three stories put a human face on both perpetrators and victims and challenge the ethnic separatism that demonizes Canaanites and sanctifies Israelites. The stories work together with summary comments that recast Israel's battles as defensive operations against increasingly aggressive kings (5:1; 9:1–2; 10:1–5; 11:1–5) and with a sophisticated reworking of the conquest narrative that gradually recasts the kings of Canaan, rather than its peoples, as the hostile force that Israel must overcome in the land.

At a fundamental level, Joshua is a narrative of origins that, on the one hand, lays claim to a homeland and a distinctive destiny and, on the other, constructs national identity over against the indigenous other (the peoples of the land). Joshua depicts Israel's encounter with difference and tests three primary identity markers: ethnicity, territory, and religious observance. In the course of the narrative each proves unable to provide a stable foundation on which to ground identity and action. Although ethnic exclusivity finds expression through Joshua's warnings that Israelites must keep their distance from Canaanites (23:1–16), the portrayals of Rahab and the Gibeonites oppose this notion of identity by presenting the reader with Canaanites who praise Israel's God and display exemplary Israelite virtues. These depictions, along with the reports of aliens within Israel (6:25; 8:30–35; 9:27), counter the sense that the nation is or should be ethnically homogenous. A similar dynamic holds true for territorial identity. Although boundaries define the extent of Israel's land and enclose tribal inheritances, few areas exhibit territorial integrity. Multiple references to unoccupied land and surviving peoples belie a simple correspondence between people and land. Finally, instances of Israelite disobedience and bickering over right religious practice counter depictions of meticulous obedience to divine commands, highlighting the difficulties involved in interpreting them correctly (e.g., 7:1–12; 22:10–34).

The difficulty of discerning divine priorities amid conflicting imperatives comes to a head when Joshua, twice, must decide whether to honor an oath to spare the lives of Canaanites (2:12–14; 6:22–25; 9:15–27). In both cases Joshua rules that Israel must keep the oath, even though doing so directly violates the commands of Moses that dictate how Israel must deal with the indigenous inhabitants (cf. Deut. 7:1–6; 20:16–18). In so doing, Joshua implicitly elevates mercy above the strict application of the law. As the narrative moves toward its conclusion, devotion to the one God emerges as the sole defining characteristic of the people of God. Joshua concludes with a climactic scene of covenant renewal (24:1–28), which portrays Israel as a people who choose the God who has chosen them.

Joshua as a Resource for Ethical Reflection

Joshua is a difficult and problematic book for Christians living in an age haunted by memories of genocidal conflicts and programs of colonization. It has, in many cases, directly or indirectly shaped the thinking and action of those who identify with biblical Israel. Given Christian complicity with such enterprises, grounded in declarations that "God is with us," would it not be safer to ignore this book's account of a warlike God who commands extermination and ethnic cleansing?

Modern theological reflection on Joshua generally has attempted to defuse its violent theology by placing the book within a historical and developmental framework. This allows one to read the book as a primitive expression of Israel's religious thought that has minimal relevance when set against other biblical texts that reflect a more mature ethical sensibility. It has also been argued that the prosecution of war in Joshua reflects a more thoughtful and humane prosecution of war when set against the brutal societies of the ancient Near East. Within a theology of progressive revelation, God's participation in the conquest has been viewed as a necessary divine accommodation that no longer applies in light of God's full revelation in Jesus Christ. These and other similar approaches effectively discredit strategies that use Joshua in support of violent or exclusionary agendas.

Recent study of Joshua has opened new trajectories by recognizing its narrativity and taking seriously its conflicting theological perspectives.

Postcolonial readers of Joshua have seen in the book a biblical portrayal of the violence and dispossession that they have experienced at the hands of imperial powers. Other readers have noted the interplay of opposing perspectives within the book, one that advances claims to territory by right of conquest and another that undercuts these claims and exposes the rhetoric of militant nationalism. Read as narrative, Joshua does not so much constitute a template for the extraction of moral principles as it does a testimony of God's involvement in the life of a nation, one that draws readers into a long and contentious conversation about what it means to live as God's people in a violent world.

The patristic metaphor of Scripture as a mirror, which reflects our beauty and ugliness, offers a powerful point of reference for reading Joshua in the contemporary context. In this sense, Joshua reflects a nation that both constructs and critiques a narrative of origin configured by convictions of divine election and destiny. Joshua does not mute the militant triumphalism that infuses Israel's memories of violent origins, as the convictions it articulates had become fundamental components of Israel's national identity. It does, however, bring these sentiments under a subtle and powerful criticism that unmasks the perspectives, commitments, and rhetoric that emanate from them. Joshua therefore constitutes a vital theological resource for every nation that, like Israel, seeks to come to terms with the violence of its past and to rethink its own narratives of exclusion and imperialism.

Bibliography

Creach, J. *Joshua*. IBC. John Knox, 2003.

Goetz, R. "Joshua, Calvin and Genocide." *ThTo* 32 (1975): 263–74.

Hawk, L. "Conquest Reconfigured: Recasting Warfare in the Redaction of Joshua." Pages 145–60 in *Writing and Reading War: Rhetoric, Gender, and Ethics in Biblical and Modern Contexts*, ed. B. Kelle and F. Ames. SBLSymS 42. Society of Biblical Literature, 2008.

———. *Joshua*. Berit Olam. Liturgical Press, 2000.

Nelson, R. *Joshua*. OTL. Westminster John Knox, 1997.

Polzin, R. *Moses and the Deuteronomist: A Literary Study of the Deuteronomistic History*. Seabury, 1980.

Prior, M. *The Bible and Colonialism: A Moral Critique*. BibSem 48. Sheffield Academic Press, 1997.

Warrior, R. "A Native American Perspective: Canaanites, Cowboys, and Indians." Pages 135–43 in *Voices from the Margin: Interpreting the Bible in the Third World*, ed. R. Sugirtharajah. 3rd ed. Orbis, 2006.

◆ Judges ◆

L. Daniel Hawk

The book of Judges portrays the disintegration of a nation that has lost its center. In vivid contrast to the unified Israel that triumphs and occupies the land described in Joshua, Judges begins with a depiction of a nation fragmented into tribes, each preoccupied with its own territory (1:1–36). It then moves immediately to a divine rebuke for covenantal disobedience (2:1–5), the death of the leader who has unified the people (2:6–10), and a programmatic introduction that presents the era as a constant cycle of apostasy, chastisement, and deliverance (2:11–23).

The core of the book comprises accounts of the judges that God raised up to deliver Israel (3:1–16:31). The term *judge* does not here necessarily entail judicial authority but rather refers to the individual's mission to bring justice via deliverance to oppressed Israel. The first of these, Othniel, is rendered as the paradigmatic savior but without elaboration (3:7–11). Subsequent judges exhibit a quirk or flaw that, with each one, becomes increasingly grotesque and destructive. Ehud is left-handed (and thus, suggestively, sinister), which enables him to assassinate a Moabite tyrant behind closed doors (3:12–30). Deborah is a "mother in Israel" who gloats in bloodthirsty detail over the death of Sisera at the hands of Jael, a woman who sheltered the Canaanite commander, gave him milk, tucked him in, and then shattered his skull while he slept (4:1–5:31). Gideon arises from humble beginnings but barely averts intertribal conflict, constructs an ephod that leads Israel into idolatry, and sires a son, Abimelech (meaning "my father is king"), who attempts to make himself king (6:11–9:57). Jephthah, the son of a prostitute, sacrifices his daughter to fulfill a vow and participates in intertribal warfare (11:1–12:7). Samson is an impetuous loner, obsessed with danger and forbidden women, who rallies no one to the cause and enacts his deeds of deliverance out of a desire to get revenge on the Philistines (13:1–16:31).

The book ends with two narratives that depict the dissolution of the fundamental social bonds that configure tribal Israel. The first begins with Micah, a man who steals a huge sum of silver from his mother. The story then relates the dedication of silver to the Lord in the form of an idol and the installation of a family member as priest, and features a Levite who sells his services to the highest bidder and a dispossessed tribe (Dan) that wipes out a town outside its allotted territory (17:1–18:31). The second reports a mob attack on travelers, the gang rape of a young woman and her dismemberment by her Levite lover (he is hardly a lover [husband instead?]), she is a secondary wife), the near annihilation of Benjamin by the other tribes, the destruction of an Israelite town for its nonparticipation in the conflict, and the kidnapping of women who are celebrating a religious festival (19:1–21:25).

Judges concludes with a comment that summarizes the spirit of the times: "In those days there was no king in Israel; all the people did what was right in their own eyes" (21:25 [cf. 17:6; 18:1; 19:1]). The statement is provocatively ambiguous. Does it imply that a tribal society was unworkable and thus infer that monarchy is a preferable social configuration? Or does it comment on the anarchy that ensued when Israel rejected the Lord as king (cf. 1 Sam. 8:7)? Viewed as social commentary, the statement illumines the contesting perspectives about Israel's polity (the kin-based society of tribal Israel and charismatic leadership versus the mediating institutions of dynastic monarchy) that constitute an important dynamic throughout the book. Viewed as theological commentary, it links Israel's persistent refusal to accord the Lord his rightful place at the center of communal life with the degeneration of Israelite leadership and society.

Faced with Israel's recalcitrance, the Lord repeatedly displays his supremacy by accomplishing his saving purposes in spite of the failings of his chosen deliverers. Difficult for many readers is the fact that imbuement of the Lord's spirit empowers judges to deliver Israel but does not result in the transformation of their moral or spiritual dispositions. Moreover, none of the judges succeed in restoring Israel to long-term devotion to God. Rather, the judges themselves are enmeshed in the nation's persistent attempts to chart its own destiny apart from the claims of the Lord. God is also drawn into the cycle through repeated attempts to restore Israel and, it seems, must even use surreptitious means to initiate deliverance through his chosen leaders (a case in point being the narrator's comment that Samson's infatuation with a Philistine woman "was from the LORD; for he was seeking a pretext to act against the Philistines" [14:4]).

The social consequences of "doing what is right in one's own eyes" (as opposed to the Lord's) are portrayed in stark and often symbolic terms. The perversion of fundamental values figures prominently in many accounts, with shocking effect. Deborah and Jael express their "motherly" attributes in bloodthirsty ways. Gideon the idol-destroyer becomes an idol-maker. Jephthah kills his own daughter. A Levite throws his concubine to a threatening mob after tenderly wooing her. (Women, it should be noted, bear the brunt of the violence that breaks out as the fabric of Israelite society unravels.) The symbolic threads converge in Samson, the personification of Israel, whose story is propelled by the interplay of forbidden sex, danger, and death.

As a whole, Judges draws an inseparable and reciprocal connection between devotion to God, strong central leadership, and national unity and well-being. It thus presents modern secular societies with a cautionary tale about the central importance of religious faith and the consequences that may ensue when faith in God is shunted to the periphery.

Bibliography

Bal, M. *Death and Dissymmetry: The Politics of Coherence in the Book of Judges.* CSHJ. University of Chicago Press, 1988.

Block, D. *Judges.* NAC. Broadman & Holman, 2002.

Brettler, M. "The Book of Judges: Literature as Politics." *JBL* 108 (1989): 395–418.

Exum, J. "The Centre Cannot Hold: Thematic and Textual Instabilities in Judges." *CBQ* 52 (1990): 410–31.

Schneider, T. *Judges.* Berit Olam. Liturgical Press, 2000.

◆ Ruth ◆

Jacqueline E. Lapsley

The book of Ruth tells the story of Naomi, an Israelite woman living in Moab whose husband and two sons have died, and of her faithful daughter-in-law Ruth, who forsakes her Moabite homeland and religious traditions for the uncertainties of life in Judah. Through a series of events, both fortuitous and orchestrated, Ruth ends up marrying Naomi's kinsman Boaz and bearing a son. At the end of the story both Naomi and Ruth are restored to the fullness of family and community life, with Naomi cradling the child considered her grandson.

Like most stories, the book of Ruth does not engage ethics explicitly; rather, the ethics espoused and affirmed must be discerned within the narrative itself. Engaging the book of Ruth by means of narrative ethics allows one to perceive that this short story is surprisingly rich in its ethical vision.

Unlike much of the rest of the Bible, God's role in the story is muted—only Ruth's conception of a son at the end is directly attributed to God's action (4:13); the story focuses instead on the actions of human beings. Nonetheless, the characters consistently invoke God's blessing on others in prayer, and these prayers are crucial for understanding the connection between life with God and life lived in community. Most of the characters lead God-centered lives, and the richness of that fundamental relationship empowers them to enact blessings for others through their own works of loving-kindness. The health of the community depends quite directly on the health of the people's relationship with God.

The story begins with famine and death and ends in the bounty of the harvest and the birth of a child who represents the hope of the future. Boaz and Ruth's acts of loving-kindness redeem Naomi; taking initiative to enact God's blessings, they weave her back into a full life, surrounded by a community marked by care and joy for all generations.

The story connects intertextually with OT legal material. Boaz keeps the laws that allow the poor to glean after the harvesters (Lev. 19:9–10; 23:22; Deut. 24:19–22) and keeps the spirit of the laws of levirate marriage and land redemption (see Sakenfeld 57–61). Many commentators posit a postexilic date for the book and have observed that the inclusion of a Moabite woman in the ancestral line of David flies in the face of postexilic laws against intermarriage (Ezra 10; Neh. 13), thus creating an intertextual conversation about the role of foreign women in Israel.

In the OT, the book immediately follows Judges, and the contrast in ethos is startling. Whereas Judges ends with a vision of the devastation effected when the community of faith is disconnected from God, Ruth offers a vision of the redemption possible when the community centers its prayers on God and its acts of loving faithfulness on those in need of restoration.

Bibliography

Lapsley, J. *Whispering the Word: Hearing Women's Stories in the Old Testament.* Westminster, 2005, 89–108.

Sakenfeld, K. D. *Ruth.* Interpretation. Westminster, 1999.

◆ 1–2 Samuel ◆

Bruce C. Birch

The books of Samuel were one book in the ancient Hebrew manuscripts, and they narrate the stories that move Israel from a loose tribal association to a small monarchy in the eleventh century BCE. Modern scholars understand these books as part of a larger edited narrative that tells Israel's story from entry into the land of Canaan to the destruction of Jerusalem and the start of the Babylonian exile in 587 BCE—that is, the books of Joshua through 2 Kings (excluding Ruth, which was placed after Judges in later Bibles). This narrative is edited together from multiple sources to form a continuous narrative. The process for this was complex and its description disputed, but almost all agree that some materials date close to the events of the period described, and that the process of editing and collecting was completed by editorial comments and shaping from a Deuteronomistic editor responsible for the final collection from Joshua to 2 Kings seeking to explain and interpret the end of Israel's history in exile.

The books of Samuel open in a time of internal and external crisis in Israel. The closing stories and final verse of the book of Judges suggest a situation of moral anarchy, as "there was no king in Israel" (Judg. 21:25). This is compounded by a story at the beginning of 1 Samuel that tells of corruption in the house of Eli, who with his impious sons served as priests for the sanctuary of the ark of the covenant in Shiloh (1 Sam. 2:11–17). The internal moral crisis is related to a crisis of leadership, and the birth of the prophet Samuel and the song of his mother, Hannah (1 Sam. 1:1–2:10), suggest that God is at work to answer the central question of the books of Samuel: "Who will lead Israel?"

The internal crisis is matched by an external threat in the form of the Philistines, Israel's aggressive and militaristic neighbors on their southern coast. This becomes a crisis threatening Israel's extinction when the Philistines invade Israelite territory, capture the ark, and occupy all of Israel's territory west of the Jordan River (1 Sam. 4–6). Such a threat is a factor behind the elders' demand for Samuel to "appoint for us . . . a king to govern us, like other nations" (1 Sam. 8:5) and the call and anointing of Saul to lead Israel against the Philistines (1 Sam. 9–10).

The remainder of 1–2 Samuel is dominated by three major figures whose stories are intertwined and overlapping: Samuel, the prophet who anointed the first two kings of Israel; Saul, Israel's first king, whose story ends in a tragic suicide; and David, Israel's second king, described as the "man after God's own heart" (1 Sam. 13:14) who later betrays his own promise by committing adultery and murder to satisfy his own desire (2 Sam. 11). Especially in 1 Samuel some stories seem to reflect a negative attitude toward kingship as a sinful rejection of God's rule, while other stories see kingship as the gift of God, probably reflecting the existence of a similar tension when kingship began for Israel.

The books of Samuel, like other narrative traditions in the OT, have not often been treated as material with significant theological or ethical importance. More attention has been paid to material with overt moral content, particularly if it addresses the norms of moral conduct. The books of Samuel usually are treated simply as historical narration of an important period of events establishing kingship in ancient Israel, and discussion often focuses on the reliability of its testimony.

The stories of 1–2 Samuel are actually better treated as historically realistic narrative with an intense theological testimony to God's providence as the true source of power in a transformative period of Israel's life. These narratives are not dispassionate history writing, but neither are they the saga-like narratives of the Pentateuch, where God is likely to appear and act as an overt character in the story. In the books of Samuel divine providence operates through human events and personalities, but the narration makes it quite clear that God is at work in and through the characters and events of the stories (see, e.g., 2 Sam. 5:10; 11:27b).

Several themes with theological and ethical significance can be identified in the books of Samuel:

1. In the course of transformative events in ancient Israel, God is at work subverting the usual arrangements of human power. Hannah's song at the beginning of the narrative (1 Sam. 2:1–10) and David's song at the end (2 Sam. 22:2–51) witness to God as one who overturns the world's customary power arrangements. God can allow the ark of the covenant to be captured by the Philistines and yet bring them low through the "hand of the Lord" without any human agency (1 Sam. 4–6). God can look on the heart and choose an eighth son, just a boy (1 Sam. 16:1–13), to become Israel's greatest king and the "man after God's own heart" (1 Sam. 13:14), yet who later will be confronted and judged by God's prophet (2 Sam. 12:1–15).

2. The nature of leadership of God's people requires more than personal charisma and human skill. Both Saul and David are legitimized not through their own power and authority or by the recognition of their abilities by the people. They are anointed by God's prophet and receive the indwelling of God's spirit as a result (1 Sam. 10:1–8; 16:13), so that even their achievements are understood in the narrative as manifestations of the power of God's spirit. That recognition of God's providential working through events is more crucial than human skill or power is clear in David's own statement during his retreat from Jerusalem during Absalom's rebellion: "If I find favor in the eyes of the Lord, he will bring me back" (2 Sam. 15:25).

3. There is a moral valuation attached to the contrast in the stories of the books of Samuel between the ability to receive power as God's gift and the exercise of power as a matter of grasping for oneself. David's early story shows a man of prayer constantly grateful for the providential gifts of God (1 Sam. 16–2 Sam. 10), but tragic consequences result from his use of power to grasp the objects of his own desire by taking Bathsheba

and murdering her husband, Uriah (2 Sam. 11–18). Saul comes to his tragic end largely because he, constantly pursuing his own desire to control events, falls victim to his inability to trust what God is doing. His own anger, envy, and violence are his undoing (see 1 Sam. 18).

The books of Samuel are not occupied with the ethics of conduct made explicit through commandment, law, or admonition. The expression of divine will is not overt and direct. The narratives of Samuel are reflective of an ethics of character, which focuses on the working of divine providence in partnership with the workings of personality and power. We experience the successes and failures of moral character in these appealing and all-too-human characters and come away wiser in our efforts to perceive the workings of God's providence in our own lives.

Bibliography

Birch, B. "The First and Second Books of Samuel." Pages 947–1383 in vol. 2 of *The New Interpreter's Bible*, ed. L. Keck. Abingdon, 1998.

———. *Let Justice Roll Down: The Old Testament, Ethics, and Christian Life*. Westminster John Knox, 1991, pp. 198–239.

Brueggemann, W. *David's Truth in Israel's Imagination and Memory*. Fortress, 1985.

———. *Power, Providence, and Personality: Biblical Insight into Life and Ministry*. Westminster John Knox, 1990.

♦ 1–2 Kings ♦

Craig Vondergeest

The books of 1–2 Kings recount the history of Israel and Judah from the end of David's kingship until the Babylonian exile in 587 BCE. After presenting an account of the accession and rule of Solomon and the subsequent division of the kingdoms, these books proceed to describe in varying degrees of detail the reigns of each of the Israelite and Judean monarchs, giving special attention to the kings' and people's religious practice and describing the fall of Israel to Assyria and Judah to Babylonia as the direct result of apostasy from exclusive worship of Yahweh. As part of the larger Deuteronomistic History, 1–2 Kings reflect the ethical and theological concerns of Deuteronomy.

Narrative criticism has shown significant potential in uncovering the ethical concerns and issues of narrative texts by focusing on the attitudes of the narrator or "implied author" toward characters and their actions (Wenham 5–15). This kind of analysis focuses our attention less on discussion of specific moral problems than on the characters' fundamental moral makeup and the process of their ethical formation, inviting readers to reflect on the complexity of the characters' moral lives and then on their own lives and ethical dispositions (Barton 71–74).

In 1–2 Kings the narrator gives more attention to Solomon than to any other individual, portraying him as a multifaceted character who appears to be the model of the ideal ruler yet who, in the end, is undone by his own excess. Early in the story, the new king seems almost too good to be true, not only replicating the obedience of his father, David (1 Kgs. 3:3), but also asking God for an "understanding mind" and the ability to "discern between good and evil" instead of wealth or long life (1 Kgs. 3:6–9). Thus, Solomon understands that ruling with equity, fairness, and discernment goes to the heart of what it means to be a wise leader. Undergirding these qualities is a sense of genuine humility and reliance on God, which Solomon further acknowledges in his prayer of dedication over the temple, where he asks that God forgive the people's sins when they pray in or toward the temple (1 Kgs. 8:33–34, 46–53). Finally, Solomon's wisdom leads, as promised by God (1 Kgs. 3:13), to the accumulation of great wealth, which attests to that wisdom and enables him to build a temple unparalleled for its opulence (1 Kgs. 5–6).

Ironically, though, this great wealth becomes a symbol of the excess that leads to Solomon's downfall. Right on the heels of the account of Solomon's wise judgment, the story raises a red flag with its mention of forced labor, as well as the subsequent description of the massive provisions that the royal administration must demand from its citizens (1 Kgs. 4:1–28). Because the construction of the temple requires the use of forced labor (1 Kgs. 5:13–18), Solomon's building of this magnificent house for God is accomplished only on the backs of his people. Moreover, Solomon's accumulation of horses (1 Kgs. 4:26; 10:26) points to overreliance on military might at the expense of trust in God, and his pursuit of national security through marriages to a thousand women and subsequent worship of their gods (1 Kgs. 11:1–8) leads to the Davidic-Solomonic line's loss of the whole nation except for the tribe of Judah. All this is exactly what Deuteronomy has already warned against in describing the king as a custodian of the law who is not to exalt himself above his people (Deut. 17:14–20). The story of Solomon, then, presents the reader with the opportunity to reflect on virtues in leadership such as wisdom, justice, discernment, humility, and reliance on God, especially in contrast to the dangers of excess, pride, and reliance on self.

The requirements of Deut. 17 that the king subject himself to the Torah and teach the people to do the same also lie behind the accounts of the other rulers in 1–2 Kings, even if those accounts are not as detailed as the Solomon story and generally describe the rulers as unambiguously good or bad rather than lingering over the complexities of their moral character. When Naboth refuses to sell to King Ahab the vineyard that is part of Naboth's ancestral inheritance, for instance, the king seems to accept, albeit reluctantly, that according to the law he has no recourse, but Jezebel, his wife, places herself and Ahab above the law by having Naboth falsely accused of a capital offense and put to death so that Ahab can then seize the property (1 Kgs. 21).

For the most part, though, the evaluations of Israel's and Judah's kings revolve around how well they conform to the requirements for religious practice set out in Deuteronomy, particularly the command to worship Yahweh only. Josiah, for instance, is the Deuteronomist's great hero for hearing the law and taking immediate steps to make sure that he and the people are following it, leading to his great religious reforms that centralized worship in Jerusalem and eradicated all hints of idolatry (2 Kgs. 22–23), while Manasseh reverses all of Hezekiah's reforms, leading to the downfall of the kingdom (2 Kgs. 21). More often the text includes little more than a brief formulaic evaluation of the ruler, indicating, for instance, whether he followed in the ways of David (1 Kgs. 14:8; 15:3, 11). Thus, the main concern is whether each king follows the divinely given Torah and teaches his subjects to do the same, and there is little gray area in the author's evaluations. While these accounts might seem best to support an ethic of divine command, one could perhaps also say that it is a matter of virtue and character for a ruler to subject himself to the law and thus put himself on a par with his subjects rather than simply consider himself as the giver of and authority over law.

The other important characters in 1–2 Kings are the prophets, who announce the consequences of disobedience to the Torah, speaking words of criticism to those who hold great power (e.g., Ahijah speaking to Solomon and Jeroboam [1 Kgs. 11:29–33; 14:7–14]; Elijah against the prophets of Baal [1 Kgs. 18]; Micaiah speaking to Ahab [1 Kgs. 22]). At the same time, part of what makes these prophetic narratives difficult from the perspective of ethical consideration is that the text makes no explicit remarks about the morality of acts such as Elijah's slaughter of Baal's prophets, Micaiah's initial deception of the two kings, the violence resulting from Jehu's coup (which is criticized sharply in the next century by Hosea), and Elisha's cursing of some children who had taunted him so that a bear comes and mauls them (2 Kgs. 2:23–24).

Narrative analysis seems to bear fruit in the use of 1–2 Kings for moral reflection, as it helps to highlight virtues and character, especially in the rich and multidimensional portrayal of complex characters such as Solomon.

Bibliography

Barton, J. *Understanding Old Testament Ethics: Approaches and Explorations.* Westminster John Knox, 2003.

Wenham, G. *Story as Torah: Reading the Old Testament Ethically.* OTS. T&T Clark, 2000.

♦ 1–2 Chronicles ♦

Ralph W. Klein

The sixty-five chapters of 1–2 Chronicles make this work one of the longest in the OT. Written in the first half of the fourth century BCE in Jerusalem, Chronicles urges wholehearted dedication to the second temple, its clergy, and its liturgical rites. Chronicles could also be characterized as a retelling of the history of the monarchy in Jerusalem, from David to Zedekiah, to which is prefaced a genealogy beginning with Adam and continuing to a list of the descendants of the twelve sons of Israel (Jacob). There is also a list of the descendants of King Saul and an account of his death.

David and Solomon are presented by the Chronicler in an idealized fashion. They presided over a united people of God and were responsible for the building of the first temple and establishing its regular clergy and services. David's generosity toward the construction of the temple knew no bounds and provided an excellent example for the other leaders of the people (1 Chr. 29:1–9). In his prayer at the dedication of the temple Solomon urged God to respond to calamities such as drought, famine, sickness, and especially military defeat by hearing the people when they repent and forgiving them (2 Chr. 6:24–35). In response to the prayer, Yahweh promised that if the people humble themselves, pray, seek his face, and repent, he will hear them, forgive their sin, and heal the land. This promise provides a pattern for human and divine activity in many points of Judah's history, especially in the case of Hezekiah, who serves as a second David and Solomon.

This idealized portrait of David and Solomon contrasts sharply with the description of these kings in the books of Samuel and Kings. No mention is made in Chronicles of David's adultery with Bathsheba, his murder of Uriah, his son Amnon's rape of his half-sister Tamar and David's weak response to this crime, and Absalom's revolt and his death under questionable circumstances. David's long contest with Saul (1 Sam. 16–30) is passed over in silence, and Yahweh turns the kingdom over to David in 1 Chr. 10:13 with no mention of the civil war with Ishbaal or the death of Abner and Ishbaal under questionable circumstances (2 Sam. 2–4). Similarly, the book does not discuss the seven hundred wives or three hundred concubines of Solomon, let alone their leading him astray to serve other gods (1 Kgs. 10:28–11:40). Even Solomon's journey to sacrifice at the "high place" at Gibeon (1 Kgs. 3:2–6) is cast in a different light, since according to the Chronicler the tabernacle was located at Gibeon (2 Chr. 1:3–6). Here, Solomon did not become king through the conniving of Nathan and Bathsheba, who took advantage of David's weakness in his final illness, nor is there any mention of the attempt by Adonijah, Solomon's brother, to usurp the throne. Rather, David, in full command of his powers, designated Solomon as king in fulfillment of the oracle of Nathan (1 Chr. 17:15; 22:9–10), and he cited a divine oracle designating Solomon as the king chosen by Yahweh (1 Chr. 28:6–7, 10). David's sin in regard to the census is retained, but David also acknowledged his guilt and decided to fall into God's hands because God's mercy is great (1 Chr. 21). There is no evidence that the Chronicler meant to silence the books of Samuel and Kings or even replace them. Instead, he stressed qualities of David and Solomon and of their rule of a united Israel that spoke directly to the issue that necessitated his writing. They were dedicated to the temple, generously supported it, and followed God's will in erecting it.

Hezekiah is one of several kings who reformed worship in the temple (cf. Asa, Jehoshaphat, Joash, Manasseh, and Josiah) and removed idols and other forms of syncretism. Hezekiah and Josiah also invited remnants from the north to participate in worship in Jerusalem, foreshadowing the same inclusive view of Israel that runs throughout Chronicles.

In the book of Kings, Manasseh is described as the worst king of Judah and is responsible for misleading the people to misbehave more than the nations that preceded them in the land (2 Kgs. 21:1–9 // 2 Chr. 33:1–10). Because of this behavior, exile had become inevitable, despite the outstanding behavior of Manasseh's grandson Josiah (2 Kgs. 21:11–16; 23:26; 24:3–4). In Chronicles, however, the sinful Manasseh was taken captive to Babylon, where he repented, humbled himself, affirmed monotheism, and was graciously restored to his throne by Yahweh. Back in Jerusalem, Manasseh also carried out a number of reforms and restored the altar of Yahweh and offered on it sacrifices of well-being and of thanksgiving (2 Chr. 33:11–17). Whatever one's ethical behavior, therefore, repentance and forgiveness are possible, and Manasseh is described as a model for Judah itself when it goes into exile.

The Chronicler was faced with a serious ethical dilemma as he wrote his book. The postexilic province of Yehud, in which he lived, was a small territory, about three times the size of the city of Chicago, with a population of fifty thousand or less, perhaps as small as twenty thousand. Yehud was therefore a tiny entity in the mighty Persian Empire, which extended from Libya and Egypt in North Africa in the west and to India in the east. Some in his audience no doubt wanted to throw off the hegemony of that empire, but the Chronicler recognized that the return of the exiles from Babylon to Palestine and the building of the second temple took place because Yahweh had used King Cyrus to bring these policies about. The Chronicler seems to have accepted the rule of the Persians as inevitable, at least for his time, and advocated his views on the temple, its clergy, and its rituals within this overall support for the Persian Empire. In our time, when many employ postcolonial insights in interpreting the Bible, the ethics of the Chronicler's position is debatable. The Chronicler, as in many of our own ethical choices, seems to have settled for what was realistically possible.

While in many parts of the Bible faithfulness is followed by reward or well-being and unfaithfulness by punishment, in Chronicles these rewards or punishments are more immediate and individual, normally taking place within a person's lifetime. There is no accumulated sin or merit as in the books of Kings. The doctrine of retribution places high value on moral or ethical decisions. That doctrine, of course, also has its problems, as the book of Job persuasively argues, when apparently righteous persons are not rewarded. Others argue that the doctrine of retribution can contribute to a feeling of works-righteousness. Some argue that the Chronicler is less concerned to demonstrate strict relations between acts and consequences than to emphasize Yahweh's benevolence and mercy toward the people (cf. 1 Chr. 22:12; 29:18; 2 Chr. 30:18).

The focus on temple worship and the rights of its clergy might suggest that the Chronicler had a very wooden idea of piety and the religious life. But we need to note how often the word *joy* is used in his history and how warmly he can speak of faith: "Believe in the LORD your God and you will be established" (2 Chr. 20:20).

Bibliography

Japhet, S. *I & II Chronicles*. OTL. Westminster John Knox, 1993.

Klein, R. *1 Chronicles*. Hermeneia. Fortress, 2006.

Knoppers, G. *1 Chronicles 1–9*. AB 12. Doubleday, 2004.

———. *1 Chronicles 10–29*. AB 12A. Doubleday, 2004.

◆ Ezra ◆

Michael W. Duggan

The books of Ezra and Nehemiah are considered a single volume in the Jewish canon. Ezra-Nehemiah recounts events in Judah during two distinct periods, of approximately a quarter century each, in the postexilic era. The first (538–515 BCE) covers the return of the Jews from Babylon and the subsequent reconstruction of the temple (Ezra 1:1–6:22). The second (458–433 BCE) covers Ezra's commission to teach the Torah in Jerusalem and the appointment of Nehemiah as governor (Ezra 7:1–Neh. 13:31).

The narratives of both the temple reconstruction and Ezra's marriage reform serve to identify the authentic Israel after the exile as consisting of the families of Judah and Benjamin along with the Levites and priests, who returned to Judah from Babylon (Ezra 1:5; 2:1–67; 4:1; 10:9). The "people of the land," foreigners who remained in the territory throughout the exile, must have no part in the reconstituted community. Zerubbabel, the leader, and Joshua, the priest, forbid them from working on the temple project, while Ezra demands that Judahite men sever marriage ties with foreign women (Ezra 4:1–3; 6:21; 10:2–3, 10–11). Ezra's marriage reform aims at preserving the "holy seed" by separating the exiles, who returned to Judah, from all outsiders (Ezra 9:1–2; 10:6–9, 44).

The book of Ezra invites reflection on the rights of refugees to return to their native territories and reconstitute their communities. Although underwritten by the Persian authorities, Ezra's reform is an exercise in ethnic self-determination. The text, however, sustains only one voice in a debate among various factions that claimed membership in the reconstituted Israel of the postexilic era. The author asserts the rigorist position of those "who tremble at the words/commandment of God" (Ezra 9:4; 10:3) by narrowly defining the community as consisting of the exiles from the families of Judah, Benjamin, and Levi. The reader needs to contemplate, however, the protests from the people of the land who are the subject matter of the correspondence between regional authorities and the Persian administration (Ezra 4:1–2, 7–22; 5:3–6:12). More important, a modern reader must protest the absence of any advocacy on behalf of the women and children whom the leaders banish from the community (Ezra 10:44).

Ezra's marriage reform extends beyond earlier tradition insofar as the Torah does not stipulate that Israelites must divorce their foreign wives. However, his reform appeals to the Deuteronomic laws excluding Ammonites and Moabites from the assembly of Yahweh and prohibiting Israelites from marrying foreigners who reside in the land (Ezra 9:1–2, 11–12; 10:10; cf. Deut. 7:1–4; 23:3–6).

These precepts would rule out the marriage of the Moabite Ruth into the Judahite family of Elimelech and ultimately to Boaz (Ruth 2:1; 4:7–17). Indeed, Ezra would have banished from the reformed community Ruth and her son Obed, ancestors of David. The story of Ruth suggests a vision of inclusivity in contrast to the exclusivity of Ezra's covenant community.

Bibliography

Blenkinsopp, J. *Judaism, the First Phase: The Place of Ezra and Nehemiah in the Origins of Judaism*. Eerdmans, 2009.

Grabbe, L. *Ezra-Nehemiah*. OTR. Routledge, 1998.

Williamson, H. *Ezra and Nehemiah*. WBC 16. Word, 1985.

◆ Nehemiah ◆

Michael W. Duggan

The book of Nehemiah continues the narrative about the reconstitution of Judah that begins in the book of Ezra. The stories of Ezra and Nehemiah compose a coherent narrative (Ezra 7–Neh. 13) that begins with the Persian king Artaxerxes commissioning Ezra to teach the Torah in Judah and continues with the same king appointing Nehemiah to two successive terms as governor of Judah (Ezra 7:25–26; Neh. 2:5–8; 5:14; 8:9; 13:6–7). The book of Nehemiah consists of four parts: (1) Nehemiah rebuilds Jerusalem and its walls while releasing Judahite debt slaves (1:1–7:72a), (2) Ezra and the Levites lead the people in a covenant renewal ceremony (7:72b–10:40), (3) Nehemiah oversees the repopulation of Jerusalem and the dedication of the city walls (11:1–12:43), (4) Nehemiah later enforces some of the covenant stipulations (12:44–13:31). The narrator interweaves the careers of the protagonists by noting Nehemiah's support for Ezra's Torah teaching, on the one hand, and Ezra's participation in Nehemiah's dedication of the city walls, on the other (8:9; 11:36).

The collaboration between Ezra (mission in 458 BCE) and Nehemiah (governor beginning in 445 BCE) is a literary construct; yet by making Ezra and Nehemiah contemporaries in Jerusalem, the narrator portrays them as partners who redefined the postexilic community of Judah by separating the authentic descendants of preexilic Israel from all outsiders. Each leader establishes the community boundaries by a distinctive activity: Ezra teaches the Torah, and Nehemiah constructs the city walls. The synergy of the two endeavors is apparent when the Judahites voice their commitment to disassociate from other peoples within the confines of the walls that they had reconstructed (Neh. 6:15; 9:2; 10:29; cf. 13:3). The identification of the authentic community as consisting of the families of Judah and Benjamin who returned from exile and severed all family ties from the people of the land carries forward a central thesis from the book of Ezra (Neh. 7:6–72a; cf. Ezra 1:5; 2:1–70; 4:1; 6:16, 21; 9:1; 10:9, 11).

A first-person report, the so-called Nehemiah Memoir, highlights the social reforms that Nehemiah initiated in each term: first, his cancellation of debts and release of Judahite slaves (5:1–13), and subsequently, his securing the tithes for the Levites, closing markets on the Sabbath, and protesting marriages to foreigners (13:4–31). The covenant renewal ceremony in Nehemiah constitutes the climax of the broader Ezra-Nehemiah narrative (7:72b–10:40). The postexilic community defines itself by Torah observance. The choreography of the covenant renewal suggests a movement toward greater egalitarianism within the community even as it becomes more exclusionary toward outsiders. The Torah passes in succession from Ezra to the heads of the ancestral clans and finally to the whole assembly (8:2–3, 13; 9:2–3). The assembly consists of women and children as well as men (8:3; 10:29–30).

The covenant commitments to fallowing the land every seventh year and canceling debts are matters of social justice (Neh. 10:31). The produce of the seventh year belongs to the poor (Exod. 23:10–11). The rule governing indemnity specifically demands the release of pledges that debtors had consigned to their creditors as security for loans (Deut. 24:10). Such pledges could range from a garment to a piece of real estate (Exod. 22:24–26; Neh. 5:3–4). However, the immediate context in Ezra-Nehemiah indicates that the pledge in question is a child who works as a debt slave for the creditor in order to repay a loan that his or her parents had transacted with a creditor (cf. 2 Kgs. 4:1; Isa. 50:1). Such arrangements had precipitated the social and financial crises that provoked Nehemiah to demand the release of Judahite slaves and the cancellation of debts (Neh. 5:1–13). The covenant renewal secured the possibility of indebted Judahite families to regain their social integrity as well as the possession of their ancestral properties. The participation of children in the covenant renewal suggests the priority of enfranchising the sons and daughters who had been debt slaves (Neh. 5:5; cf. 8:3; 10:29–30). In this way, the book of Nehemiah touches on the human rights of children.

Bibliography

Blenkinsopp, J. *Judaism, the First Phase: The Place of Ezra and Nehemiah in the Origins of Judaism.* Eerdmans, 2009.

Duggan, M. *The Covenant Renewal in Ezra-Nehemiah (Neh. 7:72b–10:40): An Exegetical, Literary, and Theological Study.* SBLDS 164. Society of Biblical Literature, 2001.

Grabbe, L. *Yehud: A History of the Persian Province of Judah.* Vol. 1 of *A History of the Jews and Judaism in the Second Temple Period.* T&T Clark, 2004.

◆ Esther ◆

Linda Day

The book of Esther depicts the threatened annihilation of the Jewish population in the ancient Persian Empire. After the current queen, Vashti, is banished, the Jew Esther is selected as the new queen by King Ahasuerus. Her relative Mordecai angers Haman, the second in command, who plots in revenge to have all the Jews killed. Esther convinces the king to overturn that decree, the Jews experience victory, and the Jewish holiday of Purim is established.

The book features characters who live by a compromised code of ethics: the negligent and overindulging Ahasuerus, the egotistical and vengeful Haman. When such individuals hold high social positions, personal inadequacies are shown to have the potential for widespread deleterious impact. The well-being of large segments of society (the nation's wives, its young women, and ultimately all Jews) is sacrificed for the happiness of a few (the king, his premier, and his officials). Prejudice and discrimination are given the royal stamp of approval. Against this, the courage and moral fiber of the characters who, in spite of the personal cost, resist wrongdoing and injustice (Vashti, Esther, Mordecai) are highlighted.

Particularly challenging for interpreters of the book is the violence that it depicts; most question whether such bloodshed is necessary, whether Jewish lives cannot be preserved without the loss of non-Jewish lives. Within the constraints of a story world in which royal decrees are irrevocable, there are seemingly few narrative options. Readers must take care not to allow narrative violence to condone real-world violence. The holiday of Purim is established to celebrate not a bloody victory but instead the people's relief of no longer living under mortal threat. This remembrance engenders generosity, as the people are charged to practice charity to those in need.

Present-day concerns lead us to utilize the book of Esther for contemporary ethical discourse in matters that lie outside the story level proper. Most significant, we must acknowledge that we read the book after the Shoah as well as other acts of genocide throughout modern history that, unlike in the story, were chillingly successful in their attempts for ethnic annihilation. If twentieth-century gentiles had followed the example of the book's Persian population and had chosen to side with the Jews and the other persecuted populations, perhaps the massacres of the Third Reich would not have occurred. In addition, concern for gender equality renders problematic the clearly patriarchal and hierarchical social system depicted in the book. Lacking a view of full personhood for women, female worth is measured by how much women "please" men, and despite Esther's superior political abilities, final power rests in male hands.

Bibliography

Day, L. *Esther*. AOTC. Abingdon, 2005.

Fox, M. *Character and Ideology in the Book of Esther*. 2nd ed. Eerdmans, 2001.

Goldman, S. "Narrative and Ethical Ironies in Esther." *JSOT* 47 (1990): 15–31.

Laniak, T. *Shame and Honor in the Book of Esther*. SBLDS 165. Scholars Press, 1998.

Mosala, I. "The Implications of the Text of Esther for African Women's Struggle for Liberation in South Africa." *Semeia* 59 (1992): 129–37.

4

llllllllllllllllllllllllllllllllllllllllllllllllllllllllllllllllllllllllllllllll

WISDOM AND PSALMS

✦ Ethics of Wisdom Literature ✦

Leo G. Perdue

The ethics of wisdom literature in the OT moves in a linear direction from the traditional scribal wisdom of Proverbs, to the critical wisdom texts of Job and Ecclesiastes, to the transformation into apocalyptic and rabbinic teachings. Thus, there were transmutations in the understanding of morality among the ancient sages and scribes of Israel due to historical and social changes from the eighth century BCE to the third century CE.

The Ethics of Traditional Sages and Scribes

Although family and tribe have been viewed by some as the earliest social setting of traditional wisdom, a more likely view is that the canonical and other sacred texts originated in the royal court during the period of the first temple and continued an association with the ruling classes, kings, and, later, Zadokite priests and governors even into the rule of imperial Rome in the early centuries CE. The sages and scribes presented discourse and insights of sapiential ideology that included their views of God, the cosmos, and human nature, behavior, and society. This ideology was transmitted through

87

the generations of wisdom schools at court, then the temple, and finally the *beit midrash* (i.e., "house of interpretation") associated with the synagogue. Sapiential instruction was largely for the education of children of both the aristocracy and the bureaucrats, although by the third century BCE a more democratized wisdom emerged. While it is not true of the later texts of Sirach and Wisdom of Solomon, a more democratized wisdom characterizes the rabbinic literature that included the Mishnah, Tosefta, midrashim, and the Palestinian and Babylonian Talmuds. The social ideology that included moral teachings was routinized textually and was passed down through the generations that experienced an everchanging culture. Any possible egalitarian features of premonarchic Israel were eliminated in favor of the establishment of classes based on hierarchy and power until the last two centuries BCE.

Proverbs. Traditional sages and scribes compiled the seven collections of the book of Proverbs from the eighth to the third centuries BCE and concluded with an introductory instruction (1:2–7) and a final poem (31:10–31). They engaged in their search for knowledge in the world by beginning with the affirmation of "the fear of God." "The fear of God" represented the foundational belief that God was the Creator who established a divine cosmic and social order, brought life into existence, and oversaw and maintained this order through the principle of retribution. This did not operate automatically, but rather was orchestrated by God. All life was good—that is, was filled with blessings and joy—except for that of the wicked and the fool, who experienced punishment and at times even destruction.

The wise of Israel sought out patterns of unchanging phenomena, categories of physical, anthropological, biological, and zoological classifications in the world, and political, social, and economic systems of human construction established by divine creation and guidance. This order (*ṣĕdāqâ*), considered to be part of the cosmic structure established by the Creator to orchestrate and govern the world, became the basis for human institutions and actions. Israelite society, with political and economic control in the hands of the rulers, was understood as grounded in this divine order of the cosmos. Any disturbance of the social order by foolish or criminal behavior was condemned as threatening to disrupt the world and thus was an abomination against God and disobedience to divinely selected leaders. Wealth, especially as gained through the accumulation of property, was viewed as one of the rewards of the righteous and wise, since their actions were in harmony with the cosmic order. By contrast, poverty was generally considered to be the consequence of foolish and/or wicked behavior. This ideology of the traditional sages was understood to be self-evident and was read into their perception of God, the cosmos, and humankind. Through their writings in the various sapiential forms, the sages clearly supported the social worlds in the periods of the first and second temples.

An important metaphor is Woman Wisdom in Prov. 1; 8–9. She is an itinerant teacher who offers life to her followers, a queen of heaven who chooses and directs kings, and the firstborn of God who was present, perhaps active, at creation. She becomes the image of divine transcendence and immanence in a world where God is increasingly remote.

Ben Sira. Ben Sira (c. 200 BCE) was a scribal interpreter of Scripture who taught in an academy (perhaps a Torah school of the temple in Jerusalem or a synagogue school), a scholar of Scripture, and a sage who compiled a list of his teachings, poems, and hymns into a book that underwent later redaction, the book of Sirach. He operated a wisdom school for the children of the wealthy, scribes, political bureaucrats, and aspiring teachers and taught many of the same ethical instructions found in Proverbs' traditional wisdom, except that now he fashioned wisdom, the Torah, and salvation history into a new theological synthesis.

Ben Sira equates wisdom with the Torah and even considers himself an inspired prophet. The equating of wisdom and Torah and the sage as the teacher and interpreter of the law are strong indications that the sages are professionals under the oversight of the temple priests. Thus, he emphasizes the importance of the support of the priests and especially the high priest (notably Simon II), as well as the observance and performing of the rituals of the temple cultus.

Ben Sira likely attended and later taught in a Jewish school in Jerusalem connected to the temple or a synagogue. The synagogue became a place of assembly for the local community, a house of worship, and often, if a *beit midrash* was attached, a location for study, including a formal school. He was an interpreter of earlier texts that became Scripture and was familiar with Greek philosophy, in particular Stoicism. Ben Sira's virtuous sage is described within an aretology in Sir. 38–39 as a loyal servant to God and an ambassador to foreign lands who has cultivated speech and possesses wisdom. Further, the primary virtue is the "fear of Yahweh," expressed in piety, faith in the creator and sustainer of the cosmos, trust in the providential guide of human history, and obedience to the revealed commandments. As the divine potter who creates humanity from the earth, God fashions both the nature and destiny of humans. Making use of Gen. 1:26–28, Ben Sira tells of humans as created in the divine image who rule over the other creatures that fear them. Rulers receive from God the gift of wisdom in order to rule justly. Created to possess freedom of will, humans acquire their knowledge of the Creator through the "fear of God," which they receive in the womb and is equated with reflection on and living according to the commandments.

Personified wisdom is a dominant theme for Ben Sira. Wisdom is the first of God's acts of creation and permeates cosmic and social reality. Wisdom also is given to the sages in order to understand both God and the world. With this knowledge, the sage is able to interpret correctly the Torah and thus to live a moral life. This cosmic wisdom also becomes the divine inspiration that fills the heart of the sage and teaches youth how to behave in order to experience well-being. As the means of divine immanence, Woman Wisdom is the agent of God in revitalizing creation, while just and wise acts of humans strengthen this cosmic order.

In his encomium known as the Praise of the Pious (Sir. 46–50), Ben Sira focuses on noble heroes whose qualities enhanced their character, deeds, and prestige and thus are to be remembered. It is because of their deeds and virtues that their descendants will continue for all times.

Qumran and the moral life. The texts from the Judean Desert indicate that wisdom literature was copied, newly written, and transmitted to the members of a community whose founders, including the enigmatic Teacher of Righteousness, were opponents of the Zadokite priesthood. The Qumran community looked forward to their installation as the legitimate priests, led by a priestly messiah who would control the temple, and also to the return of a royal descendant of David who would rule as the surrogate of God from Jerusalem over the "heavens and earth."

Many of the wisdom texts found in Qumran not only teach the proper course of the moral life but also project a theological worldview from an apocalyptic perspective. Their ethos for this approaching time was shaped by study of the ancestors, the composition of commentaries on prophets, the engagement in piety and ritual cleansing designed to prepare them for worship and the final days and the restoration of the purified cosmos and temple, the knowledge of sacred things, and a prescribed moral behavior of avoiding sins of laziness, greed, impatience, and sexual promiscuity.

Their ethical emphasis was placed on the gift of divine wisdom, which enabled them to know the proper behavior that prepared them for the final conflict between the "Children of Light" and the "Children of Darkness." This wisdom could be known through study and reflection on sacred texts. The order of the cosmos is revealed to and known by only the elect, including the recipients of the instruction who are to reflect on and learn from divine revelation. These apocalyptic sages appropriate the ethical dualism of Proverbs to divide humans into two groups of good/righteous and evil/sinful. This dualism is also projected to a cosmic level. The wisdom of the sectarians is also pedagogical, for its purpose is to teach people the commandments and virtues of piety, study, meditation, sexual purity, hospitality and sharing with the poor, and control of the passions. Once actualized in speech and behavior, these virtues lead to well-being and the future exaltation of the righteous.

Wisdom of Solomon. The final sapiential, canonical/deuterocanonical wisdom book, Wisdom of Solomon, was likely written by a sage or rhetor to a Jewish audience in Alexandria at the time of Rome's control of Palestine and Egypt (30 BCE and following). The book appears to reflect a period of persecution when Egyptian Jews were experiencing a pogrom conducted by Hellenists (Greeks, Egyptians, and possibly some apostate Jews), probably in about 38 BCE.

Traditional wisdom is given new shape in the form of a paraenetic address by linking Jewish wisdom, apocalyptic, the exodus from Egypt, and Greek popular philosophy. This exhortatory speech encourages faithful Jews to maintain their loyalty to their ancestral traditions in the face of persecution, to persuade apostate Jews to return to their religion, and to convince Hellenes of the superiority of Jewish religion and the moral life. The rhetor used both Greek rhetorical and literary features and popular philosophical ideas from a variety of sources. These included the Stoic understanding of the Logos and the four cardinal virtues, the Platonic teaching of the immortality of the soul and the corruptibility of the flesh that hindered the moral life, and Wisdom's guidance of the heroic leadership of unnamed ancestors whose deeds and virtues led to salvation.

This teacher combines creation and redemption into a new theological synthesis. Central to redemption are the elements of justice and wisdom. The divine spirit (Sophia) that permeates creation and dwells within the souls of the righteous and pure (Wis. 7:27) is the architect of all things and guides and delivers the righteous throughout history (Wis. 10:1–11:1). The "good" is understood as virtue and is to be actualized in human behavior. The cardinal virtues are self-control, prudence, justice, and courage, found also in Stoicism. Reason, not the passions, is the highest aspect of human nature for both Stoics and the rhetor, and moral human beings should realize it to control the passions and to follow consistently the ordered world. The life of virtue is to conform to the natural order, which permeates the cosmos and is present in human nature.

The Ethics of the Critical Sages and Scribes

The collapse of traditional wisdom occurred due to the transformation of the sociopolitical order initiated first by the Babylonians (587–539 BCE) and then by the Ptolemies (200–31 BCE). These conquests and oppressive rules brought traditional teaching into disrepute. With the fall of the monarchy, some of the sages continued in the role of counselors, but now they advised the governors appointed by the foreign kings or the temple priests. Others provided instruction in wisdom schools, likely attached either to the temple or to local political institutions. The poetic book of Job likely was composed in the context of a wisdom school, especially since the dialogues make use of the disputation, a sapiential form in which sages debate the authenticity of a teaching. In this case, the principle of retribution grounded in the justice of God is the object of contention. Qoheleth, who was a teacher of the "people" (Eccl. 12:9–14), also likely taught in a wisdom school. This text may have been written as late as the beginning of the third century BCE for a school of scribes by a famous but unidentified sage. This teacher takes on the fictional role of being the "son of David," likely Solomon, who, like Egyptian pharaohs of the Middle Kingdom addressing their successors from the dead, instructs his students in critical wisdom.

Job. The earlier of two canonical texts representing critical wisdom is Job (sixth century BCE). The ideology of the previously uncontested values and affirmations in traditional wisdom is represented by the "friends of Job," who argue that God is a just deity, sure to reward the righteous and punish the wicked. They are inflexible dogmatists. Job, represented as a man of great wealth and status who lost everything, contends that God is a destructive tyrant who seeks capriciously to destroy both creation and the wise and righteous. The justice of God and retribution are assailed. In the concluding theophany, Yahweh first attempts to intimidate Job with power and knowledge but, failing that, admits that he struggles with chaos (Behemoth and Leviathan) for rule over the earth. This strengthening of the power of chaos into a contestant for kingship over the cosmos is a step toward the development of a satanic power.

The prose narrative is an early example story of traditional wisdom prior to the Babylonian captivity (Job 1–2; 42:7–17). This tale is taken by the exilic poet of Job and appended to the poetic dialogue as a prologue and epilogue in which the traditional Job is pious and just and maintains his faith in spite of extreme suffering. Once the poetry and prose are connected, the epilogue concludes, incidentally, that Yahweh is angry with Eliphaz and his two friends for not having spoken "correctly" about him. This rereading of the older, traditional tale of Job suggests that the poet has affirmed the authenticity of Job's repudiation of retribution and the unchallenged justice of divine rule in his speeches with his friends and in his direct challenge of Yahweh. It is unlikely that Job repents. Rather, Job continues to adhere to his condemnation of an unrighteous Yahweh and feels sorry for humankind, who must suffer under the divine yoke. It is in the epilogue that Yahweh is the one who repents, or changes his behavior, when he condemns his three supporters and honors Job with his restoration.

Qoheleth. Several centuries later, in the book of Ecclesiastes, a sage who came to be known only by his office, "Qoheleth" ("one who assembles"), argues against any assertion that the political and social order are ruled over by righteous rulers, and that cosmic rule is presided over by a just deity. His opponents probably were temple scribes and apocalyptic sages, the former of which looked to the past and the Jerusalem cultus as the guarantee of divine favor, while the latter looked to the future as a time of a "new heaven and new earth" when divine salvation and the exaltation of Israel and the righteous would occur. For Qoheleth, any hope in a just social and political order in the present world is repudiated by his own experience. This sage teaches that the behavior of the unknown God is unpredictable, even capricious, although he remains a power to be feared (Eccl. 5:7). The one teaching that Qoheleth offers about God is that one should "fear him." Yet this is actual terror, not faith in a just God of creation. For Qoheleth, it is better to go to the temple to listen than it is to offer the sacrifices of fools and to make unwise vows. Qoheleth does not totally negate the validity of temple worship, but he does stress the fear and trembling that should accompany any who engage in its activities.

Qoheleth argues not only against the justice of God, the principle of retribution, and cosmic and social embodiments of order, but also against a final judgment in which the righteous will be vindicated and the wicked punished. He also denies the teaching that wisdom will enable one to know when and how to act successfully. For him, both the righteous and the wicked, along with the wise and the foolish, face the same fate: death. From death there is no escape, and the tomb is humanity's eternal home. The one boon of human existence, provided by God to anesthetize the pain of suffering and despair, is the joy that one may experience. Joy becomes the basis of Qoheleth's moral system, occurring seven times in the literary structure: joy in one's activities and labor, eating and drinking (a symposium?), and one's spouse. But joy and life are quickly fleeting. Qoheleth does not articulate a program of social justice, but rather is resigned to passive acceptance.

Conclusion

As wisdom transitioned to apocalyptic, the direction of history finally became the end of the present order and the beginning of a "new heaven and new earth." As wisdom's teachings were incorporated into rabbinic texts, they supplemented ethical instruction. Wisdom's social location moved from the court, to the temple, to the synagogue, to the apocalyptic community. The tradition developed from an elitist one for behavior in the court and service to the monarch to a more democratized setting in which the marginalized, such as the Essenes of Qumran, became the elect of God.

◆ Job ◆

Choon-Leong Seow

The question of ethics is implied at the outset of the book of Job as the narrator speaks of Job's character: he is a man who is "blameless and upright" and who "fears God and turns away from evil" (1:1, 8; 2:3). This fourfold affirmation suggests that Job was the quintessential faithful and ethical person—personally (blameless) and socially (just), religiously (fearer of God) and morally (one who avoided wrong). Despite Job's meticulous actions to ensure that nothing ever goes wrong (1:5), however, a capricious agreement in heaven leads to a series of misfortunes that befall him and his family (1:6–2:9). In particular, he is afflicted "with loathsome sores . . . from the sole of his foot to the crown of his head" (2:7), a poignant spectacle because that precise affliction is found elsewhere only as a curse for those who violate the covenant (Deut. 28:35). The rest of the book then debates two key issues: the relevance of the doctrine of retribution in this case, and the proper response in the face of such suffering.

Job's afflictions lead his friends to suspect that something must be amiss in his conduct, even if they do not know what that might be. Their best response is that he should not blame God but rather look deeper within himself, and even if he fails to discover the problem, he should turn to God anyway in praise and in hope of divine forgiveness and restoration. It is the traditional response that we find already in the various "exemplary sufferer" texts from elsewhere in the ancient Near East. The premise is that it is impossible that anyone be without sin, so in the face of unexplained suffering, one should simply count on divine mercy (cf. 1 John 1:8–9). One must look beyond oneself, beyond any efforts to prove one's faithfulness and just conduct, and count instead on God's faithfulness and just conduct.

The reader knows from the prologue, though, that Job is suffering not because of any wrong that he has committed. Job himself, while not denying the possibility that he might have erred, is unwilling to simply accept the premise of traditional doctrine. He sees his friends not as comforters but as tormentors. In his rebuke of them he offers a profound ethic of friendship: "To one who is discouraged, steadfast love comes from one's friends, even if that one may have abandoned the fear of Shaddai" (6:14 [all translations mine]). For Job, God has seemed like an enemy. Whatever "steadfast love" (the biblical term for unwavering loyalty) Job will experience now, therefore, will come not from the deity directly; it will have to come from friends, if it comes at all. In times of deep despair, when God seems utterly inimical, when faith seems impossible, true friendship that does not depend on one's confessional stance, friendship that does not depend on one's theology, may be the very manifestation of grace. In Job's view, though, the friends are not true and cannot be trusted: "Surely you are not [confounded? trustworthy?], for you see trauma and you feared" (6:21).

The allusion to fear harks back to the "fear" in 6:14, where Job speaks of a friendship that manifests steadfast love to one who is desperate, even if that one should forsake "the fear of Shaddai." Job is suggesting that his friends are the ones who fear, not in the sense of being pious, but in the sense of being timid. They fear simply because they have seen Job's trauma, meaning not just his physical condition, but, even more, his apparent abandonment of piety. They fear the blatant theological contradiction that Job embodies in his broken self. Job has portrayed himself as a theological "whistleblower," who is not afraid to face the truth and "tell it like it is," whatever the consequences of doing so (6:10). In that sense, he is not a fearer, and perhaps because of that the friends might have regarded him as impious, one who does not fear. To Job, however, people who are afraid of confronting the tough, faith-shattering questions are not fearers of God. Rather, they are simply fearers, theological cowards, for they fear the truth.

There are profound theoethical reflections like this scattered throughout the book. The most important passage in this regard, though, is Job's oath of innocence in chapter 31, where he goes through a detailed list of crimes that may be committed by anyone, and he denies them all. Yet what is important is not the list itself, what one should or should not do, but how Job goes about his ethical reflection.

He begins with a series of possible sexual offenses, beginning with lust. He claims that he not only has been proper in his conduct, but he even has covenanted with his eyes not to desire (31:1). He speaks thus not only of guilt that is visible, exterior; he speaks rather of interiority (cf. Matt. 5:27–28). Importantly, the basis of such a profound commitment is theological: "What is the portion of God above? What is the lot of Shaddai on high?" (31:2). That is, God has assigned each individual a portion, an area of responsibility (so the Hebrew term implies), and one must honor that assignment.

What Job sets forth in 31:1–12 is his defense of his integrity. He is, therefore, unwittingly corroborating the narrator's and God's judgment that he is blameless. Yet he is also "just"—that is, proper as regards his treatment of others (31:13–18). He speaks of not rejecting the just cause of his male or female servants when they bring a complaint, and he makes it clear that his is a theological ethic: "How shall I act, since God will arise; since God calls one into account, how shall I answer Him?" (31:14). It is an ethic grounded in creation theology: "Surely in the belly the Creator of me created them [Job's servants], and He has formed us in the womb as one" (31:15). What this means, then, is that we must treat others justly out of respect for God's creation, since God is the Creator of all people, regardless of their class or stature. All are created in "the belly," which refers not just to the belly of a human being, but to the realm of God's cosmic rule (see Ps. 139:13, 15).

Job asserts that he has been just to the needy and the defenseless. His words in 31:16–17 are choked with emotion: "[I'll be damned] if I have turned away from the desires of the weak, extinguished the longings of the widow, eaten my morsels by myself, while the fatherless did not partake of it!" In the next verse he states, "For from my youth He has reared me like a father; so from the womb of my mother I will guide her [the widow]." In Job's appeal to creation a few verses earlier, he argues that he as a master treats his slaves respectfully because God is the Creator of them all "in the belly." Now Job moves from birth to parental nurture. He does not treat others unjustly, because God is the parent of all. Indeed, because God is father, Job has been father to the fatherless, and because God is mother, Job has been a mother, a guide to those who need guidance.

The book of Job recognizes as well that God is utterly transcendent and mysterious, and that the divine will may be unknowable. Yet, if that is the case, does human conduct, whether good or bad, matter at all? Does ethics matter if God is unknowable and God's will unknown? Job poses the question crudely, asking whether sinful conduct has negative consequences for God: "If I have sinned, what can I do to you, O guardian of humanity?" (7:20). Eliphaz later reframes the question to make an opposite point, asking how Job's good conduct might have a positive impact on God: "Is it a pleasure to Shaddai that you are righteous, or is it a benefit that your ways are blameless?" (22:3). Elihu deduces, however, as if responding to both formulations, that Job was wondering whether there is any use *for humans* to be in God's favor (34:9). These are questions of ethics when God is silent and hidden in the face of human suffering, and Elihu's own proffer is theologically profound and ethically principled:

If you sin, how do you affect Him?
If your transgressions are many, what do you
    do to Him?
If you are righteous, what do you give Him?
Or what does He receive from your hand?
Your wickedness is for people like yourself,
So your righteousness is for human beings. (35:6–8)

To Elihu, ethics has consequences not for oneself, but for others in the human race. Just as one's wickedness affects others, so too one's righteousness affects others. Thus, Elihu advocates an ethic that is not self-interested: righteous conduct is not for one's own benefit, nor is it even for God's sake. Rather, one acts ethically simply for the common good.

◆ Psalms ◆

Joel M. LeMon

The Psalter manifests the implicit connection between ethics and prayer through its explicit focus on the Torah, the law. Indeed, the very structure of the Psalter reveals a concern for the law, for the five books of the Psalter (Pss. 1–41; 42–72; 73–89; 90–106; 107–150) reflect the fivefold division of the Torah (Genesis, Exodus, Leviticus, Numbers, Deuteronomy). Thus, in its final form, one could understand the Psalter as the law of God in song. Within this framework, numerous individual psalms describe the benefits of living according to the law and the overall necessity of righteous (i.e., orderly) living. Psalm 19, for example, exhorts the faithful to act in ways that preserve the order God has established at creation (vv. 1–6). Just as God has created the world by bringing order to chaos, God created the faithful community by ordering it through the law (vv. 7–14). Individuals and communities can participate in God's creative and ordering work; by living in accordance with the law, the faithful help preserve and sustain the order that God has imposed upon the world.

Many psalms focus on the theme of living righteously—that is, keeping the law (e.g., Pss. 15; 24; 37; 73). Among them, Ps. 1 has pride of place. As the introduction to the Psalter, it sets the agenda for all that follows. The first verses of this psalm reveal that a clear choice faces all individuals regarding how they will live in relationship to God and the world. One option is to live with and like the wicked (1:1), yet such a life leads inexorably to destruction

(1:4–5, 6b). The other option is to live righteously and enjoy the rich blessings of God as a result (1:2–3, 6a). Given the extreme consequences of these options, it may seem surprising that the psalm names only one specific activity that characterizes the righteous life: meditating on the law (v. 2).

Modern readers often understand meditation as the process of entering into a state of silence, tranquility, solitude—even transcendence. However, the Hebrew verb *hāgâ* (translated "meditate" in the NRSV) actually suggests none of these connotations. Rather, *hāgâ* has a broad semantic range that includes numerous modes of speaking: uttering, reciting, growling, murmuring, and even singing (LeFebvre). To meditate on the law (Ps. 1:2) is to use a variety of forms of speech to talk to God and about God's justice. That is to say, the essence of meditation on the law is prayer; and framed this way, the entire Psalter becomes an extended meditation on the law. In light of Ps. 1, one discerns that the Psalter presents an ethic of prayer. Prayer is the sole foundation of righteous behavior, informing and shaping every action in the lives of the faithful. Right actions rely on constant dialogue with God.

In the Psalter, this dialogue appears in beautiful and arresting poetry, set in a variety of genres (individual and communal laments, hymns, songs of thanksgiving, etc.). Taken together, these prayers give expression to the profound joys and deep sorrows that accompany a life lived honestly in relationship with God. Yet there remains a significant challenge for those who seek to live out the ethic of prayer that the psalms embody. Many psalms reflect a fear of the violence of the wicked enemies and contain prayers for Yahweh to provide both salvation from and retribution against the enemies. The violent pleas of the psalmist— for example, that God slay the wicked (Ps. 139:19) or shatter the heads of the enemies (Ps. 68:21)—create unease among many modern readers, for these passages seem to blur the line between salvation from enemies and retribution against enemies. One wonders if it is right for the psalmist to pray this way.

There have been many suggestions for how Christians should understand the psalms that curse the enemies and invoke God's violent actions against them—the so-called imprecatory psalms. Erich Zenger has helpfully outlined a number of the proposals (13–22). Some interpreters have considered these psalms to reflect a pre-Christian or anti-Christian Judaism that is utterly contrary to Jesus' teaching of love for one's enemies (Matt. 5:4; Luke 6:27, 35). This supersessionist viewpoint has led to the dismissal of certain psalms altogether or at least to the practice of reading only selected verses of problematic psalms so as not to acknowledge the psalmists' desire for God to act violently against the enemies. The sad irony is that such supersessionism has actually motivated and ostensibly justified brutal acts of violence by Christians against Jews.

In response to this, an increasingly common trend is to find ways to reclaim the psalms of imprecation as appropriate and even vital elements of Christian piety. According to one line of thinking, violent thoughts that go unacknowledged can degrade and pollute the relationship between God and the faithful. Praying honestly requires voicing these feelings, so these psalms function as a form of theological catharsis for those who suffer greatly (McCann 115). Such catharsis is a necessary step in healing. Similarly, Patrick Miller has suggested that psalms of imprecation are valuable for Christian faith and practice in that they represent a simultaneous "letting go" and "holding back." The prayers validate the experience of suffering and acknowledge the need for retribution, even as the psalmists restrain their emotions by praying the violence rather than executing violence themselves (Miller 200). Thus, these psalms in fact present a radical ethic of nonviolence. By placing violence in the context of prayer, the psalmists reject the right of human retribution and trust in God alone to bring about justice (Firth 141).

These responses to the problem of violence in the psalms have merit, but questions remain. It is difficult to maintain that the psalms categorically reject any act of retribution by humans against humans. While the Psalter commonly pictures Yahweh as the one who would execute violence on the enemies, in several cases humans are the ones meting out violence (e.g., Pss. 18; 149). Whether one understands this violence as execution of divine justice or vengeance, these psalms suggest that such human violence somehow serves the will of a righteous, judging God.

A community's patterns of prayer reflect and inform its behavior. Thus, someone who prays for blessings of widows, orphans, and the downtrodden (Ps. 146:8–9) also will be inclined to minister to the needs of these people just as God does. Likewise, it is reasonable to assume that someone who prays for God to execute violence on evil oppressors may be motivated to act as God's agent and inflict violence if and when that is possible. Violent prayers may ultimately have a deleterious effect on the community if they lead to the assumption that one can act as God's agent and mete out divine retribution.

At this point, the antiphonal nature of the psalms becomes critical to understanding their ethic of prayer. In ancient Israel, as today, prayers uttered within a community prompt the community's "Amen!" (e.g., Deut. 27:19–26; 1 Chr. 16:36; Pss. 41:13; 72:19; 89:52; 106:48; Jer. 28:6); that is, the community can serve as a moderator of the prayers, confirming some prayers with its amen and withholding its amen from other prayers, when, for example, the violence of the prayer does not suit the actual situation of the supplicant. A faithful and sensitive community affirms that it is better to pray that God would act violently against the enemies than it is for supplicants to do violence and take matters into their own hands. Yet the community is also aware that prayers shape behavior. And violent prayers can be as dangerous as they are healing. Thus, for every prayer in the psalms, particularly for violent ones, a community serves a critical role, regulating and affirming the prayers with its amens.

Bibliography

Firth, D. *Surrendering Retribution in the Psalms: Responses to Violence in the Individual Complaints*. PBM. Paternoster, 2005.

LeFebvre, M. "Torah Meditation and the Psalms: The Invitation of Psalm 1." Pages 213–25 in *Interpreting the Psalms: Issues and Approaches*, ed. D. Firth and P. Johnston. InterVarsity, 2005.

McCann, J. *Theological Introduction to the Book of Psalms: The Psalms as Torah*. Abingdon, 1993.

Miller, P. "The Hermeneutics of Imprecation." Pages 193–202 in *The Way of the Lord: Essays in Old Testament Theology*. Eerdmans, 2007.

Wenham, G. "The Ethics of the Psalms." Pages 175–94 in *Interpreting the Psalms: Issues and Approaches*, ed. D. Firth and P. Johnston. InterVarsity, 2005.

Zenger, E. *A God of Vengeance: Understanding the Psalms of Divine Wrath*. Westminster John Knox, 1994.

◆ Proverbs ◆

Timothy J. Sandoval

The book of Proverbs directly addresses questions concerning ethics and the moral life. It is an anthology of "wisdom" material that includes long instructional poems (chaps. 1–9); collections of short, pithy sayings commonly thought of as "proverbs" intermingled with direct admonitions (chaps. 10–29); and other instructional material, including an acrostic poem (chaps. 30–31).

The poems in Prov. 1–9 deploy the metaphor of the "two ways" to speak of the possibilities of moral life: the way of wisdom and righteousness leads to life; the way of folly and wickedness leads to death. These poems exhort the reader to forsake the way of folly and follow the way of wisdom. Wisdom's value, or desirability, in the poems is persistently and metaphorically highlighted in terms of material riches (e.g., 2:4; 3:14–16; 8:10–11) and erotic attraction (e.g., 4:6, 8–9; 7:4). Wisdom is more valuable than wealth and offers not merely literal, material riches, but the "enduring wealth" of virtue (8:18) and is personified for the book's presumed original young, male audience as a desirable and marriageable woman (Yoder).

Yet, Proverbs recognizes that life's two divergent paths may not always appear so different from each other; it speaks of the enduring value of wisdom's way, but also of the powerful (if superficial) attraction of the way of folly and wickedness. The "sinners" who follow this way, for example, also hold out a promise of (ill-gotten) "precious wealth" to the one who would join them (1:10–19). Likewise, Prov. 1–9 not only personifies wisdom as a virtuous and desirable woman; these chapters also speak of another desirable woman: the strange or foreign woman, who, on a literal reading of the text, is best understood as an adulteress, potentially able to seduce the addressee (e.g., 2:16–19; 5:3–23). The adulteress, however, is symbolically linked with folly, which is later also personified as a woman (9:13–18). Together, the strange woman and Woman Folly constitute the mirror image of Woman Wisdom (9:1–6; cf. 1:20–21; 7:10–12). They represent all that belongs to the dangerous, wrong way.

By deploying images of desirable women and valuable material wealth in relation to the ways of wisdom and folly, Prov. 1–9 undertakes the moral task of training the desires of its addressee along the better of the two paths. Although wealth and erotic fulfillment are pleasing and can afford temporary advantage, neither, according to the sages of Proverbs, is ultimately as desirable as wisdom. The pursuit of these and other lesser goods, the text suggests, ought to be subordinated to the pursuit of wisdom and appropriately ordered by wisdom's virtues.

The precise content of the virtues that constitute wisdom's way, however, is only minimally sketched in Prov. 1–9. The short sayings, or "proverbs," and admonitions of Prov. 10–29, by contrast, address a spectrum of topics relevant to daily life that together comprised the themes of moral discourse in ancient Israelite wisdom traditions: right and wrong speech, diligence and slothfulness, wealth and poverty, the rich and the poor, and so forth.

Folklorists who have studied the proverbs of a range of cultures have demonstrated that the oral "performance" (or use) of such sayings in everyday settings regularly serves important moral purposes—in ethical instruction, decision-making, legal reasoning, and promoting the prized values and virtues of the culture in which they are current. However, the precise meaning, and hence moral import, of any proverbial saying is dependent on the concrete context in which it is uttered. When it is divorced from its oral context, a proverb becomes rootless and loses its full connotation. Wolfang Mieder has gone so far as to claim that "a proverb in a collection is dead" (Mieder 892) because, by definition, a proverb that is written in a book is devoid of its oral context.

If Mieder is correct that a proverb in a collection is dead, certain problems for understanding the book of Proverbs arise, since this text in large part consists precisely of proverbs in collections. Some commentators advocate "recontextualizing" the sayings of Proverbs for today's world (Bergant) and suggest that readers of the book today consider their own lives and apply any biblical proverbs that might prove to illumine those contexts.

Recontextualizing biblical proverbs is one way in which the contemporary ethical import of aspects of the book of Proverbs might be recognized and made accessible. Yet, scholars have long debated whether the sayings of Proverbs are the kind of oral, folk proverbs with which Mieder and other folklorists are concerned, or whether they represent the literary production of learned sages. If the sayings of Proverbs are not the kind of proverbs normally deployed in oral contexts, any recontexualizing can appear artificial and awkward.

In fact, it is likely that the sayings of Proverbs are not mere transcriptions of the oral, proverbial wisdom of the folk of ancient Israel and Judah, but rather are tropes that have been consciously shaped by the literary hand of professional scribes. Hence, they reflect and promote the virtues and moral perspectives of an intellectual elite, though not necessarily an economic or political elite.

Thus, in order to understand the moral landscape of Proverbs, it is most productive to consider the book's literary character. In this regard, the prologue in Proverbs (1:2–6) provides a hermeneutical cue for understanding both the book's moral purpose and how the text's literary features relate to the book's instruction. These verses indicate that Proverbs is concerned with instilling in its addressee intellectual virtues that it calls "wisdom," "instruction," and "insight" (v. 2); the social virtues of "righteousness, justice, and equity" (v. 3); and practical virtues such as "shrewdness" (v. 4). A close examination of 1:2–4 (see Sandoval) also indicates that v. 3 stands at the pinnacle of the passage's poetic structure, suggesting that the sages who constructed Proverbs particularly prized social virtue.

If vv. 2–4 of the prologue outline the content of Proverbs' teaching, vv. 5–6 signal how Proverbs' instruction will be presented by means of tropes (NRSV: "proverbs"), figures, and riddles. The book's moral discourse therefore is not a discourse that can be comprehended in merely literal terms; it requires readers who will thoughtfully examine its figurative dimensions.

Considering Proverbs' teaching within the literary horizon sketched by the prologue is important because the book sometimes is characterized as a simple guide to success. This understanding is largely due to an overly literal reading of the book's retributive rhetoric, which appears simplistically to promise good things to those who pursue wisdom's way and bad things to those who stray onto folly's path. The book's association of wealth with wisdom, for instance, often is thought to suggest that the one who finds wisdom should inevitably be rewarded with literal, material riches. Similarly, because the text also relates specific virtues (e.g., diligence) with images of material wealth, and certain vices (e.g., sloth) with images of material lack, sayings such as "A slack hand causes poverty, but the hand of the diligent makes rich" (10:4) sometimes are thought to "blame the poor" for their poverty and to congratulate the wealthy for their virtue. Since Proverbs also recognizes the real social advantage that wealth often provides the rich (10:15; 18:23; 22:7), many likewise believe that the book's moral bias is in favor of the economic elite. Yet, because the text also insists that the poor be treated with kindness and justice, some have characterized much of the book's moral discourse as ambiguous.

However, by recalling that Proverbs is likely the product of a scribal (intellectual) elite, and that the prologue communicates the sages' preference for social virtue or justice (1:3) via figurative language, modern readers can approach the text in a meaningful manner while avoiding the extremes of literalism or acquiescence to the book's apparent moral ambiguity.

Readers can achieve this by, on the one hand, recognizing that Proverbs' retributive rhetoric, even if it ought not to be understood in a simple, literal manner, does suggest a correlation between the attainment of wisdom and good things, or a "good life," and by, on the other hand, identifying another important moral-theological claim made in the book: wisdom's close relationship to creation. According to Prov. 8:22–31, wisdom is intimately related to Yahweh's act of creation and might be said to infuse creation itself. Hence, those who attain wisdom's virtues and thus align themselves with the genuine nature of the wisdom-infused cosmos ought not be surprised if they reap real-life well-being.

Proverbs 8:22–31 is furthermore significant because here wisdom is personified as a woman and is arguably presented as a divine being whom Yahweh "acquired" (NRSV: "created"), perhaps as a consort, at "the beginning of his work" (v. 22). She both preexists creation (8:23–26) and is present at the moment of creation (8:27–29), if not actively creating with Yahweh as a "master worker" (8:30). As an independent and creative being beside the male Yahweh, Woman Wisdom has proved a remarkably generative image for much feminist ethical and theological work.

Bibliography

Bergant, D. *Israel's Wisdom Literature: A Liberation-Critical Reading*. Fortress, 1997, 78–107.

Mieder, W. "The Essence of Literary Proverb Studies." *Proverbium* 23 (1974): 888–94.

Sandoval, T. *The Discourse of Wealth and Poverty in the Book of Proverbs*. BIS 77. Brill, 2006.

Yoder, C. *Wisdom as a Woman of Substance: A Socioeconomic Reading of Proverbs 1–9 and 31:10–31*. BZAW 304. De Gruyter, 2001.

✦ Ecclesiastes ✦

Eunny P. Lee

Moral formation is an important goal of wisdom literature, and Ecclesiastes is no exception. The title derives from the Greek translation of the Hebrew word *qōhelet*, which means "gatherer of an assembly" and functions as a pen name for the author. According to the epilogue, Qoheleth was a sage who "taught the people" (12:9 [hence the NRSV rendering "Teacher"]). But the teachings of this sage, marked by incongruities and radical skepticism, have perplexed readers, both ancient and modern. Qoheleth himself was perplexed by what he observed in the world, repeatedly declaring that "all is vanity [*hebel*]." The Hebrew word *hebel* literally means "vapor" or "breath" and is used as a metaphor for the ephemeral, incomprehensible, and unreliable dimensions of life, whatever is beyond the grasp of mortals. Because of the ubiquity of this motif (thirty-eight occurrences), many conclude that Qoheleth is a thoroughgoing cynic who despairs of finding anything good in life. Others, however, highlight the equally persistent counterpoint of joy that runs throughout his discourse with ever-increasing urgency and verve. There is a growing recognition that the book cannot be reduced to either one of these sentiments; indeed, the contradictions are part and parcel of its message.

Observation of moral incongruities leads Qoheleth to overturn all notions of human certitude. However, he does not give up his quest to determine what is good (2:3). He presses on to address fundamental questions: What does it mean to be human? How should one live in a world beyond human control?

In reconstructing his moral vision, Qoheleth critically engages traditional sources: wisdom teachings, Torah, Solomonic traditions, as well as other ancient Near Eastern literature. A hallmark of the wisdom tradition, however, is its empirical, contextual, life-centered approach to moral reflection. Qoheleth accordingly gives considerable authority to his own perception and experience. Under the guise of the wise king par excellence, he sets out on an ambitious program to investigate "all that is done under heaven" (1:13). His favorite verb is *r'h* ("to see, experience"), and he is most often the explicit or implicit subject. Qoheleth reports what he sees: injustice and oppression (3:16; 4:1; 8:9), the unpredictability of divine economy (2:26; 6:1–3), contradictions between traditional precepts and reality (7:15; 8:10–14; 9:11–13). He communicates his findings through literary vehicles that capture the imagination: memorable proverbs, gripping anecdotes, evocative poems. In short, the sage employs all the resources of the wisdom tradition, both its method and its forms, to lend weight to his teachings and to recast traditional profiles of wisdom.

Another element in Qoheleth's account of the moral life is the fear of God (3:14; 5:6; 7:18; 8:12–13; 9:2; 12:13). Rejecting sentimental religiosity, Qoheleth emphasizes the vast distance between God and humanity. Creation is ordered by God, and norms for the good life are a part of this design. But its logic is hidden from mortals, for God is wholly other (3:11; 5:2). God's inscrutable determination of events and the contingencies of an unpredictable world impinge on human agency, so that humans must relinquish control. They can respond only to what happens, moment by moment (3:1–15; 7:13–14). That is not to say that foresight is useless (10:10). Qoheleth does value wisdom, but he also exposes its limits and vulnerabilities. His teachings are therefore built on humble grounds that recognize both the tragic limitations and the joyous possibilities in humanity's "portion."

Qoheleth's ethic of enjoyment is all the more compelling because of its unflinching realism. Enjoyment entails perceiving things rightly; it is "seeing the good" or "seeing well" (2:1; 3:13; 5:17; 6:6, 9; 7:14; 11:9). The verb *r'h* connotes not only observation but also the meaningful integration of what one "sees." And Qoheleth urges his audience to encounter fully both the good and the bad (7:14a). He endorses not a hedonistic ideal that is intent on avoiding pain and maximizing pleasure, but rather an authentic and full-blooded experience of the world.

Enjoyment is described also in terms of the basic pleasures that sustain life: eating, drinking, working, sleeping, being with one's beloved (2:24–26; 3:12–13, 22; 5:17–19; 7:14; 8:15; 9:7–10; 11:7–12:1). Qoheleth thus presents a material and concrete understanding of the good life. Enjoyment is located resolutely in the fulfillment of fundamental needs, including not only physical but also vocational and relational pleasures. These are the things that God provides in order to make and keep human life human. They describe in concrete terms the desirable goals of life.

By associating enjoyment with basic needs, Qoheleth opposes the insatiability of the human appetite that can lead to destructive consumption. Enjoyment therefore has important socioeconomic implications. Indeed, the book's preoccupation with such issues is suggested by its frequent use of commercial terms. Although the debate about the book's provenance is ongoing (with recent scholarship converging on the postexilic period), Qoheleth clearly addresses an economically volatile context in which opportunities for wealth existed alongside risks of financial disaster. To hedge against possible loss, people toil away for more and more in an obsessed attempt to find some security or advantage. The acquisitive impulse that Qoheleth observes takes on a heightened virulence in contemporary culture, shaped by its technology of mass communication in service to a consumerist ethos. In contrast, Qoheleth's ethic of joy commends the habit of contentment. Enjoyment is not about the pursuit of more, but rather is the glad appreciation of what is already in one's possession by "the gift of God." Likewise, his work ethic is intimately connected with life's simple joys, not the pursuit of an elusive profit (Brown, "Whatever Your Hand Finds to Do").

Moral formation takes place in community; Qoheleth, however, seems to dwell in isolation, with communal concerns absent from his self-referential monologue. Nevertheless, a communal vision may be teased out from what he bemoans in his reflections. When he observes the plight of the oppressed, what disturbs Qoheleth is not only the fact of oppression but also that those who suffer have "no one to comfort them" (4:1). He also laments the absurdity of a solitary miser who toils away, with no companion to share in his riches (4:7–8). The focus of Qoheleth's despair is the unmitigated isolation of these individuals. In contrast, two are better than one (4:9–12).

A social dimension is also implicit in his most common metaphor for enjoyment, eating and drinking, which in the moral world of the OT takes place in the context of community. Qoheleth, admittedly, does not describe communal meals, but his rhetoric concerning the proper use of food suggests that an individual's enjoyment must never come at the expense of neighbor. He condemns irresponsible forms of feasting, which impede a person's capacity to fulfill social obligations (10:16–20). In contrast, the ethical life is characterized by a different kind of recklessness. The exhortation to "send out your bread upon the waters" (11:1–2) is a call to perform charitable deeds with abandon, and it constitutes an important expansion of Qoheleth's ethic of enjoyment. One must enjoy the bread in one's possession; one must also gladly release it for the benefit of others.

Bibliography

Brown, W. *Character in Crisis: A Fresh Approach to the Wisdom Literature of the Old Testament.* Eerdmans, 1996.

———. "'Whatever Your Hand Finds to Do': Qoheleth's Work Ethic." *Int* 55 (2001): 271–84.

Christianson, E. "The Ethics of Narrative Wisdom: Qoheleth as Test Case." Pages 202–10 in *Character and Scripture: Moral Formation, Community, and Biblical Interpretation*, ed. W. Brown. Eerdmans, 2002.

Fox, M. *A Time to Tear Down and a Time to Build Up: A Rereading of Ecclesiastes*. Eerdmans, 1999.

Seow, C.-L. *Ecclesiastes*. AB 18C. Doubleday, 1997.

———. "Theology When Everything Is Out of Control." *Int* 55 (2001): 237–49.

◆ Song of Songs ◆

Chip Dobbs-Allsopp

Of all biblical literature, Song of Songs may well be the least obvious site for an ethically oriented kind of criticism. Indeed, these poems' exquisite reveling in the erotic escapades of two young lovers outside the bounds of marriage, if anything, is likely to put Song of Songs beyond the ethical pale for many with traditionally oriented pieties. Yet, let us consider 4:1–7. In its essence this section offers a poetic rendition of a boy gazing at a girl. In the conceit of the so-called *wasf* (in Arabic literature, a genre in which an extended description of a person or other object is elaborated), the poem follows the boy's line of vision, as it were, as he admires one part of his beloved's body after another, moving from her head, topped with long, flowing dark hair, down to her gazelle-like breasts. At the very least, the poem provides a wonderful literary site from which to enter the discussion initiated by Laura Mulvey in 1975 about the "male gaze." But there is more here. This poem's staging of the "male gaze" has something positive of its own to contribute to the conversation. Gazing is never neutral, and far too frequently males looking at females even in the Bible results in violence perpetrated against the woman (e.g., Dinah in Gen. 34), though female gazing is not necessarily innocent either, as evidenced by the Shulammite's own stares in Song of Songs, which occasionally overwhelm her beloved (4:9; 6:5).

Still, not all gazing is of a kind; not all gazing, even by men, is destructive. These poems are a case in point. Here tone, however intangible and nebulous a quality, forever resisting precise specification, is absolutely critical. There is little doubt as to the loving nature of this boy's gaze. He is, after all, the one whom the girl's "soul loves" (3:1–4) and in whose eyes she finds "well-being" (*šālôm* [8:10])—a gazing, in other words, that is not only not malignant but also is judged by this girl to be life-enhancing. Here, then, in 4:1–7 we have the kind of "male gaze" that a woman can honor and enjoy, "one where the desire to discover her beauty is linked to a desire to discover her otherness, both sexually and personally" (Lambert, cited in Steiner 219). Worries over the hurt and violation that can result from the "male gaze" are real, well documented, and not to be lightly dismissed. But males are also capable of gazing lovingly, or so these poems would provoke us to believe—a not insignificant moral insight.

Song of Songs does not wear its ethics on its sleeves. After all, it is a sequence of love poems and not a treatise on the moral life. In this, it is very much like most of the Bible, in fact, where moral concerns are mostly not presented explicitly as points of textual interest. Therefore, whatever ethical sensibilities are to be gleaned from these poems require acts of reading, as in the much (too) abbreviated reading of 4:1–7 here, intent on engaging matters of ethical interest.

Not all is fair game, of course. Song of Songs, by dint of its subject matter—love—will open on to some moral issues more seamlessly, more readily, than others, and the book's own cultural particularity will itself always demand ethical negotiation. Moreover, readers will want to remain ever attuned to the lyricism of this poetry's underlying medium of discourse (see Dobbs-Allsopp), as not all that is of moral relevance is given propositionally in such poems (e.g., tone can have an ethical uptake). But in the end, the project of reading Song of Songs toward specifically ethical ends is a wonderfully open project that awaits only the decision to put these age-old love poems into conversation with the moral issues of the day. The possibility of a loving male gaze as provoked in the foregoing reading of 4:1–7 is offered as but one example of what may be achieved through such an ethically interested kind of criticism. There are many more poems in Song of Songs to read, and myriad moral concerns toward which to read them.

Bibliography

Dobbs-Allsopp, F. W. "Psalms and Lyric Verse." Pages 346–79 in *The Evolution of Rationality: Interdisciplinary Essays in Honor of J. Wentzel van Huyssteen*, ed. F. Shults. Eerdmans, 2006.

Mulvey, L. "Visual Pleasure and Narrative Cinema." *Screen* 16, no. 3 (1975): 6–18.

Steiner, W. *Venus in Exile: The Rejection of Beauty in Twentieth-Century Art*. Free Press, 2001.

5

iiiiiiiiiiiiiiiiiiiiiiiiiiiiiiiiiiiiiiiiiiiiiiiiiiiiiiiiiiiiiiiiiiiiiiiiiiiiiiiiiiiiiiiiiiiiiiiiiii

PROPHETS

♦ Isaiah ♦

Eunny P. Lee

This book takes its name from Isaiah of Jerusalem, a prophet whose ministry spanned the reigns of four Judean kings in the eighth century BCE. However, portions of the book address a much later and much different context in Israel's history, suggesting that it is a composite work. Chapters 1–39 deal primarily with the events and circumstances of Isaiah's day; because of rampant corruption and social injustice, the prophet announces that divine judgment is imminent, and that it will come at the hands of Assyria, the reigning world power. A dramatic shift occurs in chapters 40–55 ("Second Isaiah"), which proclaim a message of comfort and restoration to a people who have long been exiles in Babylon (597–539 BCE). Although stylistically similar, chapters 56–66 ("Third Isaiah") seem to presuppose yet another context, in which the exiles are back in their homeland but struggling to reestablish themselves as a viable community. Recent scholarship, however, has emphasized not only the diversity of this corpus but also its unity. Indeed, it appears that material spanning some 250 years was intentionally edited and shaped to create a thematic/theological coherence. The current form of the book, thus, has an overarching theme that highlights the drama of God's judgment of Israel for its national sin and the promise of a glorious restoration to follow.

For Isaiah, the moral life is grounded in the character and will of God, who is sovereign over all creation and passionately involved in Israel's life. Because Judah and its leaders are at odds with God, the word of the Lord, through the mouth of the prophet, confronts the wayward people with a life-or-death choice: if they forsake evil and learn to do good, they will enjoy life on the land; if not, devastation will come (1:16–20; cf. 58:1–14).

To discern and articulate God's will, Isaiah draws from Israel's religious heritage, including traditions about Zion that celebrate the supremacy of God and the inviolability of God's chosen city. In Isaiah's theological ethic God's supremacy relativizes, indeed dwarfs, all other claims to power, so that prideful rebelliousness becomes the cardinal moral offense (2:11–22; 3:16–17). Humble obedience and trust are the virtues that the prophet prizes above all (7:3; 26:3–4; 30:15; 32:17; cf. 57:15; 66:2). This fundamental orientation impacts all spheres of life, even international relations. Hence, with Assyria making its westward move, Isaiah counsels the kings of Judah (Ahab in 8:11–15; Hezekiah in 37:6–7) to trust in God, not in diplomatic relations, to protect Jerusalem (30:1–15). Indeed, Assyria is merely the rod of divine judgment (10:5–19), and Judah must temporarily submit to it. Although the Zion tradition promised that God would always defend Jerusalem from its enemies, Isaiah turns that ideology on its head, arguing that because the city had become morally defiled and unfit for God's presence, God would purify it in judgment to make it habitable once more (4:2–6; 29:1–24).

Of course, obedience to God also has implications for Judah's internal relations. Instead of caring for the poor and vulnerable members of society as Torah required, Isaiah's audience was guilty of oppression and miscarriages of justice (1:16–23; 3:13–15; 5:8–24; 10:1–2; 29:21). Land ownership was a focal issue. Family-based land was a vital source of material support, critical for the living of a good life, and Isaiah bewails the destructive conduct of those who amass property at others' expense (3:14; 5:8). Moreover, he condemns not only the exploitation of the vulnerable but also the habitual drunkenness of the ruling class, which breeds misjudgment (5:11–13, 22–23; 28:1–13). The moral failure has implications for Judah's religious life. Isaiah categorically denounces its worship practices as detestable (1:10–15), because a right relationship with God cannot be cultivated without a right relationship with one's neighbor.

Chapters 40–55 address a broken people on the other side of judgment. This corpus engages ethics less directly, and its moral vision must be discerned in the way the prophetic voice breaks through the despair of the exiles and awakens them to renewed trust. The material continues Isaiah's emphasis on God's sovereign power but declares that it is now redemptively focused on Israel. Hence, the poet employs both hymnic and disputatious forms to make a passionate appeal for the exiles to trust God instead of Babylon (40:12–31). Even Cyrus the Persian, the emancipator who would take down Babylon and release its captives, is called a servant of God (44:28; 45:1). The prophet also draws from exodus and creation traditions to construct vividly the possibility of a new beginning (see Brown). In short, he marshals his theological resources and vast literary skills to inspire faith and move the people to action (their homeward journey).

At the same time, the enigmatic figure of a humble servant who brings forth justice and healing adds an important qualification to the message of deliverance. The "Servant Songs" (42:1–9; 49:1–6; 50:4–11; 52:13–53:12) suggest that justice is established through one who is willing to suffer for others. They also suggest that Israel's release from exile is not just for Israel's sake but has a larger purpose that embraces the nations. This gives meaning to Israel's suffering. It is not a sign of divine abandonment; rather, the servant's suffering was God's surprising way of bringing salvation to all.

Chapters 56–66 reflect the crisis of a people back in Jerusalem struggling to rebuild a city and form a community. And this section of the book also makes some important ethical claims. First, it renews Isaiah's earlier insistence on obedience to Torah that rises above self-serving scrupulosity (58:1–14; 59:1–15). As before, the focus is on proper administration of justice and tending to the needs of the weak. Second, its conception of community is remarkably inclusive, so that even those formerly excluded from the religious community now share in the new life together (56:3–8).

Finally, in spite of the harsh realities of resettlement, the accent is on the gracious promises of God, surely to be fulfilled (see especially chaps. 60–62; 65:17–25; cf. 40:8; 55:11). Eschatological visions occur throughout the book (2:4; 11:6–9; 35:1–10) but are all the more pronounced at its culmination. They present an alternative vision of reality in which God's good purposes—*shalom*, security, fruitfulness, and joy—will prevail over all creation. This hope fuels the moral life. The glorious vision summons the people to a way of living that is commensurate with it and contributes to its realization.

The book ends, however, with a cautionary word of judgment against the rebellious (66:24). Jerusalem, the renewed city, is a wondrous gift from God, but it does not merely descend from heaven. It requires human agents to build it, and that inevitably entails dissension and conflict. Although the book has a decided movement from judgment to hope, the reference to corpses and unquenchable fire stands as an acknowledgment of (and warning against) human strife that continually imperils God's (re)creation.

Bibliography

Barton, J. "Ethics in the Book of Isaiah." Pages 67–77 in vol. 1 of *Writing and Reading the Scroll of Isaiah: Studies of an Interpretive Tradition*, ed. C. Broyles and C. Evans. VTSup 70/1. Brill, 1997.

Brown, W. "I Am about to Do a New Thing: Yahweh's Victory Garden in Second Isaiah." Pages 229–69 in *Ethos of the Cosmos: The Genesis of Moral Imagination in the Bible*. Eerdmans, 1999.

Brueggemann, W. *Isaiah 40–66*. WestBC. Westminster John Knox, 1998.

Childs, B. *Isaiah*. OTL. Westminster John Knox, 2001.

Goldingay, J. *Isaiah*. NIBC. Hendrickson, 2001.

Mays, J. "Justice: Perspectives from the Prophetic Tradition." *Int* 38 (1983): 5–17.

Oswalt, J. "Righteousness in Isaiah: A Study of the Function of Chapters 55–66 in the Present Structure of the Book." Pages 177–91 in vol. 1 of *Writing and Reading the Scroll of Isaiah: Studies of an Interpretive Tradition*, ed. C. Broyles and C. Evans. VTSup 70/1. Brill, 1997.

✦ Jeremiah ✦

Else K. Holt

The book of Jeremiah presents poetic oracles, sermons, and discourses in Deuteronomistic style, and narrative material from the last days of Judah and Jerusalem before the final assault of the Babylonians in 587 BCE. Chapters 1–25 contain oracles of judgment and doom, arranged in thematic collections, introduced by prose sermons (Stulman), and ending with a prose oracle of judgment against the whole world. Chapters 26–45 consist primarily of prose narratives that illustrate the kings' and the people's lack of reception of the prophetic warnings and its consequence, the fall of Jerusalem. Chapters 46–51 present oracles against the nations that surround Judah; chapter 52 repeats the narrative of the fall of Jerusalem, 2 Kgs. 24–25. Two poetic collections deserve special interest, the so-called Confessions of Jeremiah (11:18–12:6; 15:10–21; 17:14–18; 18:18–23; 20:7–18) and Book of Consolation (chaps. 30–31).

Jeremiah traditionally is dated to the late monarchic and early exilic periods. The prophet is believed to have received his calling in 627 BCE (1:5–19); his death is untold in the biblical text. The dating and authorship are disputed in recent scholarship, since a valid distribution of authentic and redactional layers is considered to be uncertain at best. The differences between the Hebrew (MT) and the Greek (LXX) versions also warrant that Jeremiah be read on the background of and as a witness to an innertextual theological discussion that ran for at least four centuries after the time of the prophet.

The basic message of Jeremiah is that the people have abandoned the covenantal relationship with Yahweh (in English Bibles, "the LORD"), their only God, and have followed foreign gods. Therefore, God will send foreign armies to wage war against them. By and large, as opposed to Amos, for example, social, cultic, or moral conduct is not the primary concern in Jeremiah. Ethical questions are subsumed under the covenantal headline, ethical or moral transgressions being viewed as consequences of apostasy.

Our primary direct source to ethics in Jeremiah is the so-called Temple Sermon in Jer. 7. The prophet urges the people to amend their ways and their doings (7:3), summed up in acting justly one with another; not oppressing the alien, the orphan, and the widow; not shedding innocent blood in this place (i.e., the temple/the land); and not following other gods (7:5–6). These recommendations represent the basic Deuteronomic ethos of protecting vulnerable social groups in society, so closely contingent with common ancient Near Eastern law. As examples of the people's transgressions, the prophet uses a short version of the Decalogue (cf. Deut. 5). He accuses the people of stealing, murdering, committing adultery, swearing falsely, making offerings to Baal, and going after other gods, and then believing that their trust in cultic observance will save them nevertheless (7:9–10). True observance of the law is manifested in keeping both the religious and the ethical commandments.

Accusations of ethical misdemeanors (e.g., greed for unjust gain [8:10]) are raised against the ruling classes, most of all the kings. In chapter 22, a collection of oracles about the monarchy, King Jehoiakim is accused of building his house by unrighteousness and injustice, making his neighbor work for nothing, and thus transgressing his social responsibility. Moreover, his house is built with excessive luxury, as a spacious house with paneling in painted cedar, in order to show off royal opulence. By contrast, his father, King Josiah, is touted as an example of good governance. He lived more modestly, and he implemented justice and righteousness and took care of the cause of the poor and needy, whereas Jehoiakim's "eyes and heart are only on dishonest gain, for shedding innocent blood, and for practicing oppression and violence" (22:17). Thus, the ethical demands made of a ruler in Jeremiah are in accordance with the Deuteronomistic ideal, which puts limitations on royal authority and admonishes the king not to acquire several wives or silver and gold in great quantity, in order to keep his heart with the Lord, "neither exalting himself above other members of the community nor turning aside from the commandment" (Deut. 17:20).

All in all, modesty seems to be an ideal in Jeremiah, and drunkenness, for example, is seen as a disgraceful state that makes the offender vulnerable to punishment, a potent display of divine rage (Jer. 25:15–29).

In the late oracle Jer. 31:31–34, the Lord promises that some day in the future he will make a new covenant with the house of Israel and the house of Judah: "I will put my law within them, and I will write it on their hearts; and I will be their God, and they shall be my people." The new covenant is aimed at creating a relationship between God and his people that is not subject to the uncertainties and damage afforded by the human propensity to sin. The knowledge of the Lord, internalized in the people, will lead to a life of justice and righteousness. In the NT, this new covenant is understood as fulfilled in the Lord's Supper (e.g., 1 Cor. 11:25), and the idiom has named the two biblical collections, the Old and New Testaments (Gk. *diathēkē*; Lat. *testamentum*).

From a modern perspective, Jeremiah can be an unpleasant book to read, given its violent and sexually offensive language. The relationship between God and God's people often is pictured in metaphors of war, cruelty, environmental catastrophes, and matrimonial violence. Israel, which once was God's wife, is portrayed as a wild ass in heat and as a whore, whose master has every right to punish her (chap. 2). For this reason, criticism is raised from both feminist and ideological-critical exegetes against some parts of the message of Jeremiah. Only in a few chapters, primarily in the Book of Consolation, do we find testimony of a forgiving God who cares for the exiled people. In the end, however, the powerful image of God crying like a mother for daughter Zion (8:18–22) adds a nuance of feminine empathy to the image of the OT God as an angry sovereign.

Bibliography

Stulman, L. *Jeremiah*. AOTC. Abingdon, 2005.

◆ Lamentations ◆

Chip Dobbs-Allsopp

In the midst of Lam. 3 (vv. 25–39), where the poem's speaker ("the man" [Heb. *haggeber*] of v. 1) considers Judah's traditional teachings about how to cope with suffering (see Dobbs-Allsopp 119–22), comes the commendation "to give one's cheek to the smiter, and be filled with insults" (v. 30). Emmanuel Levinas, perhaps the twentieth century's foremost thinker of "the other," finds in this verse (Levinas, *Otherwise*, 111) insights that prove central to his account of subjectivity and the self, which, stated simply, is "suffering for the other" (Gibbs 56). Key among these insights is the idea of vulnerability, that "aptitude . . . for 'being beaten,' for 'getting slapped'" (Levinas, *Humanism*, 63), a susceptibility to trauma and persecution that makes possible the extraordinary human capacity "to pass from the outrage undergone to the responsibility for the persecutor . . . from suffering to expiation for the other" (Levinas, *Otherwise*, 111). To suffer in such a way, "by the other," is to take care of that other, to "bear him, be in his place, consume oneself by him. All love or hatred of one's fellow man as a thoughtful attitude supposes this prior vulnerability" (Levinas, *Humanism*, 64).

As ever, Levinas is a thinker of lived experience, and here one suspects that the insight reached bears the imprint of his own survival of the Shoah, that time in which even those most cherished of Enlightenment notions of self—as autonomous, free, rational—could not deflect the embodied vulnerability that ultimately subsists and envelops the self "from top to toe and to the very marrow" (Levinas, *Humanism*, 63). This analysis of persecution, intentionally extreme, still is intended to say something about the self's ordinary relations to the other; indeed, the entire middle section of Lam. 3 (vv. 25–39) is rendered in an expansive and inclusive voice such that the poem's audience may more readily assimilate the perspective(s) on suffering being scrutinized (see Dobbs-Allsopp 122). And yet the insight gained is one that the experience of persecution would surely teach, rendering brutally apparent the outer limits of a self's autonomy, freedom, and rationality. Nevertheless, in Levinas there is no glorification or "deliberate seeking of suffering or humiliation" (Levinas, *Humanism*, 63), no drawing "from suffering some kind of magical redemptive virtue" (*Otherwise*, 111); the alluding swerve away from the "turning of the *other* cheek" in the Gospels is patent (Matt. 5:39; Luke 6:29) (see Gibbs 56–57). For Levinas, suffering in itself is "precisely an evil" and "useless" and in the other "unforgivable to *me*" (Levinas, *Entre nous*, 92–94). Indeed, it is this perspective, as achieved (in this instance) through the experience of the Shoah, that leads Levinas to proclaim the end of theodicy: such suffering—"suffering for nothing"—"renders impossible and odious every proposal and every thought that would explain it by the sins of those who have suffered or are dead" (Levinas, *Entre nous*, 98).

Levinas's choice of texts by which to think these issues through is far from serendipitous. Lamentations is one of the Bible's more antitheodic works (Dobbs-Allsopp 27–33; see also Braiterman). In fact, one of the more poignant expressions of antitheodic sentiment in Lamentations comes in 3:42. Having contemplated several traditional poses toward suffering, including the "tending of the cheek" in verse 30, the speaker confronts Judah's God, "We have transgressed and rebelled, and you have not forgiven," thus refusing, rather acutely, any suggestion that the suffering experienced by "the man" of Lam. 3 (and the community whom he personifies and ventriloquizes) is finally containable by notions of sin, guilt, or theodicy. Renewed lamentation and complaint follow, counterpointing and countermanding wisdom's presumptuous grasp of human suffering (see Dobbs-Allsopp 122–28). Levinas is adamant that the only way that suffering's "congenital uselessness" can take on meaning is when it is "suffering *in me*, my own experience of suffering," "a suffering for the suffering . . . of someone else" (Levinas, *Entre nous*, 94). This, for Levinas, is the very essence of human "subjectivity," a responsibility for the other in "the form of the total exposure to offense in the cheek offered to the smiter" (Levinas, *Otherwise*, 111).

The book of Lamentations, like so much biblical literature, does not present itself textually as a treatise on morality. And thus whatever ethical sensibilities are to be gleaned from it requires readerly interventions, acts of reading intent on engaging matters of ethical interest. Levinas's reading of (and with) Lam. 3:30 is one such act of ethically interested reading. It is a spectacular act of such a reading, in fact, as this one biblical verse lies at the "centerpiece" of Levinas's argument in *Otherwise than Being* (xlvii). But there are more verses in Lamentations—many more, in fact, and myriad contemporary moral concerns toward which to read them.

Bibliography

Braiterman, Z. *(God) after Auschwitz: Tradition and Change in Post-Holocaust Jewish Thought*. Princeton University Press, 1998.

Dobbs-Allsopp, F. W. *Lamentations*. IBC. John Knox, 2002.

Gibbs, R. *Why Ethics? Signs of Responsibilities*. Princeton University Press, 2000.

Levinas, E. *Entre nous: On Thinking-of-the-Other*. Trans. M. Smith and B. Harshav. Columbia University Press, 1998.

———. *Humanism of the Other*. Trans. N. Poller. University of Illinois Press, 2003.

———. *Otherwise than Being; or, Beyond Essence*. Trans. A. Lingis. M. Nijhoff, 1981.

◆ Ezekiel ◆

Andrew Mein

The book of Ezekiel is the third major prophetic work in the OT, attributed to Ezekiel son of Buzi, a Jerusalem priest deported to Babylonia by

Nebuchadnezzar in 597 BCE. The book falls into three parts: chapters 1–24 are mainly oracles of judgment against Jerusalem and Judah, chapters 25–32 are oracles against the nations, and chapters 33–48 are principally taken up with promises of restoration, including the visions of the dry bones (37:1–14) and the new temple (40–48). The book is punctuated by dramatic visions of God, which set the scene for the prophet's call in exile (1:1–28), then describe Yahweh's abandonment of his temple to destruction (8–11) and return to his new dwelling place at the heart of a perfected Israel (43:1–9).

Sources and Assumptions

Ezekiel's ethic is fundamentally one of obedience to God's will revealed in "statutes and ordinances" (5:6–7; 11:12, 20; 18:17; 20:11; 36:27). Ezekiel draws on a range of earlier traditions, but the priestly influence is preeminent, and Ezekiel is much more positive about worship and ritual than are prophetic predecessors such as Amos and Micah. The prophet's personal commitment to purity is evident in his claim never to have defiled himself with unclean food (4:14). His moral language is heavily dependent on priestly forms of speech; his arguments often resemble priestly case law (14:1–11, 12–20; 18:1–32 [cf. Lev. 17; 19]); and his analysis of Israel's behavior is full of ritual concepts such as defilement, profanation, and purification. From the perspective of exile, where all Judah's old certainties are crumbling, Ezekiel succeeds in keeping the temple as a focal point for communal values and aspirations (Mein). As a priest, Ezekiel places a high value on hierarchy and order (especially visible in 40–48), and honor and shame also play a significant part in the prophet's worldview. Indeed, the logic of the book (seen in a nutshell in 36:16–32) is that Yahweh has been shamed by Israel's disobedience, and that both judgment and salvation are "for the sake of my holy name" (36:22).

Moral Issues

Ezekiel's oracles of judgment condemn Judah's failings in three main areas: cultic apostasy, political faithlessness, and social injustice. However, the main purpose of these oracles is not social analysis but rather theodicy. Ezekiel's task is to persuade the exiles that the current disaster is fully under Yahweh's control, indeed that it is Yahweh's only possible response to Jerusalem's grievous sins. In turn, the oracles of restoration promise a divine re-creation of both individuals and national institutions that will preclude the possibility of disobedience.

Responsibility is perhaps the key ethical theme in the book. Ezekiel 18 over-turns the exiles' claim that their current troubles are not their fault but rather that of their parents. By setting out a test case in which each of three related individuals—a wicked father, a righteous son, and a wicked grandson—is judged on the basis of his own sins, Ezekiel challenges his hearers to take re-sponsibility for their own situation. Past scholarship saw Ezekiel as the great herald of individual responsibility, moving beyond more "primitive" notions of corporate responsibility and punishment visible in both the Decalogue and the Historical Books. Ezekiel's contribution probably is more modest than a wholesale ethical revolution; rather, he takes ideas of individual responsibility that had long prevailed in legal proceedings and applies them afresh to the matter of divine judgment (Joyce).

Jacqueline Lapsley notes a tension in Ezekiel between different understand-ings of the moral self. The calls to repent (14:6; 18:32) presuppose that human beings have the capacity to do good and to reform themselves, whereas the promise of the new heart (11:19; 36:26) is both more deterministic and more pessimistic about the possibility of human virtue. It is the deterministic view that ultimately predominates in the book, as we see a shift from Jerusalem's responsibility for judgment to Israel's passivity in the face of restoration. An-drew Mein sees this theological shift as also reflecting the social experience of Ezekiel's hearers, who have moved from positions of power and responsibility in Jerusalem to live with the much more limited moral possibilities of life in exile.

The force of Ezekiel's rhetoric at times raises its own moral difficulties. This is most true of the two chapters (16; 23) in which Jerusalem is portrayed as a promiscuous wife, guilty of adultery and murder, destined for shame and brutal punishment. The rhetoric works by placing Ezekiel's (probably male) hearers in the position of a shamed and degraded woman and thereby shocking them into accepting their guilt. At the same time, it implies that women's sexuality is wild, defiling, and in need of control, and feminist critics warn that an ethical reading of these metaphorical texts must take into account their potential to perpetuate male dominance and even to justify violence against real women.

Contribution

Ezekiel's readers have sometimes been ambivalent about the prophet's contri-bution to ethics. Recent concerns about gender follow on earlier criticism of the prophet's emphasis on ritual. However, Ezekiel's very strangeness helpfully marks the distance between our world and that of the texts and reminds us that biblical prophecy does not approach ethics in a sanitized, theoretical way.

The oracles arise out of the pain and confusion of the Babylonian deportations and the destruction of Jerusalem. Driven by an absolute conviction of God's holiness and power, the prophet articulates views of responsibility, free will, and social order that are still contested in contemporary ethical discourse.

Bibliography

Block, D. *The Book of Ezekiel*. 2 vols. NICOT. Eerdmans, 1997–98.

Darr, K. "Ezekiel's Justifications of God: Teaching Troubling Texts." *JSOT 55* (1992): 97–117.

Joyce, P. *Divine Initiative and Human Response in Ezekiel*. JSOTSup 51. JSOT Press, 1989.

Lapsley, J. *Can These Bones Live? The Problem of the Moral Self in the Book of Ezekiel*. BZAW 301. De Gruyter, 2000.

Matties, J. *Ezekiel 18 and the Rhetoric of Moral Discourse*. SBLDS 126. Scholars Press, 1990.

Mein, A. *Ezekiel and the Ethics of Exile*. OThM. Oxford University Press, 2001.

Odell, M. *Ezekiel*. SHBC. Smyth & Helwys, 2005.

Odell, M., and J. Strong, eds. *The Book of Ezekiel: Theological and Anthropological Perspectives*. SBLSymS 9. Society of Biblical Literature, 2000.

♦ Daniel ♦

Anathea Portier-Young

As war captives exiled to the court of Babylon, Daniel, Azariah, Hananiah, and Mishael are chosen for service to the conquering king, trained in Babylonian sciences, and given new names (1:3–7). Yet they abstain from the king's food and wine, relying for sustenance not on imperial patronage but on divine providence (1:8–16). Six stories portray their trials and success (chaps. 1–6). God grants them wisdom (1:17; 2:19–23) as they rise to power (2:46–49; 3:30; 5:29; 6:4, 29). Daniel interprets dreams, solves riddles, and speaks hard truth to raging, proud, and drunken kings (chaps. 2; 4; 5). The heroes give their bodies over to death rather than worship the king's idol (chap. 3) or abandon the practice of prayer (chap. 6). God delivers them (3:25–29; 6:23).

Symbolic visions follow (chaps. 7–12): a parade of beastly empires, exposing the monstrosity of warring and rapacious kings who deal out deception and death; the fiery throne of the Ancient of Days; judgment against the beastly empires; and eternal dominion given to one like a human being (chap. 7); and future persecution, when some will betray the covenant while wise teachers of

Judea fall to sword and flame (11:30–36). By their witness and self-sacrifice these teachers will make the many righteous and wise (11:33–35; 12:3). The angel Michael will take his stand in this anguished time to set the faithful free (12:1). Many of the dead will rise: some to eternal life, others to eternal disgrace (12:2).

The visions were written and joined to the stories during this persecution. In 167 BCE the Seleucid king Antiochus IV Epiphanes, ruler over Judea, banned the practice of Jewish faith, commanding Jews to sacrifice on alien altars, eat defiling foods, and profane their holy days and sanctuary. He burned Torah scrolls. Those who refused his commands he killed (1 Macc. 1).

In response, the book of Daniel promotes an ethic of nonviolent resistance and civil disobedience. Its politics is theopolitics, viewing all human rule in the light of divine rule. Daniel's critique of empire highlights its violence, greed, ambition, and deception. The vision of one like a human being promises the alternative of humane rule in which God's holy people participate in and imitate the justice of God's rule (7:13–14, 18, 27). The author's belief in God's deliverance and confidence in their angelic champions excluded the path of armed resistance. Instead, the book exhorts its readers to hold fast to the covenant and give public witness to truth even in the face of death.

Daniel is the first biblical book to articulate a belief in the resurrection of the dead, assuring its readers that God honors the covenant promises even when appearances say otherwise. God's faithfulness encourages their own. At the same time, when faced with the choice between worshiping an idol to preserve their life or dying in faithful service to God, the heroes Shadrach, Meshach, and Abednego (here called by their Babylonian names) give no consideration to outcomes (3:15–18). They do not need to believe that God will save them in order to do what is right.

The ethics of the book of Daniel draws on Israel's sacred traditions, including the Torah of Moses and the prophets (9:6–13). Daniel himself consults the scroll of Jeremiah (9:2); the author identified the wise teachers with Isaiah's suffering servant. Traditional prayers of penitence modeled appropriate confession of sins (9:3–21). Myths of the divine warrior who defeats the beasts of chaos and death provided a powerful symbolic framework for critiquing the empires and asserting God's power and will to save (chap. 7). At the same time, the book of Daniel draws on and engages traditions from other cultures. Israel adapted the divine warrior myths from Canaanite tradition. Daniel recasts the Babylonian art of interpreting dreams, drawing it within the purview of God's revelation. The apocalyptic worldview so central to the book's moral vision similarly adapts elements from Persian and Babylonian religious traditions. The visionary critique of empire borrows techniques from prophetic resistance literature elsewhere in the Hellenistic world. The multiple sources of Daniel's moral vision testify to a dynamic process of acculturation, affirming the authority of Israel's native traditions while speaking a new authoritative word into a new cultural moment.

The book of Daniel's activist stance demands engagement with the powers of the earth. While the visions engage in radical critique of empire, aiming to position the faithful outside its web of deception, the stories show the heroes enmeshed in imperial structures of power. They serve in the courts of Babylon, exercise rule, and accept the king's patronage. They participate in the moral economy of the empire and speak their critique from within. What is empire today? Does the contemporary reader stand inside or outside? How does one defend against royal and self-deception in the exercise of power?

Finally, how do those who seek to actualize Daniel's theopolitics, as many have done, avoid reinscribing structures of domination? Over the centuries, Daniel has been used to demonize nations, regimes, and religious traditions, fanning hatred and fueling violence among those who would inaugurate the eternal rule of Daniel's holy ones. The book's nonviolent ethic, recognition of our complicity in the imperial economy, and emphasis on a posture of humble penitence speak against such interpretations. Its call to martyrdom challenges believers in every age.

Bibliography

Barton, J. "Theological Ethics in Daniel." Pages 661–70 in *The Book of Daniel: Composition and Reception*, vol. 2, ed. J. Collins and P. Flint. Brill, 2002.

Fewell, D. *Circle of Sovereignty: Plotting Politics in the Book of Daniel*. Abingdon, 1991.

Goldingay, J. "Daniel in the Context of Old Testament Theology." Pages 639–60 in *The Book of Daniel: Composition and Reception*, vol. 2, ed. J. Collins and P. Flint. Brill, 2002.

Pace, S. *Daniel*. SHBC. Smyth & Helwys, 2008.

Rowland, C. "The Book of Daniel and the Radical Critique of Empire. An Essay in Apocalyptic Hermeneutics." Pages 447–67 in *The Book of Daniel: Composition and Reception*, vol. 2, ed. J. Collins and P. Flint. Brill, 2002.

Smith-Christopher, D. "The Book of Daniel." Pages 19–152 in *The New Interpreter's Bible*, vol. 7, ed. L. Keck. Abingdon, 1996.

✦ Hosea ✦

Brad E. Kelle

This OT book is associated with Hosea, son of Beeri. Hosea was a prophet active during the turbulent, final years of the northern kingdom of Israel (ca.

750–720 BCE). He is best known for the stories of his marriage to Gomer (1:2–9), and the book uses the prophet's broken family as a metaphor for the people's relationship with God. Yet the bulk of Hosea (chaps. 4–14) contains divine judgments against Israel's political and religious leaders for various kinds of wrong behavior and calls the people to return to faithfulness in light of God's love. Metaphors drawn from family, agricultural, and animal realms address the people's life before God. Ethical engagement with the book requires an exploration of these metaphors, especially the ways they fund an alternative imagination for their hearers' perception of reality.

The prophet's words focus on the moral failures of the people in their fidelity toward God and others (e.g., 4:1–3). Although often thought to be associated with the worship of the Canaanite god Baal, Hosea's criticisms are more typically concerned with the hypocrisy of the leaders of the community, especially kings (7:5–7; 8:4–10) and priests (4:4–6), accusing them of worshiping God ostensibly yet refusing to follow God's desires in the social and political dimensions of the community's life. In Hosea's view, the health of the kingdom depends on ethical leadership that comes from a sense of fidelity to God and generates faithfulness among the people. The book places these ethical demands in the broader context of God's enduring love for the people (2:14–23; 11:1–9; 14:4–8), which offers the ability to return to God for reconciliation.

The ethical discourse of Hosea poses difficulties for contemporary readers. In addition to depicting a punishing God, much of Hosea's language and imagery, especially in the marriage metaphor of chapters 1–3, is patriarchal, using female characters and experiences to represent sin and describing acts of physical abuse and sexual violence as symbols for divine judgment. In modern contexts so rife with domestic violence, such actions, even when depicted as a means toward reconciliation, can lead to views of God that produce destructive behavior, especially toward women and children. One can emphasize the ancient cultural context of these images or use other biblical depictions of God as correctives, but raising questions about such imagery and the import that it might have in contemporary society is a necessary part of ethical reflection on Hosea.

Not limited to its original context, Hosea's language and metaphors speak into any situation in which politics, economics, and religious ideology have become intertwined to serve the interests of the economically and socially advantaged. In the same way that the prophet challenged the royal and social elite of his day, the book offers an ongoing word of judgment against the co-opting of religious beliefs and practices in the service of social, political, military, and economic systems that injure the vulnerable and tear at the fabric of the community. Such a word of judgment, however, remains in the context of an enduring divine love, which permits the hopeful possibility of redemption from the destructive systems of power, greed, and violence.

Bibliography

Keefe, A. *Woman's Body and the Social Body in Hosea*. JSOTSup 338. Sheffield Academic Press, 2001.

Kelle, B. *Hosea 2: Metaphor and Rhetoric in Historical Perspective*. SBLAB 20. Society of Biblical Literature, 2005.

Simundson, D. *Hosea, Joel, Amos, Obadiah, Jonah, Micah*. AOTC. Abingdon, 2005.

⬩ Joel ⬩

D. N. Premnath

The short but complex book associated with the prophet Joel has generated much scholarly discussion on a variety of issues, such as the date of the book, the nature of the locust invasion (real or symbolic), the unity of the book, and the relevance of its message. Particularly challenging is the prophet's insistence on judgment and punishment without ever specifying the transgression of the people. The placement of the book between Hosea and Amos may be due more to its thematic affinity than chronological proximity. In the absence of specific information, it is likely that the parameters for the date of the book lie somewhere between the sixth and fourth centuries BCE. The two-part division in the book (1:1–2:27; 2:28–3:21), each part with a contrasting message, tone, or mood, need not entail different authorship. The first part may be seen as relating to a crisis and resolution as experienced by the prophet's community, while the remainder of the book may be seen as presenting the prophet's broader vision for the future.

From an ethical perspective, three themes deserve mention. First, Joel sees a close connection between people's lives and the environment. When nature/land is affected, people's lives are affected, and the reverse would be true as well. The root cause for this is the lack of proper relationship to God. The assurance of new life in terms of economic renewal (2:18–27) is the result of Yahweh's response to the crisis. Second, in the passage on the outpouring of Spirit, Joel offers a vision that is barrier-breaking. The promise of the prophet is for the empowering of "all flesh" (2:28). By further specifying the recipients—sons and daughters, old and young, male and female servants—the prophet reinforces the idea that the outpouring of the Spirit knows no discrimination based on sex, age, or class. Third, Joel goes on to say that the Spirit is given for the purpose of prophesying and receiving dreams and visions. The recipients of the Spirit will be a nation of prophets. The use of the terms *dreams* and *visions* shifts the focus to something that is essential to prophecy. Prophecy often is understood merely as social critique or ethical urging. Joel goes one step beyond in calling for a broader vision. In its fundamental sense, prophecy is the ability to see the invisible—an alternative vision. The prophet Joel's vision is barrier-breaking as it seeks to redefine social perceptions, attitudes, and structures, thereby paving the way for a new ethic.

Bibliography

Barton, J. *Joel and Obadiah*. OTL. Westminster John Knox, 2001.

Birch, B. *Hosea, Joel, and Amos*. WestBC. Westminster John Knox, 1997.

Crenshaw, J. *Joel*. AB 24C. Doubleday, 1995.

Mason, R. *Zephaniah, Habakkuk, Joel*. OTG. JSOT Press, 1994.

Wolff, H. *Joel and Amos*. Trans. W. Janzen, S. McBride, and C. Muenchow. Hermeneia. Fortress, 1977.

✦ Amos ✦

M. Daniel Carroll R.

The book of Amos perennially has generated interest because of its strong ethical message. Its strident condemnation of oppression and of religious ritual has resonated in diverse contexts over time. Many consider Amos and other prophets of that era—Isaiah, Micah, and Hosea—as the zenith of what has been called "ethical monotheism": they are champions of God's universal demand for justice. Recently, liberation theologies have found a valuable resource in Amos.

The book's heading (1:1) locates the prophet in the reign of Jeroboam II of Israel in the mid-eighth century BCE. This was a time of economic exploitation facilitated by the internal policies of the monarchy and international political and economic realities. The text is less interested in analyzing these underlying realities than in appealing to moral sensibilities concerning the plight of the needy, the arrogance of nationalism, and the nature of acceptable worship.

The book of Amos draws on various strands of theological traditions in ancient Israel. Its vocabulary and themes find echoes in the wisdom literature and the covenant demands of the law, while the concern for the sanctuaries and rituals suggests that the prophet was well acquainted with the religious world of that time. The moral voice of Amos is full of indignation and sarcasm, and the ethical realities presented in the book are complex and include every sphere of social life.

The exploitation of the poor is a key theme. They are sold into slavery because of debts and suffer undue taxation and unfair treatment in legal proceedings (2:6; 5:10–15; 8:4–6). In the midst of this injustice the comfortable enjoy abundance (3:15–4:3; 6:4–6; cf. Isa. 3:16–4:1; 5:8–25; Jer. 22:1–16). The well-to-do acquire their goods and status with violence toward the vulnerable (3:9–10; cf. Mic. 2:1–5; 3:1–4). The cruelty of the nations in warfare that is condemned in the opening chapter is evident within the borders of the people of God in the abuse of the unfortunate.

Although this socioeconomic criticism is aimed at those who take advantage of the weak, the prophet also turns his withering gaze against the nation as a whole. He mocks its military pretense. The litany of conflicts in chapter 1, the mockery of insignificant victories (6:13), and the announcement of comprehensive defeat in the near future (2:14–16; 3:11–12; 5:1–3, 16–17, 27; 6:8–14; 7:9, 17; 8:1–3, 9–10; 9:9–10) undermine Israel's confident posturing. Apparently, this pride in military power was shared by the entire populace. All crowded the sanctuaries to celebrate the national deity, whom they felt would ensure their safety. But the Lord God of hosts will have none of this worship that ignores oppression and takes his endorsement for granted (3:14; 4:4–6; 5:4–6, 18–27; 7:9; 9:1; cf. Isa. 1:10–20; 58; Jer. 7:1–11; Mic. 6:6–8; Mal. 3:2–5). The visions reveal that Israel is "so small" (7:1–6) and that its mighty fortresses actually have walls like "tin" (7:7–8 NET [not "plumb line," as in many translations]). The religious ideology that Amos so fiercely derides is defended by the high priest Amaziah (7:10–13). What made this uncritical and self-deceiving wedding of patriotism and religion even more insidious is that those who are the victims of the injustices of the nation cheer this perversion of the divine will along with the rest. They stubbornly accept that system and champion king and country (4:4–12).

The Lord desires that Israel seek and love the good and hate evil. This "good" is to be manifested concretely in the socioeconomic relationships of the community (5:10–15). It is to be the public display of righteousness and charity, which they have distorted and undermined (5:7; 6:12). God desires both just structures and a people of virtue. Ideally, they would have been nurtured in those ideals in their worship gatherings and would have had exemplars worth imitating in their leaders, but this is clearly not the case (4:1; 6:1; 7:9–10, 16–17; cf. Isa. 1:23; Ezek. 34).

The coming judgment is comprehensive. Some readers are troubled that all suffer the divine punishment. The text teaches, however, that sin and its recompense are not only individual or perfectly symmetrical. Judgments in history are not tidy. The personal and the social are interwoven, and the web of community ties complicates the nature of sin and chastisement. Transgression is systemic; it is embedded in social relationships in every sphere, and all are complicit at some level. The ideological distortions of faith also know no class, racial, or gender boundaries. Nations violate the norms of God on the international stage as well, as they go to war to acquire power, labor, and land (1:3–2:3; cf. Isa. 13–23; Jer. 46–51).

Amos teaches that everyone is guilty, especially the people of God whose knowledge and experience place them beyond excuse (2:11–12; 3:1–2; 9:7). At times, those who are innocent of some of these transgressions endure undeserved hardship. That is why the leaders are held most responsible for the plight and fate of their people. They make the domestic and foreign policies that affect everyone else and set a moral tone for society.

The broad, realistic ethical vision of Amos incorporates economics, politics, and religion. It involves individuals, social groups, and the entire nation in its censure. Yet this book also proclaims a future of peace, plenty, and a restored relationship with God and creation beyond the present injustice and the imminent wrath (9:11–15). Judgment is not God's final word. That future is an ethical hope that helps readers bear the contradictions of today and should motivate them to work to approximate that coming reality in the contemporary world.

Bibliography

Barton, J. *Understanding Old Testament Ethics: Approaches and Evaluations*. Westminster John Knox, 2003.

Brueggemann, W. *The Prophetic Imagination*. 2nd ed. Fortress, 2001.

Carroll R., M. D. *Amos—The Prophet and His Oracles: Research on the Book of Amos*. Westminster John Knox, 2002.

———. "Seeking the Virtues among the Prophets: The Book of Amos as a Test Case." *ExAud* 17 (2001): 77–96.

Dempsey, C. *Hope amid the Ruins: The Ethics of Israel's Prophets*. Chalice, 2000.

Heschel, A. *The Prophets*. Harper & Row, 1962.

Houston, W. *Contending for Justice: Ideologies and Theologies of Social Justice in the Old Testament*. Rev. ed. LHBOTS 428. T&T Clark, 2008.

O'Brien, J. *Challenging Prophetic Metaphor: Theology and Ideology in the Prophets*. Westminster John Knox, 2008.

✦ Obadiah ✦

D. N. Premnath

Two things about the book of Obadiah stand out. First, a book comprising only twenty-one verses has generated significant scholarly literature over the years. Second, part of the reason for the interest in the book, notwithstanding its anti-Edom polemic, may be the incorporation of some key prophetic themes within a span of twenty-one verses. The prophet touches on some familiar themes/motifs such as the day of Yahweh (v. 15), judgment against foreign nations (vv. 15–16), Zion theology (vv. 17, 21), retributive justice of God (v. 15), promise of repossessing the land (vv. 19–20), and the ultimate rule of Yahweh (v. 21). There are also echoes of prophecies from Joel (2:32) in verse 17 and Jeremiah (49:7–22) in verses 1–11. The imagery of the cup of wrath found in Jer. 49:12 also appears in verse 16. The relationship of Obadiah to other oracles against Edom found in Amos 1:11 and Jer. 49:7–22, among others, deserves closer scrutiny. Suggestions for the historical stimulus for the book have ranged from the preexilic conflict as reflected in 2 Kgs. 8:20–22 to a late postexilic context contemporaneous with Malachi or Joel. The most likely scenario seems to point in the direction of the catastrophe of 587 BCE.

Obadiah can be divided into two parts. Verses 1–15 describe judgment against Edom for its attitude and action toward Judah. Verses 16–21 take on a more general tone in that they are addressed to the "nations" about the impending judgment coupled with the promise of restoration for Judah. Three aspects of the Edomites' role draw the prophet's ire. First, although the Edomites did not initiate the action, they simply stood by and watched as the enemies carried out their assault against Judah (v. 11a). The ethical challenge of Obadiah here is this: we may not be guilty of inflicting oppression and violence, but have we chosen simply to watch as violence and oppression continue? Second, after being bystanders, the Edomites became participants in the act (vv. 11b, 13c, 14). Finally, to add insult to injury, they gloated over the misfortune of Judah (vv. 12a, 13b [cf. Ezek 35:10–15]).

From an ethical perspective, it is hard to condone or justify the xenophobic outlook presented in the book. But this must be put into perspective in light of Obadiah's emphasis on the sovereignty of God over not just Judah but over all nations. God's sovereignty manifests itself in the form of God's justice. God will not let evil go unpunished. As the focus shifts from Edom (v. 1) to the nations (v. 15), the message becomes broader to include all forces counter to God's purposes. Obadiah's word of hope to the victims is that in the end evil will be punished.

Bibliography

Barton, J. *Joel and Obadiah*. OTL. Westminster John Knox, 2001.

Ben Zvi, E. *A Historical-Critical Study of the Book of Obadiah*. BZAW 242. De Gruyter, 1996.

Mason, R. *Zephaniah, Habakkuk, Joel*. OTG. JSOT Press, 1994.

Raabe, P. *Obadiah*. AB 24D. Doubleday, 1996.

✦ Jonah ✦

Barbara Green

Commanded by God to proclaim divine judgment to the Assyrian city Nineveh, Jonah refuses. He flees by ship, but he is jettisoned by its sailors when they learn that he is the cause of the storm that is threatening them. Rescued when swallowed by a large fish, Jonah prays for deliverance and is deposited on dry ground. God reissues the Nineveh assignment, and Jonah obeys. His words are few but effective. The city turns from its evil ways, and the destruction threatened does not happen. The book ends inconclusively with Jonah and God discussing the nature of mercy.

The most pressing ethical questions concern relations with opponents: God with sinners (here, Ninevites and Jonah); Jews (here, Jonah) with oppressors.

The book makes clear that God threatens the Ninevites due to their (unspecified) evil. Clearer still, God responds to Ninevite repentance and defers punishment. For the ancients, God serves as explanatory factor for events poorly understood. Here, punishment is threatened, mercy shown.

Commentators vary widely about Jonah's feelings toward those to whom he preaches. Granting that he declined his assignment at first, there is no suggestion that his eventual preaching was grudging or resentful. He preaches five Hebrew words: laconic but sufficient. We are not told Jonah's response when Nineveh responded to his preaching. Any certitude that Jonah wished ill to Israel's enemy is misplaced until chapter 4. With preaching and repentance accomplished, Jonah becomes displeased, though Hebrew syntax leaves the object of his anger ambiguous. He complains to God about divine graciousness, providing it as the reason for his initial flight. Jonah takes shelter outside Nineveh, in a hut, shaded by a vine. But when a worm eats the vine and the sun beats down on Jonah, he prays in anger again. God speaks with him, asking a question, offering an analogy. God probes by analogy the nature of divine mercy, asking rather than telling Jonah how mercy may be relevant. The story ends with God's question to Jonah, whose nonresponse prompts the reader to ponder why God might show concern. Scholars confirm that the story is about compassion without agreeing on the relevance of what God has said.

Many (more Christians than Jews) hold that the book's point is that Jews ought to be more open to gentiles. But others have recently argued that the book, written plausibly after the destruction of the city of Nineveh (612 BCE), might reflect worry by the citizens of postexilic Jerusalem, who knew that their own city, like Nineveh, had been both rebuked for its sins and reprieved by God. If Nineveh could collapse even after being spared, might the same fate be in store for Jerusalem? How could they avoid a fate that might be deserved but was dreaded? How can Jerusalem's citizens learn God's ways, even if all they have are clueless prophets?

Finally, with so many questions open in a book that seems at first glance simple, readers may recognize that their interpretive choices are ethically self-diagnostic. If Jonah emerges as a disobedient cynic, grudging mercy, sulking over God's goodness, that suggests what a reader wants to see. If the prophetic character is constructed more respectfully, as someone caught amid poor choices and hoping to make the best of what falls his way while remaining in prayerful dialogue with God, that is more promising.

Bibliography

Green, B. *Jonah's Journeys*. Liturgical Press, 2005.
Sasson, J. *Jonah*. AB 24B. Doubleday, 1990.

♦ Micah ♦

M. Daniel Carroll R.

The book of Micah alludes to the specifics of societal oppression in singular ways, even as it expresses anger at such injustice in some of the most striking expressions of emotion in the prophetic literature. The heading (1:1) locates Micah in Judah in the eighth century BCE during the time of Isaiah.

The exploitation of the vulnerable took the form of expropriating land (2:2, 8–9), deceit in the marketplace (6:10–12), and the perversion of justice by the powerful (3:9–10; 7:3). The prophet deplores the social violence (7:2), at one point likening the attitudes and actions of the leaders to stripping meat off the bone for soup (3:2–3). Leaders of all kinds, political and religious, were on the take (3:11). The prophets, who should have protested, preferred to give messages that their listeners craved (2:11; 3:5). The entire social and familial order had been contaminated (7:5–6).

As in other prophetic books, acceptable worship of God is inseparable from ethics. Idolatry was but one component of a misconstrued faith (1:5–7; 5:12–14). In a hypothetical exchange with the people, God exposes their obduracy. They believed that extravagant offerings could regain divine favor, but what the good God requires is this: "to do justice, and to love kindness, and to walk humbly with your God" (6:1–8).

The mention of the "good" in 6:8 points to the fact that God seeks a people of character who would manifest those ethical commitments toward others. Yet the leaders exhibit the very opposite of what God demanded. Therefore, in the broader national judgment that had been decreed, they are especially singled out for their personal transgressions and for leading the nation to ruin (2:3–5; 3:4, 12; 6:13–16; 7:4).

The book demonstrates that a passion for justice is accompanied by deep emotions. These emotions include righteous anger at injustice, expressed in powerful imagery (e.g., 3:2–3, 6–7), as well as profound pain at present suffering and at the horror that will be endured in the judgment. As he contemplated what was coming, Micah writhed in agony (1:8; 7:1) and hoped that the repentance of the people would be equally profound (1:10–16; 4:9–10). The assurance of his integrity and mission (3:8) was inseparable from a love for the nation, and this was grounded ultimately in God's compassion (7:18–20).

The recognition that this social world had earned divine condemnation is not the final prophetic word in Micah. It looks forward to national restoration (2:12–13; 4:6–8, 13; 5:3–9; 7:11–17) and offers a compelling pastoral image of peace (4:4–5).

Bibliography

Brueggemann, W. *The Prophetic Imagination*. 2nd ed. Fortress, 2001.

Carroll R., M. D. "A Passion for Justice and the Conflicted Self: Lessons from the Book of Micah." *JPsyC* 25, no. 2 (2006): 169–76.

———. " 'He Has Told You What Is Good': Moral Formation in Micah." Pages 103–18 in *Character Ethics and the Old Testament: Scripture and Moral Life*, ed. M. D. Carroll R. and J. Lapsley. Westminster John Knox, 2007.

Heschel, A. *The Prophets*. Harper & Row, 1962.

Premnath, D. *Eighth Century Prophets: A Social Analysis*. Chalice, 2003.

◆ Nahum ◆

D. N. Premnath

Strong anti-Assyrian sentiment coupled with a nationalist fervor has been a source of discomfort and uneasiness among interpreters of this OT book. The book has one overriding concern. It prophesies and even takes delight in the impending fall of Nineveh. The deft use of diverse literary forms such as the partial acrostic poem (where each strophe begins with a letter of the alphabet) in 1:2–8, the "woe" oracle in 3:1–7, and the oracle of salvation in 3:14–20 creates a powerful impact. One is also struck by the prophet's ability to create sights and sounds through words and images (3:2).

No explicit information is provided on the date of the prophet's activity. Based on internal clues, one can assume a time frame somewhere between the fall of Thebes in 663 BCE (3:8) and the fall of Nineveh in 612 BCE, which the book predicts.

The book opens with a poem celebrating the coming of Yahweh, intended as an assurance to Judah (1:2–15). Yahweh's wrath and vengeance are directed against Nineveh. The assault on Nineveh is envisioned and rendered with graphic detail and force (2:1–13). Chapter 3 continues the indictment of Nineveh for its deceitful and wanton behavior.

From an ethical perspective, the uneasiness that many experience in reading the book and its message may stem from two things. First, God is portrayed as wrathful and avenging. Second, the divine wrath is directed against Assyria, a foreign nation. Both aspects bristle with theological and ethical questions. How does one reconcile the merciful versus vengeful depictions of God? How does one reconcile the anti-Assyrian stance and tirade expressed here with the more inclusive and merciful perspective in the book of Jonah (Jon. 4:2, 11)? These issues must be sorted out against the backdrop of Nahum's overall theological frame of reference. Nahum operates with an overarching sense of God's sovereignty over not just Judah but all nations. Anyone or anything contrary to the purposes of God will not go unchallenged. Forces that promote evil, tyranny, and violence will be brought under divine judgment. Assyria of antiquity was one such force known for its brutality and ruthlessness toward its enemies. Recognizing this helps to put into perspective Nahum's tirade. Part of the ethical challenge of the book concerns our responsibility and response to the persistence of evil, tyranny, violence, and injustice beyond our own borders. In our world of complex geopolitical realities and loyalties, a careful consideration and nuanced response may be necessary. The book of Jonah's emphasis on the merciful and redemptive purpose of God (Jon. 4:10–11) offers an alternative to divine justice and thus a different resolution to evil.

Bibliography

Brown, W. *Obadiah through Malachi*. WestBC. Westminster John Knox, 1996.

Floyd, M. *Minor Prophets: Part 2*. FOTL 22. Eerdmans, 1999.

Roberts, J. *Nahum, Habakkuk, and Zephaniah*. OTL. Westminster John Knox, 1991.

◆ Habakkuk ◆

D. N. Premnath

Apart from the reference to the name *Habakkuk*, very little personal information concerning the prophet is found in the book.

From a literary perspective, the book is striking for its incorporation of diverse materials: the dialogical section (1:1–2:4), prophetic invective in the form of the woe oracles (2:5–20), and a psalm (3:1–19). The diversity of the materials has also given rise to discussion of the literary integrity of the book. The sections, however, are arranged in such a way as to provide a coherent argument and message.

In the opening verses Habakkuk laments the condition of his society (1:2–4). The prophet sees and hears destruction and violence all around. Strife and contention are on the rise. The wicked oppress the righteous. Key to the complaint is the abandonment and perversion of justice, mentioned twice in 1:4. The response to the lament comes in the form of an assurance that Yahweh is sending the Chaldeans to take care of the situation (1:5–11). Surprised by this response, Habakkuk protests with another lament that questions how God can be silent when the wicked swallow those more righteous than they (2:1–5). The prophet is told to record the vision and wait patiently for its fulfillment. The series of five woe oracles (2:5–20) is directed at those who plunder the people (vv. 6–8), those who derive gain at the expense of others (vv. 9–11), those who build a town with bloodshed (vv. 12–14), and those who degrade their neighbors (vv. 15–17). This could very well apply to native rulers as much as foreign powers because of the open-ended nature of the references. The ethical challenge of 1:2–4 and 2:5–20 has timeless value in that these passages isolate specific actions and behaviors that contribute to injustice, oppression, and violence within a community. Chapter 3 celebrates the victorious march of Yahweh coming in rescue of Yahweh's people.

From an ethical perspective, two other issues are pertinent: first, the frustration of facing a reality where evil seems to thrive; second, the question of what a faithful person should do in such a situation. The key to handling the frustration in the former issue is the realization that God is working out God's purposes. To those pondering the latter question Habakkuk offers a word of hope for living between promise and fulfillment. One can lead a meaningful life through faithfulness only by placing one's life under God.

Bibliography

Brown, W. *Obadiah through Malachi*. WestBC. Westminster John Knox, 1996.

Floyd, M. *Minor Prophets: Part 2*. FOTL 22. Eerdmans, 1999.

Mason, R. *Zephaniah, Habakkuk, Joel*. OTG. JSOT Press, 1994.

Roberts, J. *Nahum, Habakkuk, and Zephaniah*. OTL. Westminster John Knox, 1991.

✦ Zephaniah ✦

D. N. Premnath

The genealogical introduction to this book, unusually long for a prophetic book, places the prophetic activity of Zephaniah in the reign of King Josiah of Judah (640–609 BCE). The connection to "Cushi" in the genealogy raises the intriguing possibility of an African ancestry for the prophet, which in turn may explain the longer introduction for the purpose of stressing legitimacy. For a relatively short composition, the book manages to pack a range of themes that echo the messages of some earlier prophetic figures. Readers may recognize familiar themes such as indictment against wayward religious behavior (1:4–6; 2:10–11), invectives against incompetent and venal leadership (1:8–9; 3:3–4), indignation against social injustices (1:10–13), call for repentance (2:1–3), the idea of the remnant (2:7, 9b; 3:8–13), the day of Yahweh (1:14–16), God's sovereignty over the nations (2:4–9a), and a picture of future salvation (3:14–20). Aside from these familiar themes, in arranging the materials, Zephaniah also incorporates the familiar threefold pattern of judgment against Judah (1:2–18; 3:1–8), judgment against the nations (2:4–15), and salvation for Judah (3:9–13). Like Amos and Joel, the prophet explicitly develops the concept of the day of Yahweh to frame his prophecies. But Zephaniah never loses sight of the specific reasons for God's judgment such as social injustices. Here one recognizes the prophet's affinity with the eighth-century BCE prophetic voices.

From an ethical perspective, some key emphases are worthy of note. The image in the opening lines of the book sets a powerful tone. God's wrath will sweep away the creation in its entirety. The all-inclusive nature of the destruction is indicated by references to creatures that populate the heavens, the earth, and the sea. But the ones responsible for the calamity are the humans. From an ecological perspective, the point that can be extrapolated is that the sinful and destructive behavior of humans drags down the rest of the creation.

Scholars have long recognized the paraenetic character of Zephaniah. The exhortation to embrace life-saving faith and conduct, and the admonition to abandon destructive beliefs and action, form the core of the book's emphasis. Although the prophet talks about life-saving and life-negating conducts, the primary emphasis is on turning to God. The prophet goes to the root of the issue. True devotion to God will result in proper ethical behavior. Obedience to the law may fulfill the letter of the covenant relationship, but the vitality of the relationship derives from a vibrant and genuine attunement to God. Zephaniah recognizes the deeper theological basis of the prophetic ethical urging.

Bibliography

Berlin, A. *Zephaniah*. AB 25A. Doubleday, 1994.

Mason, R. *Zephaniah, Habakkuk, Joel*. OTG. JSOT Press, 1994.

Roberts, J. *Nahum, Habakkuk, and Zephaniah*. OTL. Westminster John Knox, 1991.

Sweeney, M. *Zephaniah*. Hermeneia. Fortress, 2003.

♦ Haggai ♦

Mark J. Boda

The book of Haggai records the words of a prophet from the late sixth century BCE and the response of the community to which he spoke. The prophetic message addresses a community living in the early phase of the restoration of Judah after the devastating Babylonian era that saw the destruction of Jerusalem and the exile of Judah's elite.

At several points the book draws on the Deuteronomic theology of blessing/curse (e.g., Deut. 28–30) in which disobedience invites God's disciplinary curse (Hag. 1:1–11; 2:15–19a), while obedience God's blessed reward (2:19b). Blessing/curse is expressed predominantly in terms of present physical privation and abundance. At two places in the book (2:6–9, 20–23), however, blessing takes on a universal (approaching eschatological/apocalyptic) tone as Yahweh promises subjugation of the nations. At one place in the book the priestly ethical vision dominates as the prophet identifies the altar and its sacrifices as unclean due to past disobedience (2:10–14).

The moral issue in the book of Haggai is singularly the failure of the people to begin reconstruction on the temple in Jerusalem. In this, Haggai stands in stark contrast to other prophetic books associated with preexilic/exilic prophets where the temple was attacked as a center of Israel's disobedience and its leadership as its chief offenders. In Haggai the rebuilding of the temple so dominates the ethical vision of the prophet that the remnant concept, articulated in Hebrew tradition as that purified group that would emerge from the exile, is described as those who took up Haggai's challenge in 1:12–15.

Motivation for ethical response in Haggai has both negative and positive dimensions. On the negative side is the cessation/avoidance of curse (Deuteronomic) and uncleanness (Priestly). On the positive side is the hope of blessing through abundant agricultural provision and international hegemony (2:6–9, 15–23), the promise of God's presence (1:13; 2:4–5), and the pleasure and glory of God (1:8).

The book of Haggai expresses a balance between the human and divine dimensions of ethical response. The people's obedient response to the prophet through the fear of the Lord identifies them as the remnant (1:12), but this obedience is accompanied by a divine work of "stirring up the spirit" of both leaders and people (1:14).

Drawing on a diversity of OT ethical traditions, the book of Haggai makes temple reconstruction a moral imperative. In the early phase of restoration after exile, the first step in ethical renewal would be the creation of a place for Yahweh's manifest presence to foster the foundational covenant relationship between Israel's God and his people.

Bibliography

Boda, M. *Haggai, Zechariah*. NIVAC. Zondervan, 2004.

Boda, M., and M. Floyd, eds. *Tradition in Transition: Haggai and Zechariah 1–8 in the Trajectory of Hebrew Theology*. Continuum, 2009.

Kessler, J. *The Book of Haggai: Prophecy and Society in Early Persian Yehud*. VTSup 91. Brill, 2002.

Merrill, E. *Haggai, Zechariah, Malachi*. Moody, 1994.

Petersen, D. *Haggai and Zechariah 1–8*. OTL. Westminster, 1984.

Taylor, R., and E. Clendenen. *Haggai, Malachi*. NAC. Broadman & Holman, 2004.

Tollington, J. *Tradition and Innovation in Haggai and Zechariah 1–8*. JSOTSup 150. JSOT Press, 1993.

◆ Zechariah ◆

Mark J. Boda

The book of Zechariah presents the words of a prophet and the response of the Jewish community living in the early phase of the restoration of Judah after the devastating Babylonian exile (late sixth–early fifth century BCE).

The book draws heavily on earlier OT ethical traditions. It is dominated by intertextual links to earlier prophets (see 1:4–6; 7:7, 12), especially Isaiah, Jeremiah, and Ezekiel, while also drawing from key Deuteronomic and Priestly traditions.

The Deuteronomic vision of repentance found in Jeremiah dominates the prose sermon material in Zech. 1:1–6; 7:1–8:23. The initial call in 1:3 ("return to me") emphasizes that repentance is fundamentally a renewal of relationship between Yahweh and people, with the following citation of the earlier prophets in 1:4 ("return from your evil ways") reminding the reader that such covenantal renewal has ethical implications. The character of the misdeeds is identified in 7:9–10; 8:16–17 as social injustice through manipulation of the courts. The Deuteronomic vision of covenantal blessing/curse underlies the ardent call of both Zechariah and his predecessors, reminding the people that disobedience incites the disciplinary curse of Yahweh, while obedience results in God's blessed reward. Ethical transformation is encouraged through the threat of discipline (7:11–14; 8:14) and the promise of blessing (8:1–13, 15, 19–23) delivered through the prophetic voice (1:4–6; 7:12b–13).

The night visions in 1:7–6:15 represent the predominantly positive divine response to the people's initial repentance in 1:6b. Yahweh promises to return, rebuild the city, restore its prosperity, and renew its social structures. The cry of the angel in the first night vision expresses the Jewish community's moral outrage over the enduring destruction and seeming lack of punishment of their exilic abusers (Babylon). God's promise is to punish those nations (1:14–15; cf. 1:18–21; 2:6–13; 6:1–8). Yahweh's declaration of the election of Jerusalem and Joshua and provision of clean priestly clothing signal a new start for both community and priestly leadership. Nevertheless, there are enduring ethical concerns within the community: in particular, social injustice through manipulation of the courts (5:1–4) and idolatry introduced from Babylon (5:5–11). The flying scroll in 5:1–4 suggests a role for the written Torah in ethical transformation. Unethical behavior will be treated severely by Yahweh, as his legal curse destroys the lives of offenders (5:4) and heavenly messengers remove idolatrous objects from the land (5:9–11).

Interspersed among the main oracles in Zech. 9–14 are a series of short pericopes focusing on ethical crises within Judah, especially related to its leaders, who are accused of divining through idols (10:1–3), abusing the vulnerable (11:4–16), and deserting their leadership post (11:17). These crises reach a climax in the purging of 13:7–9, which finally produces a remnant able to embrace Yahweh in covenantal relationship. The eschatological vision of the oracles in Zech. 12–14 looks to Yahweh's punishment of the nations and their submission to his rule from Jerusalem through pilgrimage to the Feast of Tabernacles. In addition, these oracles envision the purification of Judah and Jerusalem, with the community grieving over their offenses against Yahweh (12:10–14) and eradicating false prophecy (13:3–6). This response is made possible by Yahweh's provision of a spirit of grace and supplication (12:10). Yahweh will also intervene directly, providing a fountain able to cleanse from sin and impurity and removing both idols and false prophets from the land (13:1–2). The book concludes with a vision of the ceremonial holiness usually associated with the temple, its personnel and utensils, now characterizing all of Jerusalem and Judah (14:20–21).

Zechariah expands the ethical vision beyond Haggai's limited vision of temple reconstruction to include issues related to injustice, idolatry, and imperial compromise. Its introduction is an important reminder that ethical response must be founded on covenant relationship.

Bibliography

Boda, M. *Haggai, Zechariah*. NIVAC. Zondervan, 2004.

———. "Zechariah: Master Mason or Penitential Prophet?" Pages 49–69 in *Yahwism after the Exile: Perspectives on Israelite Religion in the Persian Era*, ed. B. Becking and R. Albertz. STR 5. Van Gorcum, 2003.

Boda, M., and M. Floyd, eds. *Bringing Out the Treasure: Inner Biblical Allusion in Zechariah 9–14*. JSOTSup 370. Sheffield Academic Press, 2003.

———, eds. *Tradition in Transition: Haggai and Zechariah 1–8 in the Trajectory of Hebrew Theology*. Continuum, 2009.

Cook, S. *Prophecy and Apocalypticism: The Postexilic Social Setting*. Fortress, 1995.

Larkin, K. *The Eschatology of Second Zechariah: A Study of the Formation of a Mantological Wisdom Anthology*. CBET 6. Kok Pharos, 1994.

Petersen, D. "Zechariah's Visions." *VT* 34 (1984): 195–206.

Tollington, J. *Tradition and Innovation in Haggai and Zechariah 1–8.* JSOTSup 150. JSOT Press, 1993.

♦ Malachi ♦

D. N. Premnath

The book of Malachi provides very little information about the prophet. Even the name *Malachi* has been the subject of debate as to whether it is a proper name or a prophetic title. Most scholars assign a date in the Persian period, sometime after the rebuilding of the temple in Jerusalem (515 BCE). From a literary perspective, two features stand out. First, the book is unique within the prophetic corpus in the way it deftly employs a series of imaginary discourses to communicate its message. In this regard, the intersection of the priestly and the prophetic in Malachi is noteworthy. The priestly aspect has to do with the main message: the concern for adherence to the Torah. The prophetic aspect has to do with the mode in which it is presented. The major portion of the book (1:6–3:24) is an excellent example of priestly instruction presented in the form of a prophetic disputation. Second, the literary parallels between the opening words of Malachi and Zech. 9:1; 12:1 have raised the issue of the book's status as an independent work. But the literary integrity, prophetic creativity, and theological sophistication displayed in the materials strengthen the case for an independent status.

The book opens on an affirmative note that God still loves Israel. For Malachi, God's love is the source of renewal and sustenance for the people. God's love is the basis of hope and the reason for the proper ethical response. In the rest of the book Malachi exposes the barriers to renewal. The longest section in Malachi (1:6–2:9) is a complex piece that reflects the rivalry between priestly groups. The prophet offers an indictment on the Aaronide priests for improper ritual practices and for usurping the role of the Levitical priests as providers of instruction and judgments. Malachi's own allegiances become clear in his explicit support of the role of the Levitical priests within the society. From an ethical perspective, the book's pointed exploration of the connection between worship and ethical/moral practices is of lasting value. Of primary importance to Malachi is the preservation of the covenant relationship between God and Israel, especially the obligation on the part of Israel to follow the stipulations, whether in regard to married family life (indictment against mixed marriages and divorces in 2:10–16) or support of cultic life (insistence on full payment of tithes in 3:6–12).

Bibliography

Brown, W. *Obadiah through Malachi*. WestBC. Westminster John Knox, 1996.

Floyd, M. *Minor Prophets, Part 2*. FOTL 22. Eerdmans, 2000.

Nogalski, J., and M. Sweeney, eds. *Reading and Hearing the Book of the Twelve*. SBLSymS 15. Society of Biblical Literature, 2000.

Petersen, D. *Zechariah 9–14 and Malachi*. OTL. Westminster John Knox, 1995.

6

|||||||||||||||||||||||||||||||||||||||||||||||||||||||||||||||||||||||||||||||||||||||||||||||||||||

DEUTEROCANONICAL/ APOCRYPHAL BOOKS

♦ Ethics of the Deuterocanonical/Apocryphal Books ♦

David A. deSilva

The Apocrypha is a collection of Jewish writings dating somewhere between 250 BCE and 100 CE, written in Hebrew, Aramaic, or Greek, and composed across a wide geographic area. Although the texts were written by devout Jews, their collection into a discrete corpus is the result of Christian reading practices and positive evaluation of this material. The core of the collection includes two historical books (1–2 Maccabees), wisdom literature (Wisdom of Solomon, Sirach [also known as Wisdom of Ben Sira and as Ecclesiasticus]), additions to or rewritten versions of Jewish scriptural books (1 Esdras, Greek Esther, Greek Daniel [which includes the stories of Susanna and of Bel and the Dragon, as well as Prayer of Azariah and Song of the Three Young Men], Baruch, Letter of Jeremiah), and two edifying tales (Tobit, Judith). Current collections (e.g., the NRSV) also include two liturgical pieces (Ps. 151, Prayer of Manasseh), another specimen of historical fiction (3 Maccabees), an apocalypse (2 Esdras), and an essay promoting the Jewish "philosophy" (4 Maccabees).

The canonical status of these books has been a matter of debate from the beginning. Several of the Apocrypha have left a clear impression on the writings of the NT, though without ever being explicitly recited or referred to as Scripture. Many church fathers throughout the first four centuries of the church's history continued to read and invoke these texts, increasingly as scriptural authorities in their own right, though with famous objections being raised to such usage (e.g., by Jerome, who championed the use of the Jewish canon and the Hebrew form of the Jewish scriptural texts as the Christian OT).

Currently, Eastern Orthodox communions and the Roman Catholic Church regard at least the core collection of these books as Scripture, with the former also including Prayer of Manasseh, Ps. 151, and 3 Maccabees. The term *deuterocanonical* is used in these contexts to affirm the canonical status of this collection while acknowledging the fact that their composition and collection followed subsequently, for the most part, on the composition and collection of the Hebrew canon. During the Reformation it became a hallmark of Protestant churches to exclude these books from the Christian canon, although several leaders of the Reformation themselves were reluctant to see them fall into obscurity. Martin Luther, for example, commended (and included) them in his translation of the Bible as "both useful and good to read," though not of equal authority with Scripture, and the Church of England stipulated in the sixth article of religion that they be "read for example of life and instruction of manners." This last statement is particularly salient here, as it is precisely as ethical literature that the deuterocanonical/apocryphal books have been most widely read and valued.

The Mosaic covenant—the stipulations and terms outlined in the Pentateuch—provides the overarching framework for ethics throughout this literature. Nearly every text reflects explicitly on this covenant as a divinely given, clearly articulated matrix of specific ethical directives and of personal and corporate motivations to embrace these directives. "Wisdom," the ethical ideal in Sirach, Wisdom of Solomon, and Baruch, for example, has come to be identified with "the book of the commandments of God, the law that endures forever" (Bar. 4:1 [cf. Sir. 24:1–23; Wis. 16:6; 18:9]). The person whose behaviors and practices align with the stipulations of Torah is the "ethical" person (Sus. 3), whereas the person who transgresses the same exhibits ethical failure. As a result of the covenantal framework, the scope of concern throughout this literature tends to be particularistic, focused on the good of the Jewish people as a whole and, within it, the individual Judean. There are limited universalistic strains (e.g., Wis. 11:23–12:2; 13:1–7), but these are often swept aside (e.g., Wis. 12:10–11; 13:8–9).

The covenant curses and blessings outlined in Deut. 28–30 are a constant reference point for analyzing social and political conditions, diagnosing ethical failure, and pointing the way toward reform and restoration both of the individual and the nation. Motivations to ethical action tend to be drawn from the consequences laid out in the Deuteronomic model: obedience leads to divine blessing, disobedience to experience of divine wrath and punishment, repentance and renewed obedience to renewed experience of divine aid and restoration (see, e.g., Jdt. 5:17–20; Bar. 1:15–22; Sg. Three 5–13; 2 Macc. 4:7–17; 6:12–17; 4 Macc. 3:20–4:21; 18:3–4). Using this model, authors can appeal to individual self-interest: ethical action is a means to an end, most expedient for the doer in terms of leading to honor, advantage, and enjoyment of particular goods valued in society. This is common in Sirach and Tobit, as, indeed, it is in the advice literature of the period more generally. Authors can also appeal to the good of the nation: ethical action is most expedient for the commonwealth, whether on the basis of the covenant blessings and curses (the actions that God would take in response to the people's alignment with covenant stipulations) or with a view to natural consequences (e.g., demonstrating the nobility of the nation's way of life to others, or rallying resistance against a tyrant by a demonstration of courage and commitment). In both instances, the rewards and punishments may be anticipated in the natural course of one's lifetime or national fortune, or in the postmortem existence of the individual or eschatological future of the nation.

Ethical action, however, is also urged as a proper response to God, an expression of commitment to God and loyalty to God for the experience of God's past gifts. In 4 Maccabees, for example, a Torah-observant life productive of virtue is a means of living so as to best honor God, using the gift of human faculties well and in line with God's best intentions for it (4 Macc. 2:21–23). The commitment to do so even in the face of great hardship, even martyrdom, may be motivated by the hope for postmortem reward or fear of postmortem punishment (4 Macc. 9:8–9; 13:14–17; 15:2–3), but it is motivated also by the awareness that it is a proper and just return to God for the gift of life itself (4 Macc. 13:13; 16:18–19). Ethical action is what is due God.

The covenantal framework elevates the nation's (and the individual's) relationship with God and experience of God's favor (past, present, and future) as the ground for the meaningfulness of and motivation for ethical action. Right ethics begins with right piety. Hence, attention is given throughout the literature to debunking idolatry (see Letter of Jeremiah; Bel and the Dragon; Wis. 12:1–14:31) and maintaining commitment to the one God, the God who gave and enforces the covenant and its legal, ethical, ritual code. The author of Wisdom of Solomon explicitly reflects on the failure to experience this relationship with the one God: the filling of the religious vacuum with idolatry—creating relationships with false gods—has resulted in the moral chaos observable in gentile society at both the personal and social level (Wis.

13:1–14:31). Perversion of piety leads to perversion of thinking, feeling, craving, and action in every arena. In an earlier section of the book (possibly by a different author) the source of this ethical mayhem is sought in the failure of individuals to look beyond death to seek immortality through virtuous living, choosing instead to grasp at whatever fleeting pleasures they can, at whatever cost to others it entails. Looking at death as the end of existence elevates the wrong goals and means to their attainment (Wis. 1:16–2:24).

The Jews' commitment to monolatry and to the particular practices prescribed by Torah frequently led to tension with non-Jewish groups (and authorities) in regard to the latter's political and civic ethics (see, e.g., Add. Esth. 13:4–5; 3 Macc. 3:3–7, 21–23). The literature bears witness to strenuous debates and a significant diversity of response within Judaism regarding how to address this, many Jews advocating significant compromise, even capitulation on these points, in order to appear as "good citizens" and enjoy the benefits thereof (e.g., 1 Macc. 1:11–15; 3 Macc. 2:31–33). The deuterocanonical/apocryphal books, not surprisingly, consistently promote fidelity to the minority culture's ethical code, even where this incurs reproach or open hostility. Moreover, there are some stunning examples of innercommunal reinforcement of ethics, whether through giving assistance preferentially to the righteous poor, using charity as a means to promote alignment with the covenant (Tob. 2:2; 4:6; Sir. 12:1–7), or through enforcing the covenant violently—for example, by circumcising Jewish boys left uncircumcised by their apostate parents and lynching or executing apostate Jews (1 Macc. 2:42–48; 3:5–8; 3 Macc. 7:10–16).

Where fidelity to the covenant and the faithful performance of its stipulations are threatened, both violent and nonviolent resistance are commended as ethical responses. The books of 1–2 Maccabees are especially interested in military and diplomatic action as a component of faithful response to Torah and thus support violent resistance (see, e.g., 1 Macc. 2:15–28, 39–48; 3:1–26; 2 Macc. 8:1–16:37). Considerable space, however, is also given in these texts to commending nonviolent resistance even to the point of death (1 Macc. 1:60–63; 2 Macc. 6:1–7:42). The book of 4 Maccabees commends the ideal of the witness who resists apostasy, foreign domination, and religious repression but does so by suffering courageously in the face of repressive violence rather than by practicing violence. Although essentially advocating a violent solution to political and religious repression, the book of Judith presents a special ethical problem, celebrating the use of deceit and seduction as a valid ethical means to secure the safety of the nation (Jdt. 8:1–13:20), a means even sanctioned by God (Jdt. 9:13). Judith's strategy, however, is analogous to other uses of "craftiness" in wartime situations. Moreover, the ancient

Mediterranean world tended to regard not the use of deceit, but rather being duped by deceit, as the point of failure.

A few texts within this collection merit special note for their contribution to ethical reflection. The book of Sirach contains the essential curriculum of a Jewish sage who maintained a school in Jerusalem in the decades around 200 BCE. This sage's literary legacy gives a window into early Jewish reflection on negotiating life in the household, in the larger society, even in the international sphere to advantage. It covers a wide variety of ethical and practical topics, including ethical speech, friendship, forgiveness, etiquette, caution in regard to ambition, moderation and self-control, household management, family duties, sexual ethics, the virtue of humility, the importance of mutual accountability, generosity, and practicing charity and social justice. A critical problem in Sirach concerns his view of women, which is largely negative and derived from his culture's obsession with female sexuality. As is reflected in the views of other authors in this collection, sexual exclusivity is the sine qua non of female virtue (see Jdt. 13:16; 4 Macc. 17:1; 18:6–9 [although in these books women are clearly regarded as capable of other virtues, notably courage and unyielding covenant loyalty]). However, Sirach expresses a clear lack of faith that women will reliably keep to the ideal, bringing anxiety and disgrace upon their fathers and husbands instead (Sir. 26:10–12; 42:11). Nevertheless, on many issues Sirach makes important ethical advances. The book promotes forgiveness of others on the basis of hoping for God's forgiveness of oneself. Also, it uses the commandments as a ground for ethical reflection, extending, for example, the prohibition against murder to include other acts of social or economic violence. Finally, it commends generosity toward all, especially the poor, as a reflection of God's character and thus of the donor's kinship with the divine. In all this, the author anticipates the ethics of Jesus of Nazareth.

The text of 2 Esd. 3–14 is a Jewish apocalypse from the late first century, usually referred to as *4 Ezra* (2 Esd. 1–2 and 2 Esd. 15–16 are slightly later Christian additions, called *5 Ezra* and *6 Ezra*, respectively). The author of this text sharply poses the ethical problem of the individual's seeking to live up to the ideal of the covenant while dominated by the tendency toward transgression that seems, from lived experience, to grip the human race (both Jews and gentiles) in a stranglehold. Like Paul, he looks to the story of Adam and Eve as the beginning of sin and, indeed, as the episode that forever predisposes their descendants toward vice (2 Esd. 3:22; 4:30; 7:118–119; cf. Sir. 25:24; Wis. 2:23–24). Nevertheless, moral responsibility is not in any way abated. The contest against the evil inclination may be difficult, and the stakes indeed high, but each person must fight well in this contest so as to walk aligned with God's law and arrive at the promised blessings beyond death (2 Esd.

7:127–130). The author thus reaffirms the conclusion at which Sirach had arrived three centuries before: ethical achievement or failure remains a matter of the individual's choice and responsibility (Sir. 15:11–20).

A product of the Hellenistic Diaspora, 4 Maccabees is the text within this collection most explicitly and fully devoted to well-defined ethical issues. Addressing a common subject of Greek and Latin philosophical ethics, the author presents Torah observance as a disciplined lifestyle that promotes self-mastery in regard to the "passions"—the emotional responses, volitional cravings, and physical sensations that pose an ongoing danger to consistent ethical action—with the result that the pious Jew attains the ethical ideals prized by the Greco-Roman philosophical culture (justice, courage, temperance, prudence, piety). Martyrdom is interpreted as both the ultimate sign of such self-mastery and the realization of the freedom of the wise person from all external compulsion. Sages can be injured only insofar as they consent to depart from their moral principles. The book is a fine example of religious ethical discourse that is also fully informed by, and engaged in, the larger Greco-Roman conversation.

The deuterocanonical/apocryphal books provide essential windows into the ethical interpretation of the received tradition and the ethical developments within Judaism in the postprophetic period. As such, they also provide essential background to any study of the ethics of the early Christian writings, and, indeed, the impact of the Apocrypha on the ethics of the early and ongoing Christian movement is significant. Whatever the canonical status of these texts might be in the eyes of the interpreter, any thorough investigation of biblical ethics must take this literature into account.

Bibliography

Charles, R. *The Apocrypha and Pseudepigrapha of the Old Testament.* 2 vols. Oxford University Press, 1913.

Collins, J. *Between Athens and Jerusalem: Jewish Identity in the Hellenistic Diaspora.* 2nd ed. Eerdmans, 2000.

———. *Jewish Wisdom in the Hellenistic Age.* Westminster John Knox, 1997.

deSilva, D. *4 Maccabees.* GAP. Sheffield Academic Press, 1998.

———. *Introducing the Apocrypha: Message, Context, and Significance.* Baker Academic, 2002.

Harrington, D. *Invitation to the Apocrypha.* Eerdmans, 1999.

Helyer, L. *Exploring Jewish Literature of the Second Temple Period.* InterVarsity, 2002.

Maldwyn, H. *The Ethics of Jewish Apocryphal Literature.* Robert Culley, 1909.

Metzger, B. *An Introduction to the Apocrypha.* Oxford University Press, 1957.

♦ Tobit ♦

Micah D. Kiel

The book of Tobit tells the story of a Jewish family living during the Assyrian deportation. Tobit, the title character, is an upright man. Early in the story, Tobit gives proper burial to one of his people who has been murdered. Afterward, he must sleep outside, where bird droppings fall in his eyes, causing him to go blind. Tobias, Tobit's son, leaves to retrieve money deposited in a far-off city, accompanied by the angel Raphael, disguised as a human. Tobias, with Raphael's instructions, survives a threatening large fish, thwarts a demon, marries, and returns home with great wealth. Tobias also, using a reserved part of the fish, cures Tobit's blindness. At the end, Raphael reveals his true angelic identity, and Tobit sings a hymn about the future of Jerusalem. After Tobit dies, Tobias witnesses the destruction of Assyria at the hand of Media.

The book of Tobit contains many ethical exhortations, but at a deeper level it struggles with how God treats those who do or do not act with righteousness.

Tobit the character is an exemplar of ethical practice. Introduced as a righteous one who did many acts of charity, Tobit tithed appropriately and alone among the exiles traveled to Jerusalem for festivals. Tobit's actions, such as feeding the hungry and clothing the naked, are for those of his tribe. Tobit provides proper burial for one of his kin, a righteous act that ironically results in his blindness. The book's most pressing issue arises in the fact that Tobit suffers because of his righteousness.

The book of Tobit has two major sections of ethical instruction (chaps. 4; 14). Although the beginning of the book mentions the law of Moses (1:8), the "commandments" (4:19) in Tobit show little interest in specific laws but instead advocate boilerplate sapiential instruction such as the importance of almsgiving (4:5–11), sexual purity (4:12–13), and fair treatment of workers (4:14–19). Such admonitions recall many parts of Proverbs or Sirach and also emulate the wisdom of Ahikar, a well-known sage in the Assyrian court whom Tobit names as a relative (1:21–22; 14:10). More important than the specifics of Tobit's ethical instructions is their conceptual underpinning that God will repay a righteous life with blessing: "Do not turn your face away from anyone who is poor, and the face of God will not be turned away from you" (4:7). Such a close connection between act and consequence leads most scholars to call the book "Deuteronomic," meaning that it draws on a well-established theological formulation that finds its source in Deuteronomy.

Despite Tobit's assertions that God repays people according to their actions, the arc of Tobit's character questions such a conclusion. The trajectory of the narrative has its own rhetorical force, one that undermines confidence in such a close connection between act and consequence. At the beginning, Tobit has no recourse in explaining his predicament other than that he (or his ancestors) has sinned (3:1–6). At the end of the book, Raphael reveals his angelic identity and the "whole truth" (12:11) about Tobit's predicament: God's role in the story was different from that which Tobit had assumed. This revelation impinges directly on the purported connection between act and consequence. It may be tempting to posit that deeds, whether just or unjust, breed commensurate repayment, but reality is much more complex. Tobit's sight returns at the end, but the original problem for Tobit's family is that they live under foreign rule and are subject to the whims of gentile kings. This situation is not resolved at the end of the book. Some scholars suggest that the healing of Tobit's blindness anticipates the future restoration that is to come to the Jewish people as a whole. Such a reading is possible but not necessary. One can also suggest that the inconclusive ending intends to question the efficacy of Tobit's ethical program. In such a scenario, the book of Tobit asks a question: is righteousness really a guarantor of God's blessing? Earlier in the story, Tobit was profoundly sure that God repays people according to their actions, but at the end, after Raphael's revelation, he is less so: "Turn back, you sinners, and do what is right before him; perhaps he may look with favor upon you" (13:6). What the NRSV translates as "perhaps" might better be rendered as "who knows?" Thus, at the end, Tobit's disposition is marked by epistemological humility. The ethical norms do not wane; they are constantly upheld. They may not, however, be used to leverage God toward blessing.

♦ Judith ♦

Daniel J. Harrington

The book of Judith presents many ethical problems. In saving her people from near certain destruction, the heroine (her name means "Jewish woman") flirts with and seduces the enemy commander, tells him lies and ironic half-truths, gets him drunk, chops off his head and has it put on public display, and sets off thirty days of plundering in the enemy's camp. The book appears to be a case of the end (Israel's salvation) justifying the means (Judith's deceit and violence).

The book is best interpreted as a historical fiction. There is no record of any city named Bethulia, or anything like the crisis described in the first half of the book, or a woman named Judith who saved her people in this dramatic way. The basic text is the Greek version found in the LXX, though the book may have been composed in Hebrew or Aramaic. Although not very accurate as history, the book is noteworthy for the literary skill with which the story is told—lively characters, complex plot, intricate structure, frequent shifting of scenes, skillful use of irony, and a final hymn.

Its most obvious biblical model is the story of Jael, the woman who in Judg. 4–5 saves ancient Israel by hammering a tent peg into the head of the enemy general Sisera. The irony is that the violence committed by Israel's enemies is overcome violently by a most unlikely instrument, the hand of a woman. Also central to the story is the biblical principle that Israel will prosper as long as it avoids sin but will be punished severely when it sins (see Deut. 30:15–20).

Judith does not appear until almost halfway through the book. The first seven chapters describe the crisis facing Israel: whether to remain faithful to the God of Israel or to worship the foreign king. As part of his program to exert sovereignty over many peoples and nations, Nebuchadnezzar (a Babylonian ruling over the Assyrians) commissions his general Holofernes (a Persian name) to bring Israel and its neighbors into line. The campaign is intended to show that Nebuchadnezzar alone is worthy of worship (3:8; 6:2) and so to test Israel's faith in its God. The people of Bethulia in the meantime are engulfed in fear. When Holofernes cuts off their water supply, the only strategy that their leader Uzziah can suggest is to wait five days for "the Lord our God" to act on their behalf (7:30).

God does act dramatically through the unlikely person of the rich and beautiful widow Judith. She criticizes the people of Bethulia for putting their God to the test and assures them that she is going to do "something that will go down through all generations of our descendants" (8:32). In prayer she asks God to make her "deceitful words" bring harm upon Israel's enemies (9:13). After beautifying herself, she lies her way into the enemy's camp and leads Holofernes on with ironic promises that he interprets positively but that she uses to disguise her real intentions.

The major theological theme of the book is captured in the phrase "the hand of a woman" (16:6). This is a reversal of expectations about the right of military conquerors to abuse women as part of the spoils of warfare. Judith shows that God can foil Israel's enemies and bring about good for his people by the most unlikely of instruments, the hand of a widow. The final hymn celebrates Judith's victory over Holofernes in a graphic way: "Her sandal ravished his eyes, her beauty captivated his mind, and the sword severed his neck" (16:9).

The inclusion of the book of Judith in the Catholic and Orthodox Christian canons of Scripture has led to its frequent use as a starting point for literary and artistic representations. There are many depictions of Judith in illustrated Christian Bible manuscripts, and she has been the subject of films, opera, and poems. Her slaying of Holofernes has attracted the attention of portrait artists for whom the combination of sex, violence, and religion has proved irresistible. In some circles Judith was viewed as a prefigurement of Mary the mother of Jesus. Medieval Jewish midrashim linked her story to Hanukkah, thus anticipating modern scholarly hypotheses about its origin in Maccabean times.

Bibliography

Craven, T. *Artistry and Faith in the Book of Judith.* SBLDS 70. Scholars Press, 1983.

Harrington, D. *Invitation to the Apocrypha.* Eerdmans, 1999, 27–43.

Moore, C. *Judith.* AB 40. Doubleday, 1985.

Stocker, M. *Judith, Sexual Warrior: Women and Power in Western Culture.* Yale University Press, 1998.

VanderKam, J., ed. *"No One Spoke Ill of Her": Essays on Judith.* SBLEJL. Scholars Press, 1992.

◆ Additions to Esther ◆

Daniel J. Harrington

The Hebrew text of Esther presents theological and ethical problems. Not only is there no explicit mention of God, but it is also silent about circumcision, Sabbath observance, and food laws, which were major identifying markers in Diaspora Judaism. Moreover, Esther becomes part of the Persian royal harem and eventually enters a mixed marriage with the gentile king. These problems may partly explain why no fragments of it were discovered among the Dead Sea Scrolls.

The Greek version of Esther turns the theology implicit in the Hebrew text into an explicit theology by introducing God into the main narrative (2:20; 4:8; 6:13). It also contains six additional sections that Jerome gathered into an appendix and placed at the end of the book. These additions heighten the role of God and prayer, give greater prominence to Esther and her motivation, and ameliorate some of the ethical problems.

Additions A (Mordecai's dream) and F (its interpretation) place the crisis facing the Jews in a cosmic context and state the basic theme of the Greek version, "These things have come from God" (10:4). Also included are full texts of what purport to be the royal decree ordering the extermination of all Jews (addition B) and its cancellation (addition E). Addition A is early evidence for charges leveled by anti-Semites against Jews throughout the ages ("perversely following a strange manner of life and laws"), while addition E recognizes that Jews are "governed by most righteous laws" and are "children of the living God."

Addition C contains two lengthy prayers by Mordecai and Esther that serve to embed the story more firmly into the wider story of God and Israel. Mordecai appeals to God as ruler of the universe and the God of Abraham to spare Israel from destruction, thus linking the story to Israel's previous scriptural traditions. Esther prays to "the Lord God of Israel" for eloquence before the king. She claims to "hate the splendor of the wicked and to abhor the bed of the uncircumcised and of any alien." She swears that she has avoided the (unclean) food and drink served at the king's table. Whatever unseemly behavior she has undertaken has been done in the service of the greater good of rescuing her people from certain annihilation. Saving Israel overrides behaviors that might appear immoral to some. The emotional and psychological struggle that Esther undergoes is neatly captured in addition C when she enters the king's court unannounced and with God's help wins a favorable hearing and averts her people's crisis. Although the Greek version of Esther does not solve all the book's theological and ethical problems, it most likely was intended to make the story less morally offensive in some circles. The Greek version is part of Catholic and Orthodox Christian Bibles.

Bibliography

De Troyer, K. *Rewriting the Sacred Text*. TCrS 4. Society of Biblical Literature, 2003.

Harrington, D. *Invitation to the Apocrypha*. Eerdmans, 1999, 44–54.

Kahana, H. *Esther: Juxtaposition of the Septuagint Translation with the Hebrew Text*. CBET 30. Peeters, 2005.

◆ Wisdom of Solomon ◆

Samuel L. Adams

Wisdom of Solomon is a sapiential text composed in Greek and written in Alexandria, Egypt, perhaps in the early first century CE. The author does not identify himself, but clearly he is an educated Jew who is familiar with Greek philosophy. The book combines hortatory language in the spirit of earlier instructions with certain philosophical ideas. It also reflects the fractured relations during this period between the large Jewish community in Alexandria and the Greeks and native Egyptians. Wisdom of Solomon can be divided into three distinct sections: the "book of eschatology" (1:1–6:21), the "book of wisdom" (6:22–10:21), and the "book of history" (11:1–19:22).

The ethics of Wisdom of Solomon focuses on the promise of eternal life for the righteous and the failure of the wicked to recognize the possibility of such reward. According to the author, the wicked believe that life is fleeting, and therefore they say to themselves, "Let us take our fill of costly wine and perfumes" (2:7). The callous behavior of these sinners also involves oppressing the righteous, since the righteous ones are so overtly pious and accuse the wicked of disobeying the law (2:12–13). Yet such wicked persons have been "blinded" by foolishness and have not "discerned the prize for blameless souls" (2:21–22), which is eternal life.

The righteous ones, however, will be vindicated. Their souls are in "the hand of God" (3:1), and although they will appear deceased to the wicked category, God has "tested" them and deemed them worthy of immortality (3:1–7). The ethical dualism of Wisdom of Solomon is therefore predicated on postmortem reward for the righteous, and this is a major innovation for a Jewish instruction. Earlier works such as Ecclesiastes and Sirach had dismissed the possibility of individual immortality as fanciful (the promise of eternal life is extended in Daniel and sections of *1 Enoch*).

It should be noted that the afterlife in Wisdom of Solomon does not involve resurrection, but rather the survival of the righteous "soul" after death. The concept of the undying soul is influenced by the author's understanding of Platonic philosophy.

In the second section of the book the author praises Wisdom as a spirit "who passes into holy souls and makes them friends of God, and prophets" (7:27). Within this framework, which is indebted to Middle Platonism, the figure of Wisdom is an entity representing God on earth, "a spotless mirror of the working of God" (7:26). Only through this intervening force can humans be set on the proper path (9:13–18). This middle section culminates in a description of how Wisdom has worked through Israel's forebears. From Adam to Noah to Abraham, the author maintains, it is Wisdom who rescues the righteous on behalf of God (10:1–21). This retrospective has a didactic function: these familiar stories serve as a model that righteous believers will be saved from precarious circumstances by the gracious intervention of God.

In the concluding "book of history," the author speaks directly to God, and the central topic is idolatry. The author excoriates the ancient Canaanites and Egyptians by recounting the exodus narrative, and this is undoubtedly a polemic against the non-Jews (both Greeks and Egyptians) living in Alexandria. The polemic serves a function within the author's ethical framework, since he encourages fellow Jews to be steadfast in their convictions and religious practices, even in the face of difficult opposition. In the midst of this polemic against idolatry and infanticide, it is noteworthy that the author of Wisdom of Solomon affirms the fairness of God: "For you love all things that exist, and detest none of the things that you have made, for you would not have made anything if you had hated it" (11:24). Despite the author's palpable concern for the situation of Jews in Alexandria, he cites the philanthropic nature of God (using the Greek word *philanthrōpia*) toward all humanity.

Wisdom of Solomon is an important book for ethics because it appeals vividly to eschatological deliverance as a means of instilling righteous behavior on earth. Subsequent Jewish and early Christian texts would follow suit. This text is also a pivotal example of how Torah piety could be merged with the insights of Hellenistic philosophy. A more elaborate example of this is found in the writings of Philo, another Alexandrian Jew from the same general period.

Bibliography

Collins, J. *Jewish Wisdom in the Hellenistic Age.* OTL. Westminster John Knox, 1997, 178–221.

Winston, D. *The Wisdom of Solomon.* AB 43. Doubleday, 1979.

◆ Sirach (or Ecclesiasticus) ◆

Samuel L. Adams

Sirach (or Ecclesiasticus) is a wisdom book written by the Jewish sage Jesus Ben Sira in the late third or early second century BCE. The book did not make it into the Jewish and Protestant canons, but it is part of the Roman Catholic OT. In these reflections, Ben Sira presents pithy sayings and longer theological discourses as he addresses a group of pupils negotiating the complex circumstances of the Hellenistic age. This colorful advice constitutes the longest postexilic sapiential work.

In terms of ethics, Sirach encourages upright behavior in the tradition of the book of Proverbs, but with a major innovation: the author explicitly links wisdom and Torah. Earlier sages in ancient Israel had discussed Wisdom and the virtuous life without mentioning the Mosaic covenant, but Ben Sira brings these together. For example, "If you desire wisdom, keep the commandments, and the Lord will lavish her upon you" (1:26).

The sage includes a great deal of discussion on financial matters, offering advice on how to handle money and remain faithful to God. Favorite topics include the intricacies of the marketplace, borrowing and lending, relations between rich and poor, and the practice of almsgiving. Of particular interest is Ben Sira's belief that "riches are good if they are free from sin" (13:24). The sage is dubious of this possibility, since he also states, "A merchant can hardly keep from wrongdoing, nor is a tradesman innocent of sin" (26:29). Yet it is noteworthy that Ben Sira does not categorize material assets as inherently evil. His ambivalence about money appears to stem, at least in part, from the fact that he educated young scribes who were destined to serve the elite classes.

Family relations also receive attention in this instruction. Ben Sira affirms the Decalogue by highlighting the need to honor one's parents (3:1–16). He also has an extended discourse on the good wife and the bad wife (25:13–26:27) and emphasizes the anxiety that daughters may bring (42:11). His discussion includes harsh language that goes beyond the patriarchal ethos of Israel's wisdom tradition. For example, "Any iniquity is small compared to a woman's iniquity" (25:19). In his instruction on such matters, Ben Sira focuses on the shame that ensues from disreputable behavior, and it is likely that he was influenced by Greek ideas of honor and shame.

On the issue of moral agency, Ben Sira urges his listeners to take responsibility for their actions: "Do not say 'It was the Lord's doing that I fell away'; for he does not do what he hates" (15:11). According to certain maxims in this book, God places human beings in the power of their "inclination" (15:14), and it is up to each person to practice "fear of the Lord" by leading a righteous existence and making the correct decisions. Elsewhere, he appears to contradict this logic by claiming that wisdom is created "with the faithful in the womb" (1:14). There is an unresolved tension between free will and determinism in Sirach.

Ben Sira's ethics are also famous for his interpretation of the creation story in Gen. 2–3. When alluding to this narrative and explaining God's creative acts, the sage declares, "He filled them with knowledge and understanding, and showed them good and evil" (17:7). According to the sage's interpretation, moral discernment was not a forbidden fruit, but an essential gift imparted to the first humans. In addition, Ben Sira appears to understand human sin and death in the context of the Adam and Eve story: "From a woman sin had its beginning, and because of her we all die" (25:24). Yet he is inconsistent on this point, since he argues elsewhere that death is a "decree" from God (41:3–4) rather than a punishment for Eve's transgression.

Finally, this instruction deals extensively with death and cultivating a good name. Like the author of Ecclesiastes, Ben Sira endorses a *carpe diem* mentality (e.g., 14:16), since he does not believe in the immortality of the individual soul. At the same time, he exhorts his pupils to cultivate a positive reputation among their contemporaries. Many sayings represent the core belief that the best way to achieve happiness and to secure a lasting future for one's offspring ·is through a good name. Such a goal can be met by upright, pious behavior (i.e., "fear of the Lord").

Bibliography

Collins, J. *Jewish Wisdom in the Hellenistic Age.* Westminster John Knox, 1997, 23–111.
Skehan, P., and A. Di Lella. *The Wisdom of Ben Sira.* AB 39. Doubleday, 1987.

◆ Baruch ◆

Daniel J. Harrington

The book of Baruch is attributed to the scribe and secretary of Jeremiah, Baruch the son of Neriah (Jer. 36:27–32; 45:1–5). It is sometimes called 1 Baruch to distinguish it from the apocalypses 2 Baruch (Syriac) and 3 Baruch (Greek) as well as 4 Baruch (Paraleipomena of Jeremiah). Its Greek version appears in LXX manuscripts, though parts of it may have been composed in Hebrew. Most scholars place its composition in Palestine in the second or first century BCE, though its narrative setting is sixth-century Babylon. Its major concerns are why the exile took place and how Israel might repent and so continue as God's people. In dealing with those questions, the book adopts and develops the theological scheme of sin, exile, repentance, and return found in Deut. 28–33 and Jer. 26–33. The major ethical problem that it raises is the adequacy of that schema as an explanation of ancient Israel's national tragedy.

The four major parts of the book differ in their literary forms: the narrative framework (1:1–14), the exiles' prayer (1:15–3:8), the meditative poem about searching for wisdom (3:9–4:4), and the poem of consolation (4:5–5:9). What unifies these four pieces are the theological convictions that the exile was the consequence of Israel's sins, that what God wanted from his people was their repentance and renewed willingness to live according to the Torah, and that God would then return Israel to its great city (Jerusalem) and temple.

The narrative framework introduces Baruch and the exiles in Babylon and portrays what follows as their letter to Jews who were remaining in Jerusalem.

The community's prayer (based on Dan. 9) recognizes the exile as God's just punishment for the people's sins and appeals to God's mercy and goodness and to the glory attached to God's name as reasons why they might be allowed to return from exile to their homeland and to renew their covenant with God. The poem about searching for wisdom (echoing Job 28) reflects on how hard it is to obtain real wisdom and affirms that it can be found in the Torah. The poem of consolation (based on Isa. 40–66) acknowledges that the exile was just punishment for Israel's sins but also offers encouragement and hope about returning to Jerusalem and the renewal of God's people. Thus, the book as a whole moves from the people's confession of sin and sadness over the exile, through a meditation on God's mysterious ways and an equation between wisdom and the Torah, to hope for return from exile.

The language, images, and theological ideas in Baruch are deeply rooted in the OT. The complex of sin, exile, repentance, and return is a communal application of the "law of retribution." According to that principle, wise and righteous persons prosper while foolish and wicked persons are justly punished in this life. Though taken for granted in many parts of the Bible (especially in the Deuteronomistic History, the Prophets, and Proverbs), this "law" is criticized and contested in the books of Job and Ecclesiastes. In Baruch it is accepted as a premise and serves as the starting point for interpreting Israel's communal exile in the sixth century BCE, for urging the people's moral renewal, and for holding out hope for a national revival.

The major question raised by the book of Baruch is whether this explanation of Israel's national tragedy in the sixth century BCE is truly adequate. Modern scholars tend to explain these events mainly in political, socioeconomic, and historical terms. The book's theological appeal to the schema of sin, exile, repentance, and return can be criticized as too easily blaming the victims or can be explained away as a futile attempt to make sense out of what has happened (an example of cognitive dissonance). However one might judge the adequacy of Baruch's explanation of the Jewish exile in the sixth century BCE, attempts to apply it or something like it to the Shoah (Holocaust) of twentieth-century Europe raise difficult ethical questions. These include the lack of correlation between the Jewish people's alleged "sins" and their "punishment," and the religious claims made by some about the providential significance of Zionism and the modern State of Israel.

Bibliography

Feuerstein, R. *Das Buch Baruch: Studien zur Textgestalt und Auslegungsgeschichte.* EUS 32/614. Lang, 1997.

Harrington, D. *Invitation to the Apocrypha*. Eerdmans, 1999, 92–102.

Wright, J. *Baruch ben Neriah: From Biblical Scribe to Apocalyptic Seer*. University of South Carolina Press, 2003.

♦ Letter of Jeremiah ♦

Daniel J. Harrington

The Letter of Jeremiah provides warnings about the folly of idolatry to Jews facing the prospect of exile to Babylon. The idea that Jeremiah wrote to the exiles is found in Jer. 29. The content echoes material in Jer. 10. Its polemic against idolatry has biblical roots in Deuteronomy, Deutero-Isaiah, and various psalms. In the Greek manuscript tradition it appears as a separate composition between Lamentations and Ezekiel, while in the Latin manuscript tradition it is chapter 6 in the book of Baruch. The primary text now is the Greek version, though it may have been composed in Hebrew. It may have originated at almost any time between the sixth and the first centuries BCE.

The text purports to be a copy of a letter that Jeremiah sent to Jews who were to be exiled to Babylon. The prophet warns that in Babylon they will be exposed to "gods made of silver and gold and wood" and exhorts them to remain faithful to worship of the God of Israel. The main point is captured by the advice, "But say in your heart, 'It is you, O Lord, whom we must worship' " (v. 6).

The body of the letter (more like a sermon) consists of ten warnings against idolatry, which here is defined as worshiping what are claimed to be images of gods. The thrust of the critique is that these images are helpless, useless, lifeless, and powerless. They cannot do what the real God does, so their devotees are misguided. Each unit ends with something like a refrain that affirms that these idols are not gods at all and therefore do not deserve "fear" of the Lord.

This letter-sermon clearly was intended to encourage Jews who found themselves in settings where they were exposed to cults other than their own Jewish form of worship. It insists that participation in such cults is foolish and useless and bears witness to strong Jewish convictions about monotheism in the Second Temple period. It was written from the viewpoint of a Jew whose own religion prohibited physical representations of God (see Exod. 20:4–5; Deut. 5:8–9). The author does not pretend to give an objective picture of the cults to which his fellow Jews might be exposed. At no point does he try to get into the heads and hearts of the devotees of those cults or to imagine that the various representations of the gods might be intended as visible symbols of the divine. For this reason, this text can present problems for Jews and Christians today attempting to engage in dialogue with other religions. Yet such attacks against the folly of idolatry are common in Second Temple Judaism (e.g., Bel; Wis. 13–15), rabbinic Judaism (the *'Abodah Zarah* tradition), and early Christianity (Rom. 1:18–32; 1 Cor. 8–10; Jas. 2:19; 1 John 5:21).

Bibliography

Barton, S., ed. *Idolatry: False Worship in the Bible, Early Judaism and Christianity.* T&T Clark, 2007.

Harrington, D. *Invitation to the Apocrypha.* Eerdmans, 1999, 103–8.

♦ Additions to Daniel ♦

Daniel J. Harrington

The Greek version of Daniel contains the "Prayer of Azariah" (a communal lament/confession) and the "Song of the Three Jews" (a benediction) between 3:23 and 3:24, as well as the "Story of Susanna" (a detective story) and the "Story of Bel and the Dragon" (a parody on idolatry) at the end (chaps. 13 and 14 in most editions). The additions reflect in various ways the tensions between the two great attributes of God in the Bible: justice and mercy.

In his prayer made in the fiery furnace, Azariah addresses God directly ("O Lord, God of our ancestors") and acknowledges the justice of God in allowing Israel to be defeated and exiled at the hands of the Babylonians in the sixth century BCE. He goes on to appeal to the mercy of God and reminds God of his promises to Abraham. He suggests that "a contrite heart and a humble spirit" may now serve as an acceptable sacrifice and issue in Azariah's own (and Israel's) deliverance.

In their long benediction in the fiery furnace, Azariah and his companions, Hananiah and Mishael, first bless directly ("Blessed are you") the God of Israel and of all creation. Then they invite all creation to join in their praise ("Bless the Lord"), including what is in the heavens (vv. 36–41), what comes down from the heavens (vv. 42–51), what lives on earth (vv. 52–59), and various classes of humans (vv. 60–66). They end by blessing God for their own deliverance. The song is an eloquent statement in praise of God's mercy, and its invitation to all creation to join the chorus of praise has positive implications for ecological ethics.

The Susanna story combines sex, religion, and death. Two "dirty old men" (who are elders and judges in the Jewish community in Babylon) happen to see the beautiful, God-fearing Susanna bathing, and they lust after her. When she refuses their advances, they accuse her of adultery with "a young man." She is saved from execution only when God stirs in Daniel "a holy spirit," and he finds a way to prove the accusation false by separating the two men and showing that their testimony is contradictory. As a result, they (rather than Susanna) are condemned to death. The Susanna story illustrates the justice of God, the power of trust in God, and God's use of Daniel's wisdom. It has also initiated a long artistic tradition of erotic portrayals of the naked Susanna.

In the episode about Bel and the Dragon, Daniel engages in contests about who the living God is. Playing detective again, he exposes the folly of idolatry and affirms the sovereignty of the God of Israel, who has mercy on those who love and trust him in the midst of their sufferings. The Additions to Daniel are part of Catholic and Orthodox Christian Bibles.

Bibliography

Clanton, D. *The Good, the Bold, and the Beautiful: The Story of Susanna and Its Renaissance Interpretations*. LHBOTS 430. T&T Clark, 2006.

Collins, J. *Daniel*. Hermeneia. Fortress, 1993.

Harrington, D. *Invitation to the Apocrypha*. Eerdmans, 1999, 109–21.

◆ 1 Maccabees ◆

Anathea Portier-Young

Composed between the years 130 and 100 BCE, 1 Maccabees documents the Jewish struggle for independence from their Seleucid overlords following a brutal persecution by Antiochus IV Epiphanes. The book's drama revolves around the priestly family of Mattathias, known to history as the Maccabees or Hasmoneans. They liberate and purify the Jerusalem temple, free the occupied citadel, expand their nation's borders, and establish a new dynasty to rule over Judea. The book of 1 Maccabees aims to legitimate this dynasty's claim to the high priesthood and kingship and to unite its readers through common identity and values.

Among the moral sources of 1 Maccabees, "the law" holds a primary place. Scrolls of the law and obedience to it are proscribed during the persecution (1:56–57), but the resisters carry a Torah scroll with them, perhaps even searching in it for guidance as they prepare for battle (3:48–54). Judas musters troops "according to the law," following the prescriptions of Deut. 20:5–8 (3:56).

The law contains not only statutes (2:21) but also moral exemplars. When the king's messenger commands Judeans to sacrifice on an alien altar, Mattathias kills messenger and sacrificer alike (2:24–25). The narrator reports, "Thus he burned with zeal for the law, just as Phinehas did against Zimri son of Salu" (2:26). In his last testament to his sons, Mattathias exhorts them to imitate not only Phinehas (2:54) but also Abraham (2:52 [cf. Gen. 15; 22]) and Joseph (2:53 [cf. Gen. 39:7–10; 41:38–45]).

Mattathias similarly urges his sons to imitate Joshua (2:55), Caleb (2:56 [cf. Num. 13:30]), David (2:57), and Elijah (2:58 [cf. 1 Kgs. 19:10, 14]). Each models piety as well as military leadership or militant zeal. Mattathias also invokes the examples of Hananiah, Azariah, Mishael (2:59 [cf. Dan. 3]), and Daniel (2:60 [cf. Dan. 6]). Elsewhere, "the holy books" provide encouragement (12:9).

Among specific practices targeted in the persecution, 1 Maccabees identifies sacrifice, Sabbath and feast days, circumcision, and purity laws (1:45–49, 60–63). Regarding idolatry, Mattathias counters the king's command with God's, declaring, "We will not obey the king's words by turning aside from our religion to the right hand or to the left" (2:22). The question of Sabbath observance is more complex. Early in the persecution a thousand women, children, and men flee to the desert (2:31, 38). Seleucid soldiers prepare to attack them on the Sabbath but first call them out, promising to spare them if they will obey the king's command (2:32–33). The Jews choose death rather than obey the king or violate the Sabbath (2:34–36). Learning of the massacre, Mattathias and his friends weigh Sabbath observance against the cost of human life, resolving to fight on the Sabbath to defend their lives and laws (2:39–41).

The book of 1 Maccabees contributes to moral discourses regarding just war (*jus ad bellum*), Sabbath observance, and conflict between divine commands and laws of the state.

Morally problematic features of the text also demand serious engagement. The call to arms in 1 Maccabees exceeds the charge to defend people and laws, aiming also at vengeance (2:67–68; 9:40–42; 13:6). Defense of the law extends to killing sinners (2:44; 9:73; 14:14). Mattathias and his comrades forcibly circumcise young boys (2:46). As their wars shift from defense to offense, his sons raze and plunder neighboring cities (5:51, 65–68; 10:84; 11:61; 12:31). Labeling certain inhabitants of Judea as "lawless" justifies their extermination (2:44; 3:5–6; 7:5; 9:23, 58, 69; 11:25; 14:14), while references to the hatred and aggression of "the nations" justify expansion (12:53; 13:6). The Judeans surrender their autonomy to this rhetoric of security through radical othering, shouting to Simon, "Fight our battles, and all that you say to us we will do" (13:9). Finally, as Jonathan and Simon broker alliances with Seleucids and

Romans, they enter a world of political patronage fraught with deception and manipulation (12:43–48; 16:18–22). The favors that they exchange are costly: they kill one hundred thousand inhabitants of Antioch to aid a king who will betray them (11:41–53). They too trade moral autonomy for an illusion of power and self-determination. Readers do well to look at their own alliances and count the cost.

Bibliography

Collins, J. *Daniel, First Maccabees, Second Maccabees.* OTM 15. Michael Glazier, 1981.

———. "The Zeal of Phinehas: The Bible and the Legitimation of Violence." *JBL* 122 (2003): 3–21.

Hieke, T. "The Role of 'Scripture' in the Last Words of Mattathias (1 Macc 2:49–70)." Pages 61–74 in *The Books of the Maccabees: History, Theology, Ideology*, ed. G. Xeravits and J. Zsengellér. JSJSup 118. Brill, 2007.

Schwartz, D. "The Other in 1 and 2 Maccabees." Pages 30–37 in *Tolerance and Intolerance in Early Judaism and Christianity*, ed. G. Stanton and G. Stroumsa. Cambridge University Press, 1998.

♦ 2 Maccabees ♦

Anathea Portier-Young

The book of 2 Maccabees details events in Jerusalem between 175 and 160 BCE. Jerusalem's priests trade ancestral traditions for "Greek glories" (4:15). A tableau of horrors follows: slaughter, slavery, the temple profaned, Jewish faith outlawed (5:11–6:11). The stories of nine martyrs occupy the book's center (6:18–7:42). With God's help (8:23–24; 10:1), Judas Maccabeus and his brothers lead an army against the oppressors, liberate the city, purify the temple (10:1–5), and finally defeat the enemy general Nicanor (15:27–36).

In the moral economy of 2 Maccabees, God defended the temple and people of Jerusalem when they obeyed God's law (3:1; 8:36). When they abandoned it (4:16–17), God disciplined them (6:12–17; 7:32–33). The willing deaths of martyrs atoned for the people's sins, effecting a turning point for the nation (7:38; 8:3–5). Living and dead alike intercede with God through prayer (3:15–21; 7:37; 10:4; 12:42; 15:12–14). Sacrifice gains God's mercy for an enemy (3:32–33) and atones for the sins of the dead (12:40–46). God's justice works through human and supernatural agents (1:15–17; 3:24–34; 4:38) and through illness and calamity (9:5–11). Punishment frequently "fits" the crime (4:16, 26, 38; 8:25; 9:6, 10).

The law and ancestral traditions prescribe a way of life, including sacrificial worship, diet, Sabbath, and circumcision. For these and for "temple, city, country, and commonwealth," the book's heroes are willing to die (13:14). When the law appears secure, Judas makes peace terms with a view to what is *sympheron*, or advantageous (11:15; cf. 12:12; see also Aristotle, *Eth. nic.* 9.3 §1004b30–31). Here and elsewhere in the book (6:20, 27, 31; 7:12; 15:12) the narrator may show the influence of Greek moral philosophy.

The book of 2 Maccabees gives special attention to the moral reasoning of the martyrs. When Eleazar refuses to eat pork, he is encouraged to save his life by pretending. He refuses on the grounds that the young would mistake his action and be led astray by his example (6:24–25 [note later discourses on "scandal"—e.g., Thomas Aquinas, *ST* II-II, q. 43]). The seven brothers who give their bodies to death are emboldened by belief in resurrection, valuing eternal life over the present one (7:9, 11). Their mother encourages them with words from the Song of Moses, alluding to the belief that God will vindicate God's people "when their power is gone" (Deut. 32:36). She deduces God's power to restore life from her experience of the mystery of conception and gestation (7:22–23 [cf. Eccl. 11:5]). In a similar vein, she instructs her youngest son to observe heaven and earth and deduce from them God's life-giving power, so that he should not fear death (7:28–29). The stories of these martyrs have inspired many in multiple religious traditions and may be considered the book's most profound moral legacy.

The book also tells of Razis, a confessing Jew who took his own life when the enemy came to arrest him (14:37–46). The Donatist bishop Gaudentius cited Razis's example in support of his own plans for suicide. In a letter to Dulcitius (*Ep.* 204), Augustine countered that Razis's actions were "great" but not "good." In Augustine's view, the book offers Razis's example not for imitation but for judgment.

The book of 2 Maccabees asserts that God fought on the side of Judas and his army, in many cases claiming divine support for actions that violate modern understandings of just conduct in war (*jus in bello*). Judas sets fire to villages at night (8:6–7); burns alive an enemy who has taken refuge in a house (8:33; cf. 10:37); takes revenge by night on refugees (12:6); slaughters the people of Caspin, Carnaim (where women and children have been sent for refuge), and Ephron (12:16, 26–27); and mutilates the dead body of Nicanor to display his head, tongue, and arm as proof of God's help (15:30–35). Serious engagement with 2 Maccabees requires that we confront these and similar claims and actions not only in the text but also in the world we inhabit today.

Bibliography

Doran, R. *Temple Propaganda: The Purpose and Character of 2 Maccabees.* CBQMS 12. Catholic Biblical Association of America, 1981.

Ego, B. "God's Justice: The 'Measure for Measure' Principle in 2 Maccabees." Pages 141–54 in *The Books of the Maccabees: History, Theology, Ideology*, ed. G. Xeravits and J. Zsengellér. JSJSup 118. Brill, 2007.

Heard, W. "The Maccabean Martyrs' Contribution to Holy War." *EvQ* 58 (1986): 291–318.

Schwartz, D. *2 Maccabees.* CEJL. De Gruyter, 2008.

van Henten, J. *The Maccabean Martyrs as Saviours of the Jewish People: A Study of 2 and 4 Maccabees.* JSJSup 57. Brill, 1997.

7

SELECTED TOPICS IN OLD TESTAMENT ETHICS

♦ **Biblical Accounts of Creation** ♦

William P. Brown

There are at least five self-contained accounts of creation in the OT: Gen. 1:1–2:4a; Gen. 2:4b–3:24; Job 38–41; Ps. 104; Prov. 8:22–31. In the NT, the prologue to John's Gospel (1:1–18) also counts as a bona fide creation narrative. In addition, many other biblical texts describe creation one way or another, such as Eccl. 1:3–11 and portions of Isa. 40–55. The ethical implications of each of these texts are examined below.

Genesis 1:1–2:4a

Due to its canonical placement, Gen. 1:1–2:3 (known as the Priestly account of creation) enjoys pride of place in the Bible. Structured around seven days, the account describes a steady process of creation initiated and governed by God's word, beginning with light and concluding with life. God, moreover, does not entirely work alone: in several instances the waters or the land are enlisted to aid in the creative process (1:9, 11, 20, 24). The result is a world of ordered complexity that accommodates and sustains the rich panoply of life, each "according to its kind." Light, sky, seas, and land are established first, followed by the creation of particular agents and living creatures within these domains: stars, birds, marine life, and land animals, including humans. Some have particular functions or mandates: the sun and the moon determine the seasons and religious festivals (1:14). Marine and aviary life receive the blessing to multiply (1:22). Humans are charged with the responsibility of exercising "dominion" (1:28). The outcome of every stage in the creative process is declared "good" by God, climactically so at the completion of creation (1:31). Such approbation acknowledges creation's integrity and self-sustainability, from seeds to reproduction. The climax of creation, however, is not the sixth day, with the creation of humankind, but rather the seventh day (2:1–3), when God ceases to create, thereby allowing creation, under human "dominion," to thrive on its own. The Exodus version of the Decalogue bases the Sabbath commandment on God's resting on the seventh day (Exod. 20:11; cf. Deut. 5:15).

Creation in Gen. 1 is a cosmic temple in which the holy seventh day corresponds to the temple's holiest of holies, the inner sanctum (1 Kgs. 8:12–13; see Exod. 40:34–35). While God remains outside creation, humans, created "in the image of God," reside within (Gen. 1:27). Elsewhere in the Bible, the term *image* designates a statue or engraving that represents God, explicitly forbidden in biblical tradition (e.g., 2 Kgs. 11:18; cf. Exod. 20:4; Lev. 19:4; Deut. 4:15–18). Genesis 1, however, applies the language of *image* to humans, who bear God's presence in the world and are commanded to exercise "dominion." For an ancient agrarian society, such a command gave divine warrant to cultivate the land and harness its fertility for sustaining life, human and nonhuman (Gen. 1:29–30). Stewardship, thus, is an appropriate way of making sense of "dominion" in Genesis for today.

Genesis 2:4b–3:24

Whereas creation in Gen. 1 begins in a primordial soup (*tōhû wābōhû* [1:2]), the second creation story, known as the Yahwist account, begins with a dry stretch of land. The soil takes center stage in this narrative, for from it God, like a potter working with clay, creates a human being, the *'ādām*. From such a simple narrative beginning, a wordplay is born: the *'ādām* is created out of the *'ādāmâ*, the "ground." Just as the English word *human* is derived from the Latin *humus*, the meaning of *'ādām* carries with it the sense of "groundling." If God is king of the cosmos in Gen. 1, God is king of the compost in Gen. 2. God animates the first human being not by divine touch (contra Michelangelo), but rather by mouth-to-nose resuscitation. In Gen. 2, creation is intimately physical.

In the Yahwist account of creation, God plants a garden for the *'ādām* and gives him the task of serving and preserving it (2:15). The divine farmer entrusts the garden to the human farmer. Thus, the *'ādām* becomes the servant of the soil, in contrast to the royal, nearly divine elevation of humanity in Gen. 1. There is nothing in the garden to be "subdued." Indeed, the ground and the "groundling" form a fruitful partnership, a kinship by which the *'ādām* is sustained and the soil yields its productivity. But as fruitful as the garden is, God finds that the life of the human farmer is "not good" (2:18). The *'ādām* needs a companion, and so God creates out of the ground the animals to see if a coequal can be found. Having failed, God resorts to a more invasive procedure: the woman is created from the *'ādām's* own flesh and blood, and only then does the *'ādām* become a "man" (*'îš* [2:23]). Such a creation by no means implies subordinate status for the woman, but rather indicates coequality and mutuality with the man, hence the marriage etiology in 2:24.

Life in the garden embodies mutuality and harmony, meaningful work and intimacy. It is marred, however, by the couple's attempt to grasp divine power and wisdom. The man and the woman are deemed unfit to care for the garden and are expelled. They suffer the curse of pain and alienation (3:14–19). But God's curse, as a consequence of the couple's disobedience, is no mandate. The garden story does not command subordination and conflict any more than it mandates crop failure. Rather, it recognizes that the blessed life of mutuality, intimacy, and harmonious work is far more difficult to embody outside the garden. Nevertheless, the garden's ethos remains binding.

Job 38–41

God's answer to Job presents a vividly panoramic view of creation. Beginning with earth and all stars and concluding with monstrous Leviathan (to which a whole chapter is devoted), creation in the book of Job is testimony to God's providential care, which extends far beyond what is familiar to humans. God, for example, makes it rain "on a land where no one lives . . . to satisfy the waste and desolate land" (38:26–27). Creation's focus here is on the wilderness, where the wild things are, from ostriches to aurochs. There, each creature has its freedom and vitality, each valued and cherished by God. Unlike Adam, to whom the animals were brought to be named in the garden, Job is shown the natural habitats of these wild creatures and taught their names. Although creation extends far beyond human reach, God points out that Job is inextricably linked to the wild: "Look at Behemoth, which I made just as I made you" (40:15). In God's answer, Job discovers his link to the wild even as the wild remains untouched by him. And so it should. Creation near and far is full of vitality and variety, dignity and terrible beauty.

Psalm 104

Psalm 104 matches Job 38–41 almost animal by animal, from the lion to Leviathan (minus Behemoth). In addition, trees are celebrated, including the majestic cedars of Lebanon. The psalm's broad focus is on creation's habitational integrity. Each animal has its home, from the lion's lair to the coney's rock and the stork's juniper. Creation is not just habitat for humanity; it is habitat for diversity, including even habitat for divinity (104:2b–3a). God provides for all, and the products of nature provide joy for human beings (104:14–15). Dominion has no place in this psalm (cf. Ps. 8); humans are simply counted among the host of living creatures, all exercising their right to live in God's manifold world. The psalmist delights in the sheer variety of creatures and habitats that fill creation (104:24), a delight that God also shares (104:31b). Psalm 104 is God's fanfare for the common creature.

Proverbs 8:22–31

Wisdom presents herself as the consummate eyewitness to God's work in creation. She recounts how God constructed the world, ensuring its integrity. As for her place in creation, personified Wisdom claims to have been "brought forth" (i.e., birthed) prior to anything else created (8:24–25). Wisdom is God's cosmic child, and as a child she plays with both God and creation (8:30–31). Creation, in short, is fashioned for Wisdom's enjoyment. Humanity, on the other hand, is scarcely mentioned, except at the very end as Wisdom's play partner, the object of her delight, along with God. Humans exist for Wisdom's sake, for her delight. Wisdom's playful delight requires humans to live up to their biological name, *Homo sapiens* (the "wise human"), and also to be *Homo ludens* (the "playing human").

Ecclesiastes 1:3–11

Although not a creation account proper, the opening chapter of Ecclesiastes presents a unique snapshot of creation in perpetual motion, from rising generations and flowing streams to circling sun and blowing wind. And yet for all its frenetic activity, the earth remains the same (1:4b). There is "nothing new under the sun" (1:9). Change is a mirage. Creation, moreover, is fraught with "vanity" (Heb. *hebel*), making life futile and fleeting. As for humanity's place and role in a world of *hebel*, the ancient sage warns against getting swept up in the relentless, all-consuming quest for "gain." In Qoheleth's eyes,

creation presents a lesson, but it is a negative one. As the world is full of ex-
pended effort, all for naught, so humans cannot grasp anything permanent
and profitable, no matter how hard they try. *Hebel* always wins. Instead, the
sage commends a nonprofit existence: "There is nothing better for mortals
than to eat and drink, and find enjoyment in their toil. This also, I saw, is
from the hand of God" (2:24). To pause amid the toil and to savor the simple
gifts of sustenance—themselves the fruits of creation—is the highest good
for humans. In his own way, the sage advocates a life of simplicity and joy.
He is not a hedonist, not one to strive for pleasure as one strives for gain. No,
Qoheleth commends a life of grateful acceptance.

Isaiah 40–55

Known as Second Isaiah, this corpus of prophetic poetry is filled with references
to creation, all bound up with the prophet's bold historical pronouncements
of release for the exilic community. As much as Qoheleth denounces anything
new, the prophet of the exile heralds the new. In Isaiah, history and creation
are inseparably wedded. God stretches out the heavens as a tent or curtain
(40:22; 42:5) and hammers out the earth as a firmament (42:5b; 44:24b). God
creates both light and darkness, weal and woe (45:6b–7; cf. Gen. 1:3). Incom-
parably transcendent, God stands alone as creator of all. All in all, God did
not create the earth "a chaos [*tōhû*], he formed it to be inhabited" (45:18).
As the heavens are stretched out, so God commands Zion to "enlarge the site
of your tent" and to "let the curtains of your habitations be stretched out"
in order to accommodate Zion's lost children, the returning exiles (54:2–3).
Creation prefigures Israel's restoration in the land, inaugurated by a new exodus (43:16–23). This is indeed something "new" (42:9; 43:19; 48:6). Released
from exile, Israel will never be the same; so also creation. Indeed, the prophet
likens Israel's restoration to new botanical growth (41:17–21; 45:8; 55:10–11).
God's saving word is a creative word.

John 1:1–18

The word that initiates creation in Gen. 1 reaches its creative fullness in the
prologue to John's Gospel. Rewriting Gen. 1, especially the first three verses,
John lifts up the divine "Word" (*logos*) that was present "in the beginning" and,
at the same time, brings it down to earth, fully enfleshed (1:1, 14). Drawing
from Prov. 8, John identifies Christ with primordial Wisdom, who was "with
God" (1:1 [cf. Prov. 8:30]) and who "enlightens everyone" (1:9). As "light"

was the first of God's primordial acts in Genesis, light in John is the sign of God's glorious effulgence "coming into the world" (1:4–5, 8–9). As in Genesis, light and life are interconnected (1:4). In Gen. 1, God fashions creation by divine word, but no indication is given as to when or how God will enter the cosmic temple, if ever. For John, however, the Christ event marks God's formal entrance into creation, once and for all (1:9–10). The evangelist establishes a broad theological arc extending from Genesis to John, from the creator God to the incarnate Christ, the "light of the world" (8:12). In John, God's creative "Word" is God's incarnational presence in the world (1:14).

Each in its own way, these creation traditions claim the world as God's creation and acknowledge creation's God-given worth and integrity, its goodness and its beauty. As God's cosmic temple, creation bears a sanctity that must not be profaned. Humankind, the accounts attest, is creation's royal steward and loyal servant, its most powerful agent and most grateful recipient. As God's "images," humans are called to reflect God's life-affirming ways, to embody the God who cares for all creatures and seeks their well-being. In the biblical narrative, the one who most fully exercises divinely ordained "dominion" is Noah, who preserves the diversity of all creation. The world that "God so loved" is nothing less than cosmic (John 3:16).

Bibliography

Brown, W. "The Moral Cosmologies of Creation." Pages 11–26 in *Character Ethics and the Old Testament: The Moral Dimensions of Scripture*, ed. M. D. Carroll R. and J. Lapsley. Westminster John Knox, 2007.

———. *The Seven Pillars of Creation: The Bible, Science, and the Ecology of Wonder*. Oxford University Press, 2010.

Davis, E. *Scripture, Culture, and Agriculture: An Agrarian Reading of the Bible*. Cambridge University Press, 2009.

Fretheim, T. *God and World in the Old Testament: A Relational Theology of Creation*. Abingdon, 2005.

◆ Dead Sea Scrolls ◆

Amy C. Merrill Willis

Between the years 1946 and 1956, the caves near the Dead Sea surrendered nearly nine hundred scrolls dating from the period 150 BCE–70 CE. Of these scrolls, 222 were of biblical and apocryphal materials, and 670 were of a nonbiblical nature. The nonbiblical materials contain treatises, hymns, and commentaries on Scripture that are sectarian in origin and character, as well as some nonsectarian and presectarian materials. The consensus view holds that the Jewish sect of the Essenes, or some subset of the Essenes, lived in the nearby installation at Qumran as a priestly introversionist community and produced the scrolls as a critique of larger Second Temple Judaism, though this view has been subject to revision or outright rejection in some quarters. Sectarian works from the Dead Sea Scrolls include the *Damascus Document* (CD), which may be a narrative of the community's formation that tells of the coming of the Teacher of Righteousness and the community's self-imposed exile to "Damascus" or the Dead Sea wilderness. It also provides codes of everyday conduct for members who appear to live in scattered towns. The *Rule of the Community* (1QS being the most complete copy of the document) is a guide for the community's leader, the *Maskil*, on how to form sectarian character. Its codes of admission and conduct assume that its readers are males living communally (and perhaps celibately) with other males. A key portion of this document, the "Two Spirits Treatise" (1QS 3.13–4.26), describes the ongoing battle between two angels and their followers: the Prince of Light and the children of righteousness versus the Angel of Darkness and the children of injustice. Both of these warring angels were created by God. Other important sectarian documents include legal works such as the *Halakhic Letter* (4QMMT), which describes explicit differences between the sect of the temple cult on issues of purity; the *War Scroll* (1QM); the *Hodayot*, or thanksgiving hymns; and a commentary (pesher) on Habakkuk (1QpHab), which reinterprets Habakkuk in light of the conflict between the Teacher of Righteousness and the Wicked Priest (the high priest of the Jerusalem temple cult?).

The *Rule of the Community* expresses the ethical desideratum of the community to be that of seeking God wholeheartedly and doing what is just according to the divine commandments mediated by Moses and the prophets (1QS 1.1–3). This would seem to establish the Torah as the source for moral knowledge and deliberation. This is not an especially distinctive articulation of ethical thinking within early Judaism, but the *Rule of the Community* and other sectarian documents from the Dead Sea Scrolls define and nuance this ethical ideal in distinctive ways.

The community associated with the Dead Sea Scrolls understands the Torah to be a divinely revealed and rigorous code of covenantal demands rather than a divinely revealed narrative of Israel's origins. Narrative and story are not the chief means of character formation in the scrolls. Instead, the community prides itself on its unique ability and authority, over and against common readings of mainstream Judaism, to interpret the Torah commands according to the divine plan. This divine plan for humanity features a profoundly dualistic view of the cosmos and created order in which God has created both good and evil angels who fight for the hearts of humanity. Even the members of the community are subject to both angels, but sectarian formation is designed to strengthen the power of the righteous angel within each member.

The scrolls indicate a complex view of human virtue and character. Sectarian discourse explicitly valorizes the qualities of obedience to the covenant, moral and ritual purity, humility to the point of self-abnegation, intelligence, discreet concealment of God's mysterious plan, and hatred of the "sons of darkness" (1QS 1.1–7a; 4.3–5; 10.1–11:22). These virtues, however, are not personal; they are not a matter of individual disposition or choices. They result from the confluence of external forces, including the rivalry of the angelic forces, the divine election of the individual, and the community environment and its discipline that nurtures these virtues (Newsom). Moreover, although the individual is accountable for deeds and actions and subject to reproof, the *Rule of the Community* does not value a morally autonomous self. The self is to be submissive and receptive. The member's ability to be obedient, however, is the result of, on the one hand, God's previous allotment of the two angels within the member and, on the other hand, God's eschatological provision of a spirit of holiness, which has already been realized, in part, within the community.

This distinctive articulation of covenant ideals underwrites particular issues of ethical practice in the sectarian documents. A stringent dedication to moral and ritual purity characterizes the sectarian writings and demands the separation of the community from outsiders and their contaminated items. Outsiders include not only foreigners but also Jews not belonging to the sect— that is, all those belonging to common Judaism. This radical principle of purity goes hand in hand with the cosmic dualism of the sect and leads the community to fear and avoid others and to anticipate their destruction at the eschaton. Thus restorative justice and a concern for "the other" are not among the ethical norms of the community. Nevertheless, certain scrolls indicate the circumstances under which "the stranger" or the resident alien may become part of the community, though the resident alien is never permitted full status (Harrington).

The use of wealth and assets is a recurring theme in the sectarian and presectarian scrolls and is tied to the ideal of "covenantal fidelity" (Murphy). Both the *Damascus Document* and the *Rule of the Community* critique the economic systems of Second Temple Judaism that fostered wealth and arrogance. These documents suggest that the community was to be an alternative economic community where usury was prohibited and resources were distributed to help the poor and needy within the group in accordance with the demands of Torah. The Torah laws concerning wealth and tithes are also reinterpreted and extended. For example, the command of Deut. 6:5 to "love God with all one's strength" is understood to mean that members are to give all of their assets—property, wealth, food—to the entire community.

Marriage practices are also a concern of the sectarian materials, which resist and denounce polygamy for the sake of gaining wealth and discourage divorce. Marriage with foreign women is denounced for reasons of purity.

The contents of the *War Scroll* raise the question of whether the scrolls view war and violence as legitimate tools in the cause of purity and covenant fidelity. Certainly, there were groups within Second Temple Judaism that conceptually and actively embraced the use of physical violence for political ends, yet the view of the sectarians remains ambiguous. The *War Scroll* describes an eschatological holy war between angelic factions—the sons of light and the sons of darkness—and understands that humans will participate in this battle, at the end of which enemy factions (including the Romans) will be utterly destroyed. Moreover, this battle, which draws on "holy war" traditions, serves the purpose of ensuring the purity and righteousness of the children of light in accordance with Torah commands. Yet this battle remains future. So although the community embraced the concept of war and violence, even divine violence, as legitimate tools, the community that lived at Qumran did not necessarily directly engage in the war against the Romans that took place during the 60s CE (Elliott).

The ethical ideals of the scrolls are often important for the way in which they shed light on NT and early Christian convictions and practices such as communal property and the distribution of resources to benefit those in need (see Acts 2:42–47; 4:32–37). More generally, the sectarian attempts to build an alternative community raise for the reader's consideration both the moral promises and the problems that inhere in any radical community's attempt to resist the dominant culture of its time.

Bibliography

Elliott, M. "Retribution and Agency in the Dead Sea Scrolls and the Teaching of Jesus." Pages 191–206 in vol. 1 of *The Destructive Power of Religion: Violence in Judaism, Christianity, and Islam*, ed. J. Ellens. Praeger, 2004.

Harrington, H. "Keeping Outsiders Out: Impurity at Qumran." Pages 187–203 in *Defining Identities: We, You, and the Other in the Dead Sea Scrolls*, ed. F. García Martínez and M. Popović. Brill, 2008.

Murphy, C. *Wealth in the Dead Sea Scrolls and in the Qumran Community*. Brill, 2002.

Newsom, C. *The Self as Symbolic Space: Constructing Identity and Community at Qumran*. Brill, 2004.

Smith, B. " 'Spirit of Holiness' as Eschatological Principle of Obedience." Pages 75–99 in *Christian Beginnings and the Dead Sea Scrolls*, ed. J. Collins and C. Evans. Baker Academic, 2006.

VanderKam, J., and P. Flint. *The Meaning of the Dead Sea Scrolls: Their Significance for Understanding the Bible, Judaism, Jesus, and Christianity*. HarperSanFrancisco, 2004.

✦ Ethics of Exile ✦

Daniel Smith-Christopher

The central issue in discussions of the ethics of exile is how the ethical examples of biblical characters and the values counseled in exilic texts are inevitably contextualized in the events and setting of conquered Israel and Judah. Exilic ethics, therefore, are advised under conditions of subjugation and subordination. A preliminary illustration of the importance of this contextualizing of exilic ethics is the behavior modeled by Abram/Abraham in the famous case where Abraham feared for his life and thus advised deception (Gen. 12:13). If this passage is dated to the time of the postexilic period (so Brett), then it must be read as a "subcultural" or even "survival" ethic—that is, misinforming the authorities for the sake of survival. Such ethical behavior may not be exemplary for "institutionalized" or "mainstream" ethics (the determination of which is always the privilege of the powerful), but may well be considered wise behavior in the context of subordination to hostile power. Therefore, any discussion of the ethical significance of biblical behaviors modeled or counseled in exilic texts cannot be separated from consideration of the events themselves.

Assessing the Historical Impact of the Exile

The historic importance of the exile and its impact on the life and faith of ancient Israel have not been matters of universal agreement in the last century of biblical scholarship. Charles Torrey, for example, famously wrote that the exile "was in reality a small and relatively insignificant affair" (Torrey 285). Early in the twenty-first century, however, as a result of both new archaeological work and recent interdisciplinary study of biblical texts (especially when read in comparison with literature on refugee studies, post-traumatic stress disorder, and minority existence), the situation has dramatically changed.

In his most recent survey of archaeological work, Oded Lipschitz refers to material evidence of "Nebuchadnezzar's desire to eliminate Jerusalem as a religious and political center" and summarizes what he calls "the totality of the devastation" (Lipschitz 80). He concludes, "The demographic evidence thus supports the previous hypothesis that Jerusalem remained desolate throughout the time of Babylonian Rule" (Lipschitz 218). The total population of Judah at the end of the Iron Age is estimated at 108,000, but at the beginning of the Persian period at 30,125 (Lipschitz 270). It should not be surprising, then, that Rainer Albertz begins the most comprehensive recent summary of the exilic period in biblical history and literature with these words: "Of all the eras in Israel's history, the exilic period represents the most profound . . . [and] radical change. Its significance for subsequent history can hardly be overstated. Here, the religion of Israel underwent its most severe crisis" (Albertz 1).

A more radical transformation in biblical scholarship is hard to conceive. The events themselves are easily summarized. The short-lived "united" monarchy of ancient Israel existed from about 1020 BCE to the death of Solomon in about 722 BCE. After Solomon's death, the Hebrew tribal territories split into rival political entities: the northern "state" of Israel, and the southern "state" of Judah, based in Jerusalem. Before long, however, the assertion of power from Mesopotamian regimes to the east eroded any sense of independence on the part of these small, rival states in Palestine (not only Judah and Israel but also Damascus, Moab, Edom, Ammon, and others). The Neo-Assyrian Empire conquered the northern state of Israel in 722 BCE, and Sennacherib also devastated Judah in 701, but Judah was not fully conquered and made into a Neo-Assyrian province as the north certainly was. Still, the devastation of colonial control by Assyria had its continued impact on Israelite and Judean territories.

A century later the rising power was the Neo-Babylonian Empire. In their military attempts to possess Egypt, the Babylonians needed the corridor down the Mediterranean coast clear and under control; thus, Judah was "in the way." Judah, at first, surrendered to Babylon in 597 BCE, after a siege, and a number of prisoners of war were exiled into separate communities in the Babylonian heartland. Ten years later, the remaining Judean political vassal of Babylon, Zedekiah, tried to revolt with promised assistance from Egypt, and the results were catastrophic. The deportations associated with the Babylonian conquests of Judah are normally referred to as "the Babylonian exile." Substantial Diaspora communities were permanently planted in the eastern regions of Mesopotamian and Persian territories from the sixth century BCE onward, and remained well into the modern period. The biblical literature from the time of the Babylonian conquests consists of writings from both the homeland and the Diaspora, and often it reflects relations between the two kinds of communities (homeland and Diaspora). However, given the universal agreement that the writings that would later be canonized into the Jewish and Christian Scriptures were gathered, widely edited, and many actually written after the devastations of the sixth century BCE, the Bible as we now read it is largely the product of the conditions of Diaspora and occupation.

With regard to the Neo-Babylonian policies, David Vanderhooft surmises that Nebuchadnezzar's western ventures had monetary motivations as well (Vanderhooft 82, 209). Furthermore, following the Babylonian Empire, the Persian "economy" was also a system for the hoarding of precious metals facilitated by a massive tax and labor (Frye 114–15). These realities continue right through to the Hellenistic period under the Ptolemies and Seleucids (Green 187). Irrespective of the very real differences between the political and ideological regimes from 587 to 164 BCE and into the Roman period, any discussion of biblical ethics must be attentive to the stubborn realities of ancient imperial designs toward power and control over wealth, territory, and human resources.

Situating an Ethics of Exile

A number of ethical issues are raised when biblical literature of the period is read in a social context featuring these sociopolitical dynamics. First, there is the problem of "public transcripts" and "private transcripts" (Scott 1985; 1990), which refers to ideas that may be discussed within a minority community, as opposed to those ideas intended for public consumption. As Eftihia Voutira and Barbara Harrell-Bond illustrate, this has been an important emphasis in refugee studies: "To be a refugee means to learn to lie" (Voutira and Harrell-Bond 216). One of the most important arenas for ethical debate, therefore, is the relation of the subordinated to the powerful.

It hardly seems necessary to emphasize that such perspectives would dramatically change a modern reading of, say, the stories of Dan. 1–6. These can be read naively as mere counsels to faithfulness, but in their context they also must be read as stories of religious and social resistance to assimilation. Furthermore, the Daniel stories clearly represent a counsel to be highly suspicious of imperial power as well as a call to maintain identity in a hostile social and political environment.

Finally, the notion that the stories of Daniel suggest vaguely "positive" evaluation of emperors should not be easily taken to mean that the biblical texts reveal positive feelings about living in the shadows of empires. Even the case of Nehemiah, whose role as "cupbearer" often is cited as an example of the potential for success among Diaspora Jews, must be carefully reconsidered in historical context. How much of an honor is it to be chosen to be the taster of food for the emperor, thus the one who will die first if anyone tries to poison the emperor? This is hardly a success story; rather, it merely reveals the ambiguity of living under a regime and the expendability of minorities, and it reveals Hebrew stories that must calculate public relations as an element of domination.

In sum, the ethics of exile must be explicated in the context of oppression and fear. If not, then such ethical reflection is insufficiently biblical. With these foundational observations in place, then, the following are suggested as potentially important ethical themes arising from a consideration of exilic contexts and literatures of the Bible.

Communal Solidarity and Definition

It is widely noted that the language of the Mosaic legal tradition changes rather significantly from the earlier Covenant Code (Exodus) to the more compassionate language used in the Deuteronomic Code (dated, at the earliest, to the reign of Josiah, 640–609 BCE, but amended to include references to exile [e.g., Deut. 28:49–68]). Among the more compelling aspects of the Deuteronomic Code are counsels to mutual aid—care for fellow Hebrews (and even non-Hebrews) typified especially by a concern for the indigent (widow, orphan, foreigner). Many laws instituting care for the poor are unique to the later law code (e.g., gleaning [Deut. 24:19], provisions for hunger [Deut. 24:20]) and suggest an increased social solidarity among the Hebrew people that may well be tied directly to a sense of common threat in the Assyrian and Babylonian periods.

Another aspect of communal solidarity is the behavior of community members toward one another. There is evidence that this was an increasingly serious concern in the exilic and postexilic contexts. The specific Greek (LXX) addition to Daniel known as the book of Susanna is a clear case of internal conflict and corruption within the community. We know that such issues of internal corruption and behavior also continued to be serious issues right into the Roman period, where such concerns arguably define the conflicts between Jesus and his followers on the one side, and hostile members of his own tradition on the other, who see his teachings as inviting trouble from Roman authorities (e.g., John 11:48).

Later Persian and Hellenistic literature, such as the book of Tobit, also maintains a strong emphasis on service to others within the community (see

Tob. 4:13–18). Again, much of the context of the NT ethics of Jesus is illumi-
nated by this emphasis on communal solidarity (see Horsley and Silberman).

Solidarity and Group Identity

The importance of group cohesion in circumstances of oppression can
hardly be overemphasized. Any minority must attend to issues of identity
and definition. How are "we" to be defined in distinction from variously
identified "others"? In the exilic biblical literature, however, there are clear
signs of debate with regard to the ethics of this process of self-identity and
maintaining faithful communities. For example, Ezra's concern for the "purity"
of the exilic community (e.g., the "pure seed" [Ezra 9:2]) clearly reflected an
emphasis on maintaining separations and boundaries that maintained identity in circumstances of exile and minority existence. The matter of actually
divorcing all foreign wives, however, appears to have stirred debate, given that
we have contrary views stated in postexilic biblical literature as well, most
famously the story of Ruth (whose obvious status of acceptance in the story
is a direct violation of Ezra's own counsel against Moabites [Ezra 9:1]) and in
the counsel of the late texts of Isaiah (Isa. 56:3). Clearly, a major ethical issue
involved the definition of, and integrity of the boundaries of, the "authentic"
people of faith. The problem of conversion is obviously a related issue, and it
haunts any reading of the book of Jonah or of Isa. 19, where even Assyrians
and Egyptians will be included in the future definition of the people of God.
There are a variety of texts suggesting exilic hopes that foreigners will learn
to be well disposed toward Hebrews and Hebrew faith, even if falling short
of a campaign of conversion (e.g., Zech. 8:22–23). But actual converts did
exist, and thus how converts are to be treated (e.g., book of Ezra: rejection;
book of Ruth: acceptance) is another ethical issue of relations with foreigners
that continues to define the ethics of communal identity and integrity clear
through the Hellenistic period (e.g., in works such as the noncanonical *Joseph
and Aseneth*) and even into the NT debates between Paul and the so-called
Judaizers, as outlined in Acts 15–16.

Violence and Nonviolence in Relation to Outsiders

The issue of how "we" relate to "them" finds its utmost expression in the
problem of violence. For example, the postexilic warning in Prov. 1 about being
tempted to lives of urban crime (Prov. 1:10–19, esp. v. 13) is suggestive of the
temptations toward banditry and criminal behavior in the Diaspora or under
occupation. But this can also be expressed in the more acceptable language

of nationalism and language of "restoration" (1 Maccabees is clearly resto-rationist). How to relate to non-Hebrews when living as a minority or under occupation is a major ethical debate reflected in exilic and postexilic biblical texts. There are texts that suggest Hebrew involvement in violence, as well as texts calling for apocalyptic punishment by God and angels of destruction (the apocalyptic tradition).

Angry exilic texts calling for vengeance against foreigners (e.g., Ps. 137; Jer. 50–51; Obadiah) are not, however, the only voices of counsel in the postexilic literature. The story of Jonah profoundly holds out the hope of a transforma-tion of the enemy (and thus Hebrew nonviolent involvement in instigating that transformation), a tendency that seems closely related to the call of Isa. 49:6 to be a "light to the nations." Furthermore, Jeremiah's letter to the exiles (Jer. 29:4–23) has often been read as a counsel against fomenting revolution in the Diaspora. In this letter, Jeremiah cites the well-known exemptions from military activity (Deut. 20) to proclaim an armistice on the Diaspora com-munities, and then he concludes this section of the letter by counseling that these Jewish minority communities should "seek the peace [šālôm] of the city where I have sent you" (Jer. 29:7). It is likely that a disagreement on violent revolution versus nonviolent involvement was at the heart of the policy disputes illustrated by the public debates between Hananiah and Jeremiah in Jer. 28.

Resistance and Cooperation in Regard to Governing Authorities

How far can a member of a minority cooperate with the governing au-thorities? The positive values are continued life, potential prosperity, and even influence (1 Kgs. 8:50 clearly hopes for this) against the dangers of assimila-tion and loss of identity and thus also faith. Diaspora stories such as Esther, Nehemiah, and Daniel hold out the possibilities of some kind of advancement and prosperity even under the conquerors' regimes (even if the stories are not taken literally), but they all also raise the dangers of assimilation and loss of faith and identity. Potential for influence goes from the minimal desire to simply be left alone (thus 1 Kgs. 8:50) to the possibility of actually influencing public policy in relation to Hebrew existence (Esther).

Discovering a Common Ethical Language

Finally, it is interesting to note the widespread use of the wisdom genre in postexilic texts. The inclusion of large amounts of foreign wisdom sayings in Israelite works (e.g., Egyptian wisdom in Prov. 22–23; Platonic thought in Wis. 9:15) suggests that the writers of these works we now identify as "wisdom literature" were, at the very least, involved in dialogue with non-Hebrews. This may well explain the pious but hardly uniquely Israelite character of the ethical maxims of wisdom literature: it is, rather, universal in scope and application and represents a sector of Israelite society that was finding a common ethical language for discussion with non-Hebrews. This would further explain the common counsel of the wisdom literature to reasoned discussion as opposed to short-tempered (and ill-considered) violence (e.g., Prov. 16:7; 17:9, 14, 22; 24:5–6; 25:15; Eccl. 9:13–18a). The influence of wisdom traditions carries through the Hellenistic period and into the NT writings as well (e.g., Matt. 7:24–27; James).

The ethics of exile in biblical literature consists of a discussion of ethical models and counsels of behavior that cannot be separated from the lived realities of subjugation and occupation. Such a context helps to explain the emphasis in exilic and postexilic biblical literature on a matrix of interrelated ethical issues such as communal solidarity, relations with outsiders, and relations to the dominant power.

Bibliography

Albertz, R. *Israel in Exile: The History and Literature of the Sixth Century B.C.E.* Trans. D. Green. SBL 3. Society of Biblical Literature, 2003.

Brett, M. *Genesis: Procreation and the Politics of Identity.* Routledge, 2000.

Frye, R. *The Heritage of Persia.* Weidenfeld & Nicolson, 1962.

Green, P. *Alexander to Actium: The Historical Evolution of the Hellenistic Age.* University of California Press, 1990.

Horsley, R., and N. Silberman. *The Message and the Kingdom: How Jesus and Paul Ignited a Revolution and Transformed the Ancient World.* Fortress, 2002.

Lipschitz, O. *The Fall and Rise of Jerusalem: Judah under Babylonian Rule.* Eisenbrauns, 2005.

Scott, J. *Domination and the Arts of Resistance: Hidden Transcripts.* Yale University Press, 1990.

―――. *Weapons of the Weak: Everyday Forms of Peasant Resistance.* Yale University Press, 1985.

Smith-Christopher, D. *A Biblical Theology of Exile.* Fortress, 2002.

Torrey, C. "The Exile and the Restoration." Pages 285–340 in *Ezra Studies.* LBS. Ktav, 1970 [1910].

Vanderhooft, D. *The Neo-Babylonian Empire and Babylon in the Latter Prophets.* HSM 59. Scholars Press, 2002.

Voutira, E., and B. Harrell-Bond. "In Search of the Locus of Trust: The Social World of the Refugee Camp." Pages 207–24 in *Mistrusting Refugees,* ed. D. Valentine and J. Knudsen. University of California Press, 1996.

◆ Ethics of the Priestly Literature ◆
Jacqueline E. Lapsley

The Priestly material in the OT principally comprises the book of Leviticus, broadly understood (the "Priestly" and "Holiness" material); the framework of the rest of the Pentateuch (e.g., parts of Genesis, parts of Exodus and Numbers); as well as the book of Ezekiel, again broadly understood, since it shows considerable Priestly influence, among other texts. The Priestly material is routinely considered of little ethical import by modern readers due to its interest in the arcane details of Israelite worship of Yahweh, Israel's God, and due to its intense focus on the arrangement of time and space that supports appropriate worship. Despite these apparent handicaps, the Priestly material is of considerable interest for ethics. The Priestly writers understood a unitary cosmos in which human actions have cosmic import, and thus questions of ethics are always at least implicitly present and of vital importance.

The Priestly worldview is shaped by a particular concern for the sanctity of time and space (e.g., the emphasis on divisions of time and space in Gen. 1, a Priestly text). In the Pentateuch time is divided into three distinct periods, each of which is marked by an everlasting covenant. The primeval period is marked by the covenant with Noah in Gen. 9, the ancestral period is marked by the covenant with Abraham in Gen. 17, and the Mosaic period is marked by the Sinai covenant (see Exod. 31:12–17 for Sinai as a perpetual covenant). For the Priestly writers, worship is the central experience, and within that framework the presence of God within the sanctuary is of utmost importance. The sanctuary is a microcosm of the cosmos, which is why the details concerning the building of the tabernacle at the end of Exodus are so important (Exod. 35–40). God is present with the people by tabernacling with them—that is, being present along the journey with them in a kind of movable tent. The people are identified as a worshiping community; that is the core of their identity. They are called the ʿēdâ, the congregation that worships Yahweh.

The Priestly writers ground worship in the structures of creation as a whole; thus, each of the many details of the tabernacle is sacred and is an outward and visible sign of the invisible presence of God. It is a sacramental vision of worship that may appear to be in some tension with idolatry but is always carefully nonrepresentational. The sacred details of the tabernacle mediate the presence of God and make it possible for God to be present with the people in a way that maintains the necessary boundaries between the holy, the common, and the unholy. When the boundaries between these categories are inappropriately transgressed, God's continued presence with the community is jeopardized, and with it the welfare of the community is endangered.

In the Priestly worldview, a distinct order reigns, and when certain things (e.g., food, bodily fluids) cross boundaries without due ritual, the order of the world itself is disturbed. This attention to order helps to explain the regulations pertaining to food, sex, menstrual blood, and so forth. In Gen. 1, for example, the text records that God made the sky and things that fly in the sky, the sea and things that swim in the sea, and the land and things that crawl on the land. These things are separated from one another in the order of creation itself, and so, in the Priestly view, they should remain separate. But many things found in creation pose challenges to the Priestly worldview. Consider a lobster: it lives in the sea, but it does not look like a fish; it does not have fins and scales (indeed it looks more like a giant bug that should live on the land) (see Lev. 11:9–12). In the Priestly worldview, lobster and other shellfish break the boundaries of the "natural" order and therefore are defiling to eat. Likewise, wearing garments made of two different fabrics breaks boundaries and invites chaos (Lev. 19:19). So also with human sexuality: in the Priestly worldview, there are men and women, and all are assumed to be heterosexual (the priests did not imagine anyone being created "homosexual"), and so all sexual activity should be heterosexual; to do otherwise crosses boundaries and invites chaos (Lev. 18:22) (though the priests only address male-to-male homosexual acts; lesbian activity does not seem to be in view, though women having sex with animals is a concern [Lev. 18:23]). In working with the Priestly material ethically, it is important not to extract a topic (e.g., food, sex, clothing) from its Priestly context in order to establish an ethical norm for our own time. Rather, it is worth considering how to engage the Priestly writers in a way that respects the distance between this ancient worldview and the present but still seeks points of connection with integrity.

The world envisioned in Leviticus is an orderly world, created and shaped by God's purposes; a ritual world, in which creation itself is established, sustained, and restored through liturgies of worship (i.e., worship in the sanctuary keeps chaos at bay); a relational world, wherein God invites humanity to share in responsibility for sustaining and restoring the divine purposes for the world. A crucial question for ethics is this: how are human beings invited to participate in God's purposes for the world? As shown by Jacob Milgrom, a scholar of the Priestly material who has drawn attention to its rich potential as a resource for ethical reflection, the people's continuing participation in the sanctuary's cultic worship plays a vital role in keeping the forces of chaos at bay. Cultic ritual keeps the sanctuary clean, and the whole people are part of this effort. The specific role of the priests is to organize and officiate in worship, and also to teach the Torah to the people so they will know how to avoid sin, but it is the people who recognize when they have sinned and who bring their offerings to the sanctuary on the proper occasion.

The assumption is that God's world is subject to sin and disorder. Yet when human beings commit certain kinds of sins, it is not the sinner who becomes unclean, but rather the sanctuary itself is defiled: pollution, like an invisible, airborne miasma, adheres to the edifice. Milgrom likens this process to Oscar Wilde's story *The Picture of Dorian Gray*, in which the main character's sins adhere not to the man himself but instead to his hidden portrait. So the Israelite sanctuary is akin to the painting in the attic that is deteriorating hideously on account of the sins of the man below, who bears no outward sign of sin. The entire sanctuary, of course, is holy, but it is also increasingly holy as one approaches the most holy place, the inner sanctum where God is understood to be most present ("the holy of holies"). If what is holy is defiled by impurity, and if that builds up long enough, God will abandon the sanctuary, and so the people, and so the whole world. And if God abandons the sanctuary, the people, and the world, chaos will break in and overwhelm the whole world. Thus, maintaining category distinctions is crucial to maintaining order, keeping chaos at bay, and so keeping God with the people. If the sanctuary becomes too polluted with this miasma produced by sin, God will abandon it, with the resulting breach in the community's life with God.

The consequences of such a failure, the failure to keep the sanctuary relatively free of pollution, are catastrophic for the world. So the Priestly worldview believes that Israel is performing a service on behalf of the world (here one might recall the promise to Abraham in Gen. 12 that through his descendants all the families of the earth would be blessed). The entire community, not just the priests, must participate in keeping the sanctuary as pollution-free as possible; the life of the community depends on the extent to which this responsibility is shared. When they sin, the people must bring their gifts to the priest at the sanctuary, and through their sacrifice the sanctuary can be adequately cleansed of the miasma, and the community will thrive.

In order to see what Priestly ethics might look like with a specific text, consider the case of Lev. 4 and the problem of unintentional sins. Leviticus 4, like most of the book, is taken up with the problem of sin and its effects. Leviticus 1–3 deals with voluntary gifts brought to the sanctuary, whereas Lev. 4–5 prescribes mandatory gifts for the expiation of sin. These chapters are addressed to the entire people, not simply to the priests. In Lev. 4 the issue is unintentional sins, unwittingly committed. What can be done about them? The chapter moves through these on a case-by-case basis: when a priest unknowingly sins (4:3–12), a certain sacrifice is prescribed (bull); when the whole congregation unknowingly sins (4:13–21), there is another sacrifice (bull, but with elders involved); and so on, until, at the end of the list, bringing up the rear, is the ordinary person who sins unknowingly (4:27–31). This case, the ordinary person who sins unknowingly, is of particular interest for ethics.

As noted above, sin is not about what it does to the individual; it is the sanctuary that requires attention. The blood of the sacrifice is the ritual detergent, cleansing the altar. Forgiveness is a byproduct of the sinner's effort to address sin, but the sinner's forgiveness is not of primary importance. The sinner brings a gift to the priest in order to repair the relationship with God and to help the community to prosper. So in Leviticus, sin is not individual in the first instance; it is about the health of the life of the community, about whether the community as a whole will thrive. The sinner is forgiven for the sin, but the need for forgiveness arises from the effect of the sin on the sanctuary, not from impurity of the self. This focus on the welfare of the community and the ethical import of unintentional sins led Milgrom to this comment about the purification offering of Lev. 4: "If only this ritual were fully understood and implemented, it could transform the world" (*Leviticus: A Book of Ritual and Ethics*, 33).

Bibliography

Balentine, S. *The Torah's Vision of Worship*. OBT. Fortress, 1999.
Milgrom, J. *Leviticus 1–16*. AB 3. Doubleday, 1991, 253–63.
———. *Leviticus: A Book of Ritual and Ethics*. CC. Fortress, 2004, 8–16, 30–33.

◆ Law ◆
Dennis T. Olson

The Bible often portrays God as issuing commands and laws, beginning already in the book of Genesis. God's first acts of creation involve commands to all creation, "Let there be light" (Gen. 1:3), and specifically to humans, "Be fruitful and multiply, . . . have dominion" (Gen. 1:28). The first divine command that humans disobey is the prohibition against eating the fruit of the tree of the knowledge of good and evil in the garden of Eden, leading to the expulsion of the humans from Eden (Gen. 2:17; 3:14–24). God's law and commands continue throughout the Bible, functioning both as a vehicle of divine blessing and as an instrument of divine judgment.

Law in the Pentateuch

The Bible's legal material is concentrated in the Pentateuch (Genesis through Deuteronomy), the first five books of the Bible. The terms used for laws include "statutes and ordinances" (Lev. 18:5), "commandments" (Exod. 20:6), "decrees" (Deut. 6:20), and "law," *tôrâ* (Deut. 4:44). The term *tôrâ* came to be an important and inclusive term within the biblical understanding of law. Deuteronomy used the term to designate the laws within its book (4:44) and then even more expansively to include the entire book and its wide variety of genres: narratives, speeches, curses, blessings, poems, and legal material ("the book of the law [*tôrâ*]" [31:26]). Jewish tradition eventually used the word *tôrâ* as a designation for the whole of Genesis through Deuteronomy (Neh. 8:1–2; Sirach, prologue; cf. Matt. 5:17).

The core meaning of *tôrâ* includes not only "law" but also "instruction" or "teaching." The teaching function of biblical law is illustrated by the frequent inclusion of motivational clauses along with the laws that seek to persuade and provide good reasons why the reader or hearer ought to obey the law in question (Exod. 20:8–11; 23:9; Lev. 19:2; Deut. 7:12–16).

The Bible locates the primary giving of God's law to Israel at Mount Sinai, the "mountain of God," in Exod. 20–Num. 10. At Mount Sinai, God established a covenant with the Israelites as God's chosen people, forming them into "a priestly kingdom and a holy nation" (Exod. 19:6) as they traveled from the slavery of Egypt to the freedom of Canaan. God's covenant obligations or laws functioned as expressions of gratitude to God for the good things that God had done for Israel. Thus, the narrative prologue to the Ten Commandments reminds Israel of what God had already achieved for Israel: "I am the LORD your God, who brought you out of the land of Egypt, out of the house of slavery" (Exod. 20:2). The ten commands that follow constitute the basic obligations of Israel, teaching Israel how to live into its already established identity as the freed people of God (Exod. 20:3–17).

A number of law codes follow the Ten Commandments within the Pentateuch:

1. the so-called Book of the Covenant or Covenant Code, which contains case law with significant parallels to other ancient Near Eastern law, especially the Code of Hammurabi, but also contains important adaptations that reflect ancient Israel's experience and theology (Exod. 20:22–23:19);

2. a set of cultic laws given by God after Israel's rebellious act of making a golden calf that mark a new covenant, rooted in the mercy and forgiveness of God (Exod. 34:6–7), and repeat certain laws from the

Covenant Code focused on the proper worship of God and the avoidance of idolatry (Exod. 34:10–26);

3. the Priestly Code, which focuses on maintaining the holiness of the tabernacle or tent of God's presence in the midst of the Israelites as well as the holiness of the priests and the proper qualities and quantities of the sacrifices that they regularly offered to God (Lev. 1–16);

4. the Holiness Code, which expands the expectation of holiness beyond the Priestly Code to include the whole Israelite camp (not just the tabernacle), the whole land of Canaan when they live there, and the entire Israelite people (Lev. 19:1–2), both priests and laypersons (Lev. 17–26);

5. miscellaneous laws in Num. 1–10 (while still at Mount Sinai) and other laws in Numbers given by God as Israel left Sinai and continued its wilderness journey (Num. 15; 18; 19; 28–30; 35);

6. the Deuteronomic Code, which is presented as Moses' last words that he taught to a new generation of Israelites before his death and includes new laws as well as reinterpretations of the several earlier laws from the Covenant Code in Exod. 20:22–23:19 (Deut. 6–26).

Although these varied collections of biblical laws contain numerous parallels to other law codes in the ancient Near East, they also reflect many unique features. They are unique in mixing together laws concerning everyday social, political, and economic life (Exod. 22:1–14) with laws concerning religious life and worship (Exod. 23:12–19). In the context of a largely polytheistic culture surrounding Israel, biblical laws are unique in their strong emphasis on the worship of Israel's one God alone and the prohibition of the worship of images or idols (Exod. 20:3–6; 22:20; 23:13). The biblical laws originate as words from God, whereas other ancient Near Eastern law codes typically originate not with the gods but rather with human kings.

In the conclusion of the book of Deuteronomy, Moses wrote down the "book of the law" and instructed the Levitical priests to read aloud the book of the law in the hearing of all Israel every seven years (Deut. 31:9–13). This ongoing life of the "book of the law" in Israel's history is suggested by the narrative of the finding of the "book of the law" during temple renovations in the reign of King Josiah, likely some version of the book of Deuteronomy (2 Kgs. 22) and Ezra's public reading of the "book of the law of Moses" after the exiles' return to Jerusalem (Ezra 8). The ongoing role of the law in Israel's family life is also suggested by the instruction to parents to recite and teach the laws of Deuteronomy to their children every day "when you lie down and when you rise" (Deut. 6:6–9). Daily meditation on God's law became a practice of religious devotion associated with joy, delight, freedom, mercy, and blessing (Pss. 1; 119).

Law in the Prophets

The OT prophets rarely cited specific laws in their announcements of the coming judgment of God upon Israel and its leaders. However, the prophets clearly based God's judgment on Israel's repeated disobedience of God's will as generally embodied in God's law, especially focused on the worship of false gods and on social injustice (Isa. 5; Jer. 7:8–11; 11:1–17; Hos. 4:1–3). The prophets criticized Israel's life of worship, sacrifice, and ritual when it was not combined with concern for God's justice for widows, orphans, and the poor (Isa. 1:10–17; 58:6–12; Amos 5:21–24; Mic. 6:6–8). As a result, the prophets blamed Judah's exile to Babylon and the destruction of Jerusalem and its temple on Israel's disobedience of God's law (Isa. 42:24–25).

Law in the New Testament

In the NT, "law" usually refers to the commandments and laws that were given to Moses at Mount Sinai, although at times it also refers to the Pentateuch as a whole ("the law and the prophets" [cf. Matt. 5:17; Luke 24:27]) or even to the whole of Jewish sacred Scripture (John 10:34; 12:34; 1 Cor. 14:21). The NT witness affirmed that the law and the prophets found their fulfillment in Christ (Matt. 5:17; Luke 24:44). Indeed, the law (the Pentateuch) itself testified to righteousness by faith "apart from law" (Rom. 3:21). In the NT, one focus of the call to obedience included the commandments of Moses (especially for the Gospel of Matthew), but more important, obedience involves "believing in" and "following" Jesus, who carried forward but also reinterpreted Mosaic law. An inner biblical dialectic exists between Jesus as fulfilling the law of Moses (Matt. 5:17–19) and Jesus as one who is sovereign over the law and able to reinterpret it (Matt. 5:21–48; Mark 2:23–28; Luke 6:1–11; John 7:22–24). For example, Jesus declared that what makes someone impure or unclean is not what goes into the person (a reference to the food laws in Lev. 11) but rather what comes out from the human heart in words and actions (Matt. 15:11, 17–20; Mark 7:19). Jesus challenged the Jewish scribes and their interpretation of the Sabbath law, declaring himself "lord of the sabbath" (Luke 6:1–11). Jesus reinterpreted a number of OT commandments in his Sermon on the Mount (Matt. 5:17–48).

According to Rom. 1:16, the core of the apostle Paul's mission was to proclaim to gentiles the gospel of "the power of God for salvation to everyone who has faith" in Christ alone apart from works of the law (i.e., apart from observing all the laws of Moses in the Pentateuch, including circumcision [cf. Rom. 3:21–26; see also Acts 15:1–35]). For Paul, God's law functioned to guard the welfare of human beings as a temporary custodian or "disciplinarian" until Christ came (Gal. 3:25). The law continues to serve as a mirror by which God convicts all humans, both Jews and gentiles, as sinners, since "all have sinned" against God's law (Rom. 3:23). Even gentiles had requirements of the law "written on their hearts," so that no one has an excuse (Rom. 2:15; cf. 1:20). The law reveals sin and drives the sinner to trust not in works of the law but instead in God's forgiveness and mercy through the death of Jesus, who "died for the ungodly" (Rom. 5:1–11).

Yet Paul could also speak positively about the continuing role of the law in terms of obeying "Christ's law" (1 Cor. 9:21), which was summarized by the command to "love your neighbor as yourself" (Rom. 13:8, 10; Gal. 5:14). Although those who follow Christ are in one sense free from living under the law, they are in another sense bound in obedience to Christ and the law of love. All things may be lawful, "but not all things are beneficial" (1 Cor. 6:12; see also Rom. 14:1–15:13).

Law and Ethics

The biblical traditions of laws, commandments, and instructions offer a complex and varied set of resources for reflecting on the relationship of law and ethics. A few observations may be made. The biblical witness affirms God as the source of biblical law. Yet the variety of law codes and their distinctive and sometimes conflicting content invite caution and careful interpretation, sensitivity to narrative context, and comparison with other biblical laws, narratives, wisdom material, prophetic oracles, and the combined witness of both Testaments before making definitive pronouncements about the clear will of God. The Bible itself also testifies to the need for ongoing interpretation of laws and customs in the face of new circumstances and contexts (Num. 27:1–11; Matt. 5).

Moreover, the laws and commandments of the OT often represent the minimum expectations of obedience to God and boundaries of behavior beyond which God's people should not go (the prohibitive commandments, such as "You shall have no other gods," "You shall not murder," and the like). But these minimum legal standards within the OT do not fully encompass the deeper and more positive ethical ideals that both OT and NT witnesses urged upon their communities of faith: to love God with passion and urgency in every aspect of one's life (Deut. 6:5–9; 10:12; Mark 12:30), to love one's neighbor as oneself (Lev. 19:18; Luke 10:25–37; Gal. 5:14), and "to do justice, and to love kindness, and to walk humbly with your God" (Mic. 6:8 [cf. Col.

3:12]). The OT and the NT also testify that whatever human love of God and neighbor humans can muster is itself a gift of God (Deut. 30:6), motivated by the prior and overflowing love, generosity, and mercy of God (Deut. 30:6; John 15:1–17). "We love because God first loved us" (1 John 4:19).

Bibliography

Dunn, J. D. G. *Jesus, Paul, and the Law: Studies in Mark and Galatians*. Westminster John Knox 1990.

Levenson, B. *Deuteronomy and the Hermeneutics of Legal Innovation*. Oxford University Press, 2002.

———. *Legal Revision and Religious Renewal in Ancient Israel*. Cambridge University Press, 2010.

Sanders, E. P. *Paul, the Law, and the Jewish People*. Fortress, 1983.

Schreiner, T. *The Law and Its Fulfillment: A Pauline Theology of Law*. Baker, 1998.

Thielman, F. *The Law and the New Testament: The Question of Continuity*. Crossroad, 1999.

Wenham, G. "The Gap Between Law and Ethics in the Bible." *JJS* 48 (1997): 17–29.

Wright, D. *Inventing God's Law: How the Covenant Code of the Bible Used and Revised the Laws of Hammurabi*. Oxford University Press, 2009.

♦ Poetic Discourse and Ethics ♦

Chip Dobbs-Allsopp

W. H. Auden once remarked that of the two questions that interested him most when reading a poem, one was "broadly speaking, moral" (51): What kind of person inhabits the poem? What notion of the good life is on display? Yet, in the fifty-plus years since Auden's statement very little attention has been given to the general topic of poetry and ethics, and even less to the subject with respect to biblical verse more specifically. What follows, then, is by necessity a precursory statement on the topic, distinctly probative. And, in fact, the focus here is considerably narrower still. Ethical thinking over the years has preferred the expanded space afforded by narrative, philosophical discourse, and the like, and poetry has been commonly thought of as an irrational genre; yet there can be no doubt that poems often have proved an especially effective medium for asserting knowledge, for thinking (Vendler 1–9; von Hallberg 105–42). The nexus of poetry and wisdom is quite old, as the most cursory of encounters with the biblical book of Proverbs will attest. But such assertions of truth or knowledge or wisdom are not the primary interest here. While biblical poetry, like all language arts, cannot do without semantics, without propositional content, it is the potential differences of poetry's *way(s)* of saying, especially in its lyric mode (see Dobbs-Allsopp), and how these can affect ethical thinking that hold most of the attention in this article. My claim, echoing Robert von Hallberg (107), is that the (lyric) poetry of the Bible has at its "ready disposal" resources (figures, dialogue, line play, rhythm) that are conventionally less accessible to other genres and thus provide biblical poems with the capacity to open on to and stage ethical thought differently. Several examples may be offered by way of illustration.

We begin by focusing the potential gains to be had from nonlinear, non-epistemic thinking. In counterdistinction to a process of thinking in which a chain of ideas is marshaled into a "single steady trend moving toward a unified conclusion" (von Hallberg 110), lyric poems in the Bible (as elsewhere) often proceed by fits and starts, intuitive surmise, leaping over gaps, moving via juxtaposition and paradox, and generally following prosodic structures of one kind or another. And as a consequence, happily, thinking is as often as not led in directions that otherwise might not be explored, and auditors are provided with warrants for valuing certain dispositions other than by a chain of argument (see Altieri 267; von Hallberg 120).

The poetry of Lamentations is strongly paratactic in nature, which the poet exploits to good effect in shaping a response to the radical suffering caused by the 586 BCE destruction of Jerusalem. Ideas and images are routinely juxtaposed to each other without being logically linked or scripted. This forces readers to consider each idea on its own and then in relation with those most contiguous to it. Individual claims are allowed to surface and be experienced on their own, but they are also ultimately required to be considered as a part of a larger whole, which acts as a strong deterrent to the domination of any single perspective. In Lam. 1:5 we read, "Yahweh has made her [Jerusalem] suffer." The line break after "suffer" ensures that the reader contemplates this startling statement. Yahweh did not "punish" or otherwise "reprimand" personified Jerusalem, but rather intentionally caused her pain. The second line of the couplet then shifts the perspective slightly: "for the multitude of her transgressions." In other words, Jerusalem's "transgressions" precipitated Yahweh's actions, and thus our original aversion to Yahweh's behavior is mollified somewhat, but only somewhat, as we are still haunted by Yahweh's suffering-causing activity. The last couplet exploits this slippage one final time: "her children have gone away, captives before the foe." Yahweh's infliction of suffering on Jerusalem ultimately results—though the link is only implicit in the concatenation of lines—in the exile of the city's children. The image of children (however figurative) being forcefully taken into captivity evokes feelings of empathy and compassion and, ultimately, anger. Whatever guilt there is on Jerusalem's part cannot, ever, rationalize the suffering of innocent children (figures matter ethically too).

Here, then, is a wonderful example of how the poet's paratactic style shapes the ethical outlook sponsored. The attribution of sin and the reality of suffering both have their own claims to make, but neither can ultimately be considered in isolation from the other. Human responsibility must ultimately be owned and the consequences of past actions assumed, but sin, no matter how severe, can never justify human suffering. Beyond the unique perspective on the question of suffering and sin achieved through this manner of putting things (it is neither wholly Deuteronomistic nor prophetic in ideology), such a paratactic style, especially when employed regularly as throughout Lamentations, has the potential to habituate in readers a process of reflection and thinking that demands constant attention to, and interpretation and reinterpretation of, individual details, words, images, propositions; it stresses responsiveness and attention to complexity and discourages the search for single and all-encompassing answers. The time and circumstances of the poet of Lamentations likely did not permit the formulation of simple and singular solutions, and the poet's paratactic habit of thought is generally reflective of and isomorphic to this. But such a style and the view of life and learning that it sponsors may hold attraction even for those of us who read these poems belatedly. At the very least, it exemplifies a productive way for thinking (even ethically) other than through logic and abstraction.

In the short but rich Ps. 133 there is, on a certain reading (Dobbs-Allsopp), a strong valorization of family—kindred dwelling together (v. 1). But this is never argued for logically. Instead, it is simply declaimed. The only warrants provided are aesthetic (what is "good" and "beautiful" about family is likened to "precious oil" [v. 2] and the most bountiful dewfall [v. 3]) and theological— the poem's one bit of significant sound play (*gam*, *šām*, *hāʿōlām*; *nāʿîm*, *ʾaḥîm*, *ḥayyîm*; *mah-*, *mah-*, *habbĕrākâ*) linking the opening couplet (v. 1) and closing triplet (v. 3b) and in the process identifying family as the premier site (the literal "there" [*šām*] of v. 3) of Yahweh's blessing. Here, then, we have a good example of how a poem's prosodic structures can give way to ethical insight just as productively and effectively as logic or narrative. Of course, much also depends on our readerly decision to ask ethical questions of this psalm, to embed it, for example, in a larger discussion about what constitutes a good life. There is no such thing as a given or neutral ethical point of view. All ethics, in the end, are cultural constructs. And while the positive ethical evaluation often conveyed by *ṭôb* ("good" [e.g., Gen. 2:17; 3:5, 22; 1 Kgs. 8:36; Isa. 7:15]) might be taken to invite a certain ethical curiosity about this psalm, there is otherwise nothing explicitly moral about it.

And this is true too of most poems in the Bible. In these cases, whatever ethical sensibilities are to be derived from their reading(s) is the responsibility of the reader, the decision to think the psalm (in this instance) through with ethical matters chiefly in mind. And even in those places where it seems that biblical poems may be advocating specific ethical positions—as, for example, in the valorization of family life—such approbations are themselves culturally and historically motivated, and taking them up into other cultural contexts requires, at the very least, negotiating the differences that always accompany historical existence, differences, say, between what constituted a typical family household in Iron Age Israel (Meyers) and what constitutes the same today in North America—the two are by no means identical. So even when contemporary readers are won over to a perspective advocated in an ancient biblical poem, as well we might be in the case of Ps. 133, there will always be more ethical work to do should we also then want to bring that perspective (e.g., a valuing of family) to bear on our own lives. If ethics is always a constructive endeavor, it is also never-ending.

A final example to consider is the general topic of the emotions. That emotion and passion—whether in the agonizing (and angry) cry of radical suffering (Ps. 22:2), or the expressed ecstasy of sublime devotion (Ps. 9:3), or the irresistible desire of one newly in love (Song 4:6)—figure prominently and frequently in biblical poems is readily apparent (see Ryken 123–24). I would add only that this being so is entirely consistent with the strong propensity of lyric poems the world over and throughout the ages to traffic in the emotions. The ethical implications of such lyric prizing of emotion are not insignificant. Two stand out. First, there is a tacit validation of the emotional, the affirmation that the passions are part and parcel of our makeup as human beings. Indeed, we as readers are forced to engage this poetry at an emotional level, and so emotions are made visible as topics for critical discourse and thinking. Second, one of the truths toward which emotionally charged and evocative verse spurs us is the recognition of how impoverished would be our thinking and reasoning were it unaccompanied by feeling and emotion. Emotions "embody some of our most deeply rooted views about what has importance" (Nussbaum, *Fragility of Goodness*, 69–70), views that could be easily lost if we fail to attend routinely and intentionally to the emotional. Philosophers and scientists alike are now beginning to (re)appreciate how crucial the emotions are for the health and well-being of the human creature (Damasio; Nussbaum, *Upheavals of Thought*). To have a discourse, therefore, so routinely charged with emotion, where engagement with the passions is easy and comfortable (however unessential), as with so many moments in Psalms or Lamentations or the Song of Songs, is also a very good thing, something to cherish and nourish. Cold, hard logic is no guarantee of right thinking, ethical or otherwise.

If there has been little attention recently given to the general topic of biblical poetry and ethics, it is not for the lack of substantive material with which to work. Even this necessarily abbreviated consideration of a small handful of examples is sufficient to make clear the wealth of still mostly untapped potential that awaits any ethical line of inquiry into this poetic corpus. In the "how" of a biblical poem's saying there are resources for ethical thinking not so readily available to other genres or modes of discourse. Formal and stylistic choices are matters, as Alan Shapiro observes, "fraught with extraliterary judgments, biases, commitments that have moral as well as aesthetic implications" (1). In fact, to ignore "the sound and evocative power of words . . . and other rhythmic devices, associated images, repetitions, archaisms and grammatical twists" (Langer 259) in biblical poems is to miss much of how this predominantly nonnarrative kind of poetry (see Alter 27) means and to settle, ultimately, for a much impoverished moral worldview.

Bibliography

Alter, R. *The Art of Biblical Poetry*. Basic Books, 1985.

Altieri, C. "Taking Lyrics Literally: Teaching Poetry in a Prose Culture." *New Literary History* 32 (2001): 259–81.

Auden, W. H. *The Dyer's Hand, and Other Essays*. Vintage Books, 1989.

Damasio, A. *Descartes' Error: Emotion, Reason, and the Human Brain*. G. P. Putnam, 1994.

Dobbs-Allsopp, F. W. "Psalm 133: A (Close) Reading." *JHS* 8 (2008). http://www.arts .ualberta.ca/JHS/Articles/article_97.pdf.

———. "The Psalms and Lyric Verse." Pages 346–79 in *The Evolution of Rationality: Interdisciplinary Essays in Honor of J. Wentzel van Huyssteen*, ed. F. Shultz. Eerdmans, 2006.

Langer, S. *Feeling and Form: A Theory of Art Developed from Philosophy in a New Key*. Routledge & Kegan Paul, 1953.

Meyers, C. "The Family in Early Israel." Pages 1–47 in *Families in Ancient Israel*, by L. Perdue et al. Westminster John Knox, 1997.

Nussbaum, M. *The Fragility of Goodness: Luck and Ethics in Greek Tragedy and Philosophy*. Cambridge University Press, 1986.

———. *Upheavals of Thought: The Intelligence of Emotions*. Cambridge University Press, 2001.

Ryken, L. *The Literature of the Bible*. Zondervan, 1974.

Shapiro, A. *In Praise of the Impure: Poetry and the Ethical Imagination; Essays, 1980–1991*. Northwestern University Press, 1993.

Vendler, H. *Poets Thinking: Pope, Dickinson, Whitman, Yeats*. Harvard University Press, 2004.

von Hallberg, R. *Lyric Powers*. University of Chicago Press, 2008.

♦ Ten Commandments ♦

Jacqueline E. Lapsley

Although brief, the Ten Commandments (sometimes called the "Ten Words," from the Greek *deka logoi* [Exod. 34:28; Deut. 10:4 LXX], hence also the "Decalogue") have been crucially important in the history of ethical reflection in the Jewish and Christian traditions, and they continue to have significant normative power in most Jewish and Christian communities today. They occur twice in the first five books of the Bible, in both cases as a series of commands said to be authored directly by God (Exod. 31:18; Deut. 4:13). They are the first and only commandments that the whole people of Israel hear directly from God, as opposed to the rest of the Sinai legislation, which is mediated by Moses (Deut. 5:4, 22). The commandments are numbered slightly differently in various traditions. For example, Jewish traditions include as the first commandment (or word) what in Christian traditions is identified as the prologue ("I am the LORD your God, who brought you out of the land of Egypt, out of the house of slavery"), and the Jewish, Lutheran, and Catholic traditions combine into the first commandment (no other gods) what the Reformed tradition has taken to be two separate commands (no other gods, and no images).

In the first appearance of the Decalogue (Exod. 20:1–17), Israel is being formed as a people at Sinai, whereas later Moses is recalling that formative moment for the people just before they enter the land of Canaan (Deut. 5:6–21). The text makes no claim that the Ten Commandments constitute the complete will of God, but their placement within the narrative suggests that they possess an ethical priority. In both contexts the Decalogue is set apart from the rest of the legislation that follows it. Furthermore, many readers have long understood the Book of the Covenant in Exod. 20–23 and the legislation in Deut. 12–26 as a kind of explication and unfolding of the Ten Commandments, which precede them. These larger bodies of legal material show how the commandments actually function in the life of the community—that is, how they work in real-life situations that the community encounters.

Within the history of interpretation of the Ten Commandments, many scholars and interpreters have understood them as a summary of the moral law. As early as the first century CE, Philo of Alexandria, for example, understood the Torah (i.e., all the laws) to be an elaboration of the Ten Commandments. The Reformers in the sixteenth century paid special attention to the Decalogue as a source for ethical reflection. Martin Luther organized his commentary on Deuteronomy around the Ten Commandments because he understood that book to be an elaboration of them, and John Calvin understood each commandment broadly, interpreting each of the so-called negative commandments positively. The commandment against killing, for example, is appropriately understood as a command to promote the neighbor's well-being. In this way, the Ten Commandments come to exert their moral force on nearly every aspect of life. In a similar way recently, Patrick Miller proposes that a moral "trajectory" emerges from each commandment, thus indicating the broad swath of the moral life that the Decalogue encompasses.

The so-called prologue (the first "word" in the Jewish tradition) is crucial to understanding the Ten Commandments, even though typically it is not considered part of the Decalogue by most Christians: "I am the LORD your God, who brought you out of the land of Egypt, out of the house of slavery" (Exod. 20:2; Deut. 5:6). This divine self-presentation reveals the character of God as one who saves, who is gracious. Its position at the head of the commandments is vital to understanding them as coming not from an abstract deity, but rather from Yahweh, with whom Israel is already in relationship and whose character has already been revealed as one who acts for his people. The prologue is, then, intimately connected to the first commandment ("You shall have no other gods before me"). Based on the truth of the prologue, of who this God is, the people are not to have any other gods. And the first commandment, together with the prologue, serves as the foundation upon which all the others stand. They affirm unequivocally that the vertical, divine-human relationship is prior to, and sustaining of, all horizontal relationships among human beings. Given the importance of the prologue to a correct understanding of the rest of the commandments, excising it (for purposes of posting in public places, for example) violates the intent of the commandments. And it is in light of God's gracious action to save that human moral action to fulfill the commandments becomes intelligible. The twentieth-century theologian and ethicist H. Richard Niebuhr, for example, outlined an understanding of human moral action as the "response to God's redeeming action." People are set free from past bondage, and this is how they respond to that new freedom. So the commandments describe how a free people respond to freedom in that new identity.

The people are to obey the Ten Commandments not simply because God commands them to do so, but rather because obeying them is beneficial; that is, adherence to them makes it possible for the community to flourish. The commandments are meant to be not a burden, but a gift. The mere presence of the motivation clauses (e.g., persons are to honor their parents "so that your days may be long in the land that the LORD your God is giving you" [Exod. 20:12]) suggests that the commandments are neither arbitrary nor designed for the sake of having people obey. The motivation clauses suggest, rather, that from God's point of view, the commandments are not self-evident. God seeks to persuade the people that this way of life is attractive. Some tension thus exists between the deontological approach to ethics, with its emphasis on duty, and the motivational clauses in the commandments. It is good and valuable to obey these commandments, not simply a duty to do so. The commandments are also rational and sensible in and of themselves; that is, they are good for human life. In short, by giving these laws, God seeks to persuade the people that this way of life is a good one; obedience to the commandments is not only a recognition of the claim laid upon the people and an appropriate response to the gracious activity of the one who commands but also is inherently life-giving (they are "for our lasting good" [Deut. 6:24]).

The first commandment, "You shall have no other gods before me," is the foundation upon which all the other commandments rest, and also is the one that is automatically violated when any of the others is violated. The first commandment requires total and undivided trust and commitment to Yahweh, Israel's deity. Other potential claimants for meaning, value, and devotion are numerous ("other gods") and seductive, but they must be resisted. Patrick Miller spells out some of the implications of the first commandment: "The oneness of the reality that grounds existence, God, is what keeps life from being chaotic and divided beyond the limits of human management. In the face of the multiple pulls and dimensions of human life and experience, human existence is held together and in order by that one and absolute object of our allegiance and loyalty" (Miller 23). The commandment is intelligible only in light of the prologue; that is, it is only after God has acted graciously on Israel's behalf that God makes this claim of obedience. Grace precedes the law. But the first commandment is also closely connected to the prohibition on images that follows in the second commandment (in Reformed numbering) insofar as it has the double meaning of prohibiting the fashioning of images of Yahweh and also of other gods. The latter is subsumed under the first commandment; the former, however, is likely where the emphasis lies: human-made images of the divine being are excluded forever. God alone chooses the mode of divine revelation.

This section has insufficient space to deal with each commandment in turn, but here a few observations about the sixth commandment are offered because it has proved especially fascinating yet nettlesome to interpreters, with important implications for ethics. The commandment is variously translated somewhat narrowly as "You shall not murder" (e.g., NRSV) or more broadly as "You shall not kill" (e.g., RSV). Yet neither of these is entirely appropriate to the Hebrew text; indeed, there is no way to satisfactorily translate the Hebrew verb *raṣaḥ* into English, as it came to mean different things in different contexts over the course of time in ancient Israel (see, e.g., Num. 35:6–34; Deut. 19:3–13; Josh. 20:3–9; and related narratives, especially 1 Kgs. 21). Lengthy analysis of these and many other related texts reveals that the commandment against killing prohibits not just these acts of violence but also the prior emotions and attitudes that feed them. So while Jesus explicitly interiorizes the commandment in the Sermon on the Mount (Matt. 5:21–26), control of one's passions in service to the preservation of life was already in view in the original context(s) of the sixth commandment. "You shall not hate in your heart anyone of your kin" (Lev. 19:17).

In giving Israel the commandments at Sinai (and they are a gift), God seeks to form a community that will thrive in its relationship with God and with one another. But to achieve this end, the commandments cannot simply be promulgated; they must be taught and interpreted for each new generation. When the young are taught the commandments, they are first reminded of the gracious character and identity of the God who commands, and then they are instructed in the commandments themselves (Deut. 6:20–25). The centrality of the commandments for the life and faith of the community is indicated by the way in which Scripture equates the covenant itself with the commandments (Deut. 4:13; 9:11). Many interpreters understand them to function in a way akin to the US Constitution, as a founding document that must be reinterpreted by and for each new generation. In the NT, Jesus offers an authoritative interpretation of the Ten Commandments so that their radical intention, with their true force and compass, is made clear for all to see.

Bibliography

Braaten, C., and C. Seitz, eds. *I Am the Lord Your God: Christian Reflections on the Ten Commandments*. Eerdmans, 2005.

Brown, W., ed. *The Ten Commandments: The Reciprocity of Faithfulness*. LTE. Westminster John Knox, 2004.

Miller, P. *The Ten Commandments*. IRSC. Westminster John Knox, 2009.

INDEX OF SCRIPTURE AND ANCIENT WRITINGS

INDEX OF SUBJECTS